Mex-Ciné

Mex-Ciné

*Mexican Filmmaking,
Production, and Consumption
in the Twenty-first Century*

Frederick Luis Aldama

The University of Michigan Press
Ann Arbor

Published in the United States of America by
The University of Michigan Press
Manufactured in the United States of America
♾ Printed on acid-free paper

2016   2015   2014   2013   4   3   2   1

A CIP catalog record for this book is available from the British Library.

Library of Congress Cataloging-in-Publication Data

Aldama, Frederick Luis, 1969–
     Mex-Cine : Mexican filmmaking, production, and consumption in the twenty-
first century / Frederick Luis Aldama.
         pages   cm
     Includes bibliographical references and index.
     ISBN 978-0-472-07193-7 (hardback) — ISBN 978-0-472-05193-9 (paper) —
ISBN 978-0-472-02912-9 (e-book)
     1. Motion pictures--Mexico.   I. Title.
PN1993.5.M4A43   2013
791.430972—dc23
                                                                    2012047392

Contents

✄

Foreword

CARLOS SALCÉS

A pesar de todo, en especial de la catástrofe capitalista neoliberal, el cine mexicano sobrevive. Por ello, cada década se hace un *refrito* de la denominación "*Nuevo Cine Mexicano.*" El esfuerzos de los realizadores y técnicos que trabajan en esta arte-oficio-mercancía es milagroso. Milagroso y trágico.

Las películas son reflejo de las posibilidades expresivas de sus directores, y también de las tantas limitaciones del sistema para contribuir cultural y artísticamente al medio y al país. Durante los últimos años, los directores mexicanos que más filman son quienes se imponen como productores, es decir, los capitalistas más hábiles. Aquellos que ganan espacios políticos en un esquema en el que los presupuestos privados y gubernamentales se otorgan de forma caprichosa, sin tomar en cuenta a los cineastas que tienen una voz más personal e interesante.

Las películas que se realizan son tan importantes como las que se han dejado de hacer, las cuales, tienen un espacio pendiente en nuestras pantallas.

Abundan las películas que tratan, podría decirse que obcecadamente, de deshacerse de una mirada política o crítica de la realidad mexicana, y con eso dejan clara esa posición política, simplista, frívola y neoliberal, que no deja nada, más que algunos pesos, bastante pocos por cierto, en manos de exhibidores que justifican un espacio cada vez más escaso para el cine mexicano en las pantallas del país.

El cine no escapa de ser parte de la red del dominio mediático que ejerce el imperio capitalista sobre las mentes de los que habitamos en este mundo. Sólo en raras y valiosas oportunidades los autores del cine mexicano, logramos rebelarnos contra este y mostrar nuestra idiosincrasia y un propósito humano.

Desafortunadamente, con un sistema que premia la banalidad por encima de todo, siempre quedan fuera los que más tienen que decir. Únicamente en casos excepcionales, colados, podemos observar la mirada bella de nuestra perspectiva original y compartir el placer de la empatía y de la reflexión en las pantallas del mundo que vivimos.

La reflexión de Frederick Luis Aldama, en este libro, penetra en el universo de la proyección del mexicano cinematográfico con una mirada aguda. Mas allá de la crítica y las valoraciones objetivas y subjetivas de las películas realizadas al inicio del milenio, Aldama nos pone a la vista caminos por explorar para la realización de un cine nacional más identificado con su pueblo y congruente con su historia.

In spite of everything, especially the neoliberal capitalist catastrophe, Mexican cinema lives on. Thanks to this survival, in each decade we witness a rehash of a so-called new Mexican cinema. The efforts of the moviemakers and technicians that work in this art-profession-commodity are miraculous. Miraculous and tragic.

Films reflect the expressive possibilities of filmmakers, but they also reflect the many obstacles that the system places on the cultural and artistic contribution that can be made to the medium and the country. In the last few years, the Mexican directors that make more films are also the ones that become producers, that is, the most skilled capitalists, those that gain political spaces within a system in which budgets from private and official sources are furnished in a whimsical way, without taking into account those filmmakers that have a more personal and interesting voice.

The films that are made are as important as those that are not made and that have left a blank space on our screens. There are a large number of films that try, one can say obstinately, to omit a political or critical vision of Mexican reality, and in their place they exhibit a political, simplistic, frivolous, and neoliberal position that generates nothing but some pesos, quite a few by the way, for the exhibitors who provide an ever shrinking space for Mexican cinema on screens all over the country.

Cinema does not escape being part and parcel of the media network that capitalist power exerts on the minds of all those who inhabit the planet. Only in rare but valuable occasions do we authors of Mexican cinema manage to rebel against this power, showing what is unique in us, as well as the human purpose generally.

Unfortunately, in a system that rewards banality above all, those who have the most to say are always left out. As if sneaked in, only in exceptional cases can we experience the beautiful vision of our original perspective and share the pleasure of our empathy and reflection on the screens of the world in which we live.

Frederick Luis Aldama's sharp eye in this book penetrates into the universe of Mexican cinematography. Beyond the criticism and the objective and subjective evaluations of films made since the beginning of this millennium, Aldama puts in our view those roads that should be explored in order to make a national cinema more identified with its people and more coherent with its history.

Carlos Salcés is a filmmaker living in Mexico City.

Preface and Acknowledgments

I wrote this book after years of teaching contemporary Mexican cinema, and by "contemporary" I really mean contemporary: Mexican films made mostly in the first decade of the twenty-first century. This focus required me to grow the course in organic syncopation with films newly scripted, shot, spliced, or released. There is something strongly compelling and kinetic about working with the new, and I hope this book conveys the same urgency.

My interest in contemporary Mexican cinema, or Mex-ciné, focuses on three key areas: the industry as an industry, the constructedness of films, and viewers' reception of the finished works. The first area comprises issues of production, distribution, and exhibition histories, as well as conventions of Mexican film storytelling within global cinematic traditions and prototypical patterns. The second encompasses ingredients or elements such as lens type, camera placement, lighting, scene composition, actor/character look and type, costuming, motion, and editing. All films are made according to recipes, algorithms, or blueprints made up of such ingredients, and I find that the tools and concepts of film theory help me understand how the elements of such blueprints work individually and collectively. Moreover, the concept of the blueprint here aims to capture not only all the ingredients that make up the film—from technical devices and structures used to plots, events, and character dialogue and action—but also to convey the sense that all these elements that make up a film are not the result of a single entity. While a filmmaker may have a greater and lesser degree of willfulness involved in the way the elements cohere, the total product is the result of many skilled people: from producers to cinematographers and editors, from light engineers to costume and sound designers, from set and location designers to casting agents and actors, and many many more.

Of course, the ways in which directors—along with the many involved in the filmmaking process—orchestrate lighting, editing, sound, camera position, and the like when drawing up these blueprints also work to guide their ideal audiences' thoughts, emotions, and interpretations. This leads to my third interest, the consideration of the cognitive and emotive faculties involved in making and consuming such blueprints. Useful tools in this regard include advances in the cognitive and social neurosciences that deepen our understanding of human memory, emotion, perception, thought, and language. I am especially interested in the way this knowledge helps us to understand the choices made in creating Mex-ciné blueprints, to assess their effectiveness, and to see how this improved understanding can shed light on other aspects of the filmmaking and consuming experience.

I am interested, that is, in the mental faculties directors use to imagine and then (through their choices of actors, sounds, lenses, edits, styles, and genres) make a film that will in turn be processed visually and aurally by the ideal audience in ways that trigger specific thoughts and feelings. Here neuroscience and cognitive science have much to teach us about the workings of our faculties of counterfactual thinking, memory, perception, and emotion.

My approach, then, centers on the means that directors use to imagine and then make a film with the goal of triggering specific thoughts and feelings in viewers when they process the film visually and aurally. Findings from cognitive science and neuroscience provide ancillary tools for understanding this process globally, as a unitary whole resulting from the use of our faculties of causal inference, memory, perception, and emotion.

With paths carved by the likes of David Bordwell and Noël Carroll, who long ago began cutting against various psychoanalytic flora and fauna of earlier decades, and with new technologies available for research in the brain sciences (e.g., functional magnetic resonance imaging [fMRI], which allows research on active brains, such as those of subjects watching film sequences), I move with cautious confidence forward in my analysis of Mexican films.

I mention this last point with a certain caution because there is a tendency in current cognitive, neurophysiological, and evolutionary psychological approaches to film analysis to conflate the perceptual, emotive, and cognitive processes of living, breathing directors and audiences with the fictional constructs in the blueprint. As I've written elsewhere, film (like literature, comics, video games, etc.) is not real life, and filmic characters are not the same ontological beast as real events and people.

Yes, research showing how human emotions and cognition work can help explain how we *make* and *consume* films, but we ought not extrapolate the findings to fictional constructs as if they were real, autonomous beings.

Characters in cinema are realized by actors carefully directed to *act* in ways that may elicit "preordained" feelings and thoughts in audiences. In fictional cinema (but not nonfiction films), any theory of mind (the intersubject attribution of intentions or other mental states based on, say, others' facial expressions, body language, or movements) results from a carefully calibrated *representation*. Such attributions are scripted events in fictional cinema, an occurrence that takes place at a precise moment and in a specific way as part of a previously willed series of related events that form the script.

Fiction in any of its guises and means of expression is a materialization of a goal (an end or purpose) previously conceived by a human brain. In other words, fiction results from intention; it is a mental construct first and a material result later. But fiction is not only that. It is not a mirror reflection of reality, not a copy or an imitation (or a simulacrum) of anything in the real world. Fiction is only and exclusively an invented reality. Indeed, in a world made of lawlike processes and structures stretching from the inorganic, through the organic, to the social, humans *create* fictions by using their knowledge of causality and their capacities for imagining different effects or causal results by mentally projecting outcomes. Mario Vargas Llosa and other writers have termed this activity a form of deicide, a replacement of God, for to create fiction is to create something new, an addition to the world, not its replica. Admittedly, the building blocks of fiction, no matter how fantastic and strange, are always taken from the real world, but the result is nonetheless a new world where the criteria of true or false do not apply, for in this new (invented, fictional) world, "anything goes" as long as its creator (its author) wishes it so.

As a result of this carefully maintained distinction between reality and fiction, I restrict my use of scientific findings to the real world, the one inhabited by directors, scriptwriters, editors, cinematographers, and audiences, and I try to avoid the categorical (and ontological) mistake of conflating fictional events and characters with real-life events and people. On a popular view of the matter, in any event, a scientific theory is true only if the entities and events it posits exist. In a cinematic work of fiction, all events and entities are constructs; everything is posited as a product of the imagination, an imaginary narrative or story. Far from being an imitation or a reflection of the world, fiction in all its guises brings to the world a radically and qualitatively (and ontologically) new reality.

This book aims to make visible the twenty-first-century Mexican film industry, its blueprints, and the cognitive and emotive faculties involved in making and consuming its corpus. It aims to enrich our understanding of the way contemporary Mexican directors use specific technical devices, structures, and characterizations in making films—from script to image to reel images—in ways that guide the perceptual, emotive, and cognitive faculties of their ideal audiences. It aims to enrich our understanding of the historical contexts and industry in which these films are made and consumed.

A final point. In the academy, this "making visible" impulse tends to shy away from evaluative criticism. My book does not share that tendency. To analyze the variety of Mexican filmic blueprints is to consider whether they succeed on their own terms. Some do; some do not. I would consider it a job half done if I were to do no more than unpack blueprints; consider issues of production, distribution, and exhibition; and tease out the emotive and cognitive processes involved in the making and consuming. Sleuthing out how a given film is made and how it generates thoughts and feelings in audiences *should* include evaluative criticism, for at every step in any creative work, the author (or director or composer, and so on) must choose between alternatives, and such choices presuppose valuation and therefore values. To show those acts of valuation and to comment on those values is not only a proper but a necessary part of filmic analysis.

Whether we want to admit it or not, for a myriad of reasons, some Mexican films are simply better made than others. Off the cuff, I think of Alfonso Arau's hacked-up and clichéd magical realist structure used in both *Como agua para chocolate/Like Water for Chocolate* (1992) and *Zapata: El sueño del héroe* (2003; Zapata: The dream of a hero) and the overreliance on pop-star actors and corny computer-generated (CG) scenery to carry the weak story in Alejandro Gamboa's *El Tigre de Santa Julia* (2002; The Tiger of Santa Julia).

And while some are well done, they might not appeal to one's particular taste. I'm not a big fan of Arturo Ripstein's theatrically staged historical melodramas, no matter how skillfully they are done. I appreciate his craft in choosing lenses, arranging composition, and directing camera movements to convey the loneliness and hollowness of his characters, but the genre just doesn't do it for me.

Like any of us, then, I have my personal likes and dislikes. As I intend to demonstrate, however, there is taste and there is *taste*—that is, knowing why the blueprint fails. I will thus seek to deploy this latter sort of taste, assessing films not according to my merely personal taste—chocolate more than vanilla, say—but according to the way a given director assembles his or her filmic blueprints and goals to produce a coherent composition that achieves a unity of affect.

That is to say, I have no problem following an interpretive path in and through a given film that leads to understanding why it doesn't work, why we should give it a thumbs down. This is, after all, what we all do one way or another anyway when we watch films. In this sense, then, I hope this book will act not only as a guide to contemporary Mexican films but also as a how-to guide for understanding why some of these products do or do not succeed—and the reasons can be myriad yet still identifiable and verifiable. Unabashedly, this is a book of meditation, interpretation, theory, *and* critical evaluation of contemporary Mexican films.

I have written *Mex-Ciné* in the form of a book-length essay, a format I have found to be more conducive to offering important critical insight into the industry, the creative process, and the consumption and reception of contemporary Mexican film within a global cinema-making context. Subheadings will indicate different moments in the ebb and flow of the discussion, interpretation, analysis, and critical evaluation of the films. They will, for example, signal moves among discussions and analyses of the deep neurophysiological processes involved in making and consuming films, of the auditory and visual ingredients used in making film blueprints, and of issues of distribution and exhibition, as well as trends and conventions of the industry. In this way, I hope both to provide a guide to contemporary Mexican films and to sketch a theoretical approach for analyzing any and all films, any and all forms of storytelling that involve the visual and aural in motion-photographic form.

This book was made possible with support from the Ohio State University's Department of English and its College of Arts and Humanities. I would especially like to thank Associate Dean Dr. Sebastian Knowles for help in securing support for my project. I would also like to thank my acquiring editor at the University of Michigan Press, Tom Dwyer, for seeing the value of this project in an earlier, less integrated incarnation. I am grateful to the director, screenwriter, and former director of Mexico City's FIDECINE (Fondo de Inversión y Estímulos al Cine), Victor Ugalde, for taking the time to discuss the Mexican film industry today and yesterday. I wish to thank all my thoughtful students of Mexican cinema. I send out big *abrazos* to Robert Reyes and Christopher Gonzalez, PhDs at the University of California, Berkeley, and Ohio State University, who keep me on my toes and my mind dizzy with insights and ideas. And a special thanks to Samuel Saldívar at Michigan State University for bringing my attention to the audio bridge function in Mex-ciné and for plumping up the filmography.

Lights, Camera, Action

With a few nods to earlier moments in Mexico's film history, the discussions in the following pages focus entirely on the twenty-first century. In many ways (and journalists have been quick to notice this), the first decade of this century marks a massive rebirthing moment in the making of Mexican films. Some argue that this moment involves not only increased production and distribution but also the emancipation of form and content. With respect to content, such emancipation shows up not just in films that run counter to Catholic ideology, such as Carlos Carrera's *El crimen del padre Amaro/The Crime of Padre Amaro* (2002), but also in the nascent rise of a queer art-house and mainstream Mex-ciné, as exemplified by Rene Bueno's bubblegum *7 mujeres, 1 homosexual y Carlos* (2004; Seven women, one homosexual, and Carlos); Julián Hernández's black-and-white queer odysseys set in Mexico City and rooted in indigenous culture, *El cielo dividido/Broken Sky* (2006), *Rabioso sol, rabioso cielo/Raging Sun, Raging Sky* (2008), and *A Thousand Clouds of Peace* (2002); and Leopoldo Laborde's Buñuel-influenced *Sin destino* (2002; Without destiny).

There are many reasons for this rebirth, and Mexico is not alone in experiencing such a renaissance. Both Argentina and Brazil have enjoyed a filmmaking boom in the twenty-first century, as have other Latin American countries. A report in the February 23, 2009, issue of *Variety* reads, "Powered by government funding and co-production, pic productions and investment tripled over the past decade in Mexico, Argentina and Brazil—to 267 films made with $358.3 million in financing."[1] This boom resulted partly from shifts in the way films have been funded, as well as from pressure on various governments to loosen hitherto tight restrictions on the kinds of films they allowed to be made and exhibited.

I will discuss this boom at greater length later on, but for now it suffices to note that by the mid-1990s the state-funded Instituto Mexicano de Cinematografía (IMCINE, established in 1983), which sponsored the production and distribution of Mexican films, had trimmed its funding of filmmaking from an already slim dozen or so films a year to only five. Under the directorship of Ignacio Durán (1988–94), IMCINE had moved increasingly toward privatization, and it continued to demolish its protections for the industry's workers, from directors, cinematographers, and costume and set designers to carpenters and janitors, leading to a violent standoff between workers and higher-ups in 2003, under the Vicente Fox administration. Filmgoers and filmmakers attending the seventh Morelia International Film Festival, in October 2009, were more than agitated when the director of the El Consejo Nacional para la Cultura y las Artes (Conaculta) declared that the Calderón administration was supportive of the Mexican film industry, claiming that it had doubled the budget for IMCINE.[2]

Despite this tension between the state and the film industry in Mexico, directors have managed not merely to maintain, but even to increase film production. During 2000, for instance, only a handful of films were made. A decade later and we see over a hundred films made. (For a better sense of this upswing trend, see the filmography at the end of this book.) Similarly increasing is the number of films in genres and storytelling forms atypical for Mexican cinema, including animations (e.g., Juan Manuel and Figueroa Vega, *La prepa/The High School* [2006]; Ricardo Arnaiz, *The Legend of Nahuala* [2007], and Gabriel and Rodolfo Riva Palacio Alatriste's *Una película de huevos y un polo/A Movie About Eggs and a Chicken* [2006] and *Otra película de huevos y un pollo/Another Movie About Eggs and a Chicken* [2009]), science fiction (e.g., Carlos Salcés's *Zurdo* [2003] and Alex Rivera's *Sleep Dealer* [2009]), and fantasy or horror (e.g., Guillermo del Toro's *Pan's Labyrinth* [2006]; Andres Navia's *La llorona/The Wailer* [2005], and Rigoberto Castaneda's *KM31: Kilometre 31* [2006]). In sum, the twenty-first century's first decade saw the Mex-ciné film industry begin to rise from its own ashes, producing films for audiences both at home and abroad.

Of course, this and any other justification for my focus are on another level rather arbitrary. To study Mexican cinema of this particular period is to carve a scholarly slice out of reality. My slice does not include Mexicans who make other kinds of cultural objects for consumption, such as literature, sculpture, comic books, and the like. It does not include Mexican American (Chicano) directors working in the United States. It does not include films by Mexican directors from periods before 1999. It *does* include films from today's Mexican directors making films by and about Mexicans. It does include

Mexican directors who live part- or full-time in other countries but continue to make films set in Mexico. (e.g., Alfonso Cuarón lives full-time in Italy, Guillermo del Toro lives full-time in the United States, and González Iñárritu splits his time between Los Angeles and Mexico City). It does include Mexican directors who make films set in other countries.

More specifically, I delimit my territory by asking several questions.

1. What is a Mexican film? What, for that matter, are the ingredients that make up an essential Mexicanness, or *mexicanidad*? Should we buy the definitions offered by Octavio Paz, José Vasconcelos, José Gaos and his disciple Luis Villoro, and Sam Ramos, who variously turn psychological categories into ontological ones, such as an ostensible Mexican fixation on death and an inferiority complex as a bastard (*hijo de la chingada*) race?[3]

2. Does Mexican cinema differ from, say, that of the United States, Brazil, Argentina, Cuba, France, Germany, Britain, or India, and if so, how does it differ?

3. What qualifies a film to be Mexican? Are we to include in the Mexican cinematic canon Alfonso Cuarón's adaptation of *Great Expectations* or Guillermo del Toro's *Hellboy* because the directors are Mexican? Do we include films that star Mexican actors and are set in Mexico but are directed by Spaniards (Luis Buñuel), Britons (Alex Cox), or North Americans (Cary Joji Fukunaga)?

4. How do Mexican audiences differ from, say, audiences in other Latin American countries, North America, and Europe? Do Mexicans respond differently to Mexican films than do U.S. filmgoers?

5. Do some Mexican films have, built into their blueprints, specific cultural and historical information that draws lines between audiences: Mexican mainstream versus Mexican art-house audiences, for example, or non-Mexican mainstream versus non-Mexican art-house audiences? If so, how do we identify the type of ideal audience for any given film? And is it a zero-sum game, that is, does a film aimed at the mainstream necessarily mean it cannot use an art-house style or content, and vice versa?

6. At what point do Mexican films operate on a deeper level of narrative prototypicality? Does a film lose its ideal audience when it includes a high degree of cultural specificity yet follows story structures that are universally recognizable as comic, heroic, or tragic?

7. Do some Mexican movies appeal to non-Mexican audiences more than others do? If so, how and what kind of audience—mainstream or art-house?

These are the kinds of questions I ask when slicing reality to identify this entity called contemporary Mexican cinema.

I acknowledge the artificiality of these questions. After all, I am cutting a slice out of a much larger pie, one that is global in scope. This is a scholarly slice—and we will learn much about what constitutes this slice—but a slice always seen as a part of a larger, planetary whole. This is why, even as I carve out my particular piece, I pay attention not just to the way Mexican cinema is always idiosyncratic and particular (a specific expression of faculties used to imagine and create an aesthetic form in time and place) but also to the way it is a particularized expression of our universal capacity to think, feel, and symbolically represent our experiences in our one world.

Other Ways to Slice

I am by no means the first to characterize Mexican cinema. Other scholars writing in both Spanish and English have been doing this for quite some time. Each of these scholars has used specific criteria for defining the contours of Mexican cinema, and, although the criteria differ, they often overlap. I'm including a sample (available to English-reading audiences) of like-minded approaches to sketch the lay of the scholarly land.

Some scholars try to construct the genre of Mexican cinema around Mexican film archives and contemporary canons. Paulo Antonio Paranaguá, for example, seeks to archive the Mexican cinema of yesterday; in his edited volume *Mexican Cinema*,[4] he offers a series of critical film histories of early Mexican cinema, from the early sound cinema to the studio system and the ever-popular genre *comedia ranchera*.

The archivist Rogelio Agrasánchez Jr. examines the distribution, exhibition, and reception of Mexican films across the northern border in *Mexican Movies in the United States: A History of the Films, Theaters, and Audiences, 1920–1960*.[5] By 1951 there were 683 screens (100 in Texas alone) in 443 U.S. cities playing Spanish-language films. Agrasánchez discusses how these establishments included venues designed as theaters, as well as those converted to the purpose, with some devoted exclusively to Spanish-language entertainment and others integrating Mexican films into their programs with varying frequencies; how Spanish-language films in the United States fostered both ethnic pride (in most cases, a sense of *mexicanidad*) and "Americanization"; and how many theaters offered hybrid programs, with Mexican films sharing their screens with Hollywood features. Doyle Greene's *Mexploitation Cinema* attends to the way shifts in the industry and Mexican filmgoing culture generated a flood of *luchador* (masked wrestler) films with no aesthetic pretense.[6]

Jason Wood's *The Faber Book of Mexican Cinema* and *Talking Movies: Contemporary World Filmmakers in Interview,*[7] as well as Jethro Soutar's *Gael García Bernal and the Latin American New Wave,*[8] focus on today's Mexican film industry and canon in various ways. Soutar writes, for instance, that "recounting the tale of Gael García Bernal introduces and encourages the telling of the Latin American New Wave. . . . It also charts the course of the twenty-first century's first major film movement and puts it in its historical and cultural context."[9]

In *Splendors of Latin Cinema,* R. Hernandez-Rodriguez engages the film traditions that make up the cinema of Latin America generally and Mexico specifically. For Hernandez-Rodriguez, this is especially important today with the "emergence of a new, exciting, more sophisticated cinema."[10] And Paul Julian Smith's regular contributions to film journals, as well as his book-length study of *Amores perros,* focus on contemporary Mexican cinema. In the prologue to his book *Amores Perros* he states, "A place of extreme contrasts, Mexico City is also a prize location for a cinema of extremes."[11]

Some scholars who pursue a Mexican film archive see it as tied directly to political or historical contexts. These scholars tend to link periods of Mexican filmmaking to the policies of particular administrations and their cycles of six-year (*sexenio*) terms, as well as to trade and tax policies and nation-state agendas generally.

In *Magical Reels,* John King uses a big brush to paint a portrait of the way in which historical, economic, and political shifts controlled the ebb and flow of Mexican films made from the 1940s through the 1980s.[12] In *Mexican Cinema: Reflections of a Society, 1896–2004,* Carl J. Mora reconstructs, for instance, how the 1990s North American Trade Agreement (NAFTA) trade and tax policies pulled the rug out from under Mexican filmmakers by declaring state-funded support to be an unfair trade practice.[13] For Mora, this dammed the flow of monetary support for Mexican filmmakers from such state-funded mainstays as IMCINE, the National Film School, the Center for Cinematic Preparation, and Estudios Churubusco Azteca, a film studio and lab that the RKO studio built in the 1940s. In "Developing History/Historicizing Development in Mexican *Nuevo Cine* Manifestoes around '*la Crisis,*'" Scott L. Baugh links Mexican film with a sociopolitical epoch in his analysis of the 1960s Nuevo Cine Group's manifesto.[14] In "The French New Wave," Timothy Dugdale links Mexican film to a given sociopolitical moment in his analysis of *Y tu mamá también,* interpreting, for instance, the movement of Julio and Tenoch from city to countryside as representa-tive of "the larger existential crisis of national 'development' in a globalised economy."[15] According to Dugdale, when the Oaxacan countryside "resists development" and "confounds the fetish of development,"[16] at the same time its presence infiltrates and destroys the lives of the two friends.

Other scholars focus on representations in Mexican cinema that reflect (critically or otherwise) the social, political, and national issues of Mexico. Such scholarship clusters around issues like modernity, the legacy of the Mexican Revolution, indigeneity, masculinity, and patriarchy, as well as the U.S.-Mexico border, as does Andrea Noble (e.g., in *Mexican National Cinema*).[17] Sergio de la Mora questions essentialist notions of a macho and patriarchal *mexicanidad* by attending to the queer and feminist representations in Mexico's so-called Golden Age films. In *Cinemachismo* de la Mora argues that the highly sexualized and macho identities circulated during the Golden Age (1940s–50s) both inform a national cultural identity and offer a parodic critique of an essentialist *mexicanidad.*[18]

Miriam Haddu explores how Carlos Salinas de Gortari's six-year term opened doors (wittingly or not) for Mexican directors to represent "the concerns, issues, politics, hopes, and fears of the Mexican people in an era of transition."[19] According to Haddu, films such as Cuarón's *Sólo con tu pareja* (1991), Jorge Fons's *Rojo amanecer* (1989), Gabriel Retes's *El bulto* (1991), and Luis Estrada's *La ley de Herodes* (1999) reflect a Mexican film industry searching for a "visual identity and for the country's reassertion of a sense of hybrid national and post-colonial identity."[20]

In *Women Filmmakers in Mexico,* Elissa J. Rashkin attends to more feminist-oriented films created by Mexican women directors. For Rashkin, Mexicana filmmakers critically engage with a patriarchal-based *mexicanidad* by making films that demand "the transformation of the existing nation into one which not only permits but actually emerges from the diverse subject positions of its constituent populations—women, religious minorities, social and sexual dissidents, indigenous peoples, the urban poor."[21] (In one way or another, this scholarship aims to identify *otro cinema* that challenges stereotypes and clears, as Rashkin nicely sums up of her own goals, "a space of collective identification."[22])

In *Cinema of Solitude,* Charles Ramírez Berg traces a shift in national identity. He argues that contemporary Mexican cinema moved away from an identity based on a sense of *mexicanidad* as being in crisis and caught between "Old World roots and New World locations."[23] Armed with this new vision, directors no longer represent virginal women as being out of time and place or *indios* as being pure repositories of a past frozen in time; rather, they put complex women at center stage and complicate the representation of *indios*.[24]

Scholars have also analyzed and critiqued representational trends. In *Latino Images* Charles Ramírez Berg, for instance, points to a tradition in Mexican (and Mexico-based) cinema that dates back to Serge Eisenstein (*¡Que Viva México!*), followed by Emilio "El Indio" Fernández and Gabriel Figueroa, wherein the image of the *indio* mirrors Mexico's (postrevolution) official administrative policies: culturally affirming the presence of *indios* while instituting economic, education, and health care policies that have led to their annihilation.[25]

In *Mexico City in Contemporary Mexican Cinema*, David William Foster looks at fourteen Mexican films and how they create an opposition between the urban (Mexico City) and the rural. While many Mexican films set in rural areas implicitly critique a fragmented and alienating Mexico City, Foster contends that these films simultaneously reinforce representations of the rural as primitive.[26]

In a like vein, Emily Hind sets into high critical relief the ongoing urban versus rural (*provincia*) thematic in Mexican films. Many Mexican films set their stories in the rural provinces, where transgression of social, gender, and racial hierarchies takes place. For Hind the rural functions as a space that "facilitates social freedom."[27] For instance, in her reading of María Novaro's *Lola* (1989), Hind locates much of the violence and stifling gender and generational hierarchies in Mexico City and considers *provincia* to be the place of gender and generational empowerment and emancipation. Like Berg, Hind tempers her affirmative reading of the representation of *provincia,* carefully analyzing how it functions to romanticize the countryside and its people. While Mexican films do sometimes portray the countryside as a place to escape from class- and gender-inflected struggles, it also functions as a place for Mexican, middle-class, urban characters (and filmgoing audiences) to experience a transgressive thrill.

Among scholars of Mexican and Latin American cinema generally, some seek to identify the uniqueness of a given film tradition marked by cultural, historical, and national particularities. For example, Freya Schiwy identifies "a cultural politics of decolonization" at work in Quechua, Zapotec, and Moxeña film productions.[28] She considers how indigenous filmmaking (funded by the multiethnic Organization of Indigenous Audiovisual Communicators in Bolivia) stands against mainstream and art-house films, such as those by Alejandro González Iñárritu, Hector Babenco, and Walter Salles. Such scholars approach "indigenous" film production (making and worldview) as important repositories of cultural memory and knowledge.

Some scholars seek to trouble claims of a unique content informing Mexican cinema. These scholars go against the grain of earlier scholarship, which sought to identify a Mexicanness in opposition to the U.S. mainstream film industry and instead look for common ground. For instance, Laura Podalsky complicates our understanding of the way Mexican films do or do not create a *mexicanidad*. She thus demonstrates that, while at first blush González Iñárritu's *Amores perros* may appear to convey a contemporary Mexicanness, a closer inspection reveals how it expresses a U.S.-identified neoliberal ideology; resting on an ideology less Mexican revolutionary than U.S. imperialist, the film does little to disrupt and disturb audiences comfortably ensconced in a middle-class complacency.[29]

In a book focused on a single director, *Alejandro González Iñárritu,* Celestino Deleyto and María del Mar Azcona "interrogate the validity of the concept of Mexican national cinema and explore the extent to which the texts originate from and illuminate the extremely porous nature of that concept."[30] Along with examining González Iñárritu, they mention Alfonso Cuarón and Guillermo del Toro as directors who redefine the concept of *mexicanidad* in their films, all of which appeal to "local spectators," as well as an "international audience."[31]

A number of scholars who locate Mexican films within the global explore the circuits of production and distribution of Mexican films as a particularized expression of world cinema. For instance, Paul Julian Smith traces the global economic links formed between Mexico and Spain both in production (Altavista and Anhelo, respectively) and in the casting of Spanish actors and actresses in Mexican films.[32] In *Screening World Cinema,* Catherine Grant and Annette Kuhn discuss the importance of identifying Mexican cinema, or "Third World cinema" more generally, *not* according to geopolitical boundaries but rather in terms of a continuum between mainstream and experimental alternative film.[33]

The Nuts and Bolts of
Mexican Film

Like all cinematic narrative, Mexican films are first and foremost built of movement: of objects and characters within the frame, of the camera focus and angle, and in the juxtaposition of shots. More precisely, it is a double-structured ordering of movement (within the frame and in its composition) that allows Mexican filmmakers to reorganize the building blocks of reality (and experience within this reality) in an infinite number of ways to engage viewers. Such devices are used to create meaning and stir emotion in us, sometimes harshly so, as with sonic blasts or radically surprising image juxtapositions.

Like all film narrative, Mexican films operate according to a double chronology: the time of the thing told (story events, characters, and so on) and the time of the telling (devices used to arrange and rearrange elements of the story so as to stretch or shrink story time and story space). Another way to think of this is to consider how a director uses elements and structures to modify the chronology of the represented world in ways that trigger thoughts, feelings, moods, and possibly new perspectives on the world in his or her audiences. In this sense, then, Mexican films that do engage audiences do so less at the level of the story than at the level of the manner in which the story is filmed.

The camera-narrator (or discourse level) determines the order in which the audience receives the narrative events, characters, and so on contained within the story. The typical manipulation of temporal order arises in flashback (looking back, or analepsis), flash-forward (anticipation, or prolepsis), and combinations of the two, as in a flash-forward within an extended flashback and vice versa. Of course all this pushes against the narrative's natural movement forward in time. This is why Seymour Chatman argues that true description (which entails a pause in the temporal flow of the narrative) is

9

not possible in a storytelling medium such as film, which necessarily reels forward in time.[1] In this sense, films cannot describe. They show and present.

However, not all is lost. The double-structured ordering, together with filmic devices, allows directors to manipulate their stories in ways that project an illusion of slowing down or speeding up time (and expanding or shrinking space) in a physical medium that is by technological necessity always moving forward in time, illusions Alejandro González Iñárritu uses in *Amores perros* and Carlos Reygadas employs in *Japón* and his follow-up films.

The combination of both the story (content) and the way this content is presented visually and aurally by way of editing, lensing, sound recording and mixing, and the like gives a film its distinctive audiovisual style. Some directors, such as Reygadas, play with this expectation of forward movement by repeatedly reprinting a frame so that it plays out over time. This gives the effect of separating that particular image from the rest of the moving images and the illusion that we are viewing a photographic still. This is just an illusion, however. The film hasn't stopped moving forward in time.

Of course today we can hit the pause button and impose a static image on this necessarily forward moving series of images. But this is physically imposed after the fact, not an inherent possibility in the technology of the forward-moving media.

Mexican film directors recognize that this storytelling medium operates at its most fundamental level on the possibilities offered by this double chronology. They also know that it is not the same as a ballet or theater production, a painting, a comic book, or a novel. This is not to say that directors don't employ techniques from these other aesthetic forms. They do. Arturo Ripstein uses his camera in a way that makes his motion photography feel staged and theatrically mannered. And at certain moments in *Amar te duele* (2002; Loving you hurts) Fernando Sariñana cuts in sequences that move the story forward through comic-book panel grids and graphics.

Different media use different (albeit sometimes overlapping) devices and structures. Thus, directors realize that, for instance, the use of a voice-over to present an omniscient third-person narrator or a narrator who is also a character in the story offers only a pale imitation of such narrators in novels or short stories. They are aware that the careful direction of a character's intentional movement within a scene can lead us to infer an interiority of mind, and that this is not the same movement we see choreographed in ballet. They understand that in film a series of reels of stitched-together stills necessarily moves the images forward sequentially and temporally without pause. They understand that the final, edited product will be run across a light in a cinema to project the illusion of a three-dimensional storyworld space.

In *Cinematic Storytelling* Jennifer Van Sijll succinctly states, "A well-crafted film uses everything to contribute to story."[2] In fact one might argue that the stories generally are finite in number and rather typical in plot features (e.g., epic, tragic, or comic). Indeed, a viewer's interest is captured not so much by the story per se as by the way the story is told. This includes the director's decisions about camera placement, lighting, composition, motion, editing, and sound to shape and give texture and rhythm to the story's plot, actions, and characters. Of course, whether the film is a romance, epic, tragedy, or comedy, or any hybrid combination of these, it helps to have a good script, but this means not just one that tells a good tale but also one that is written for the medium of film, with its palette of audiovisual techniques clearly in mind.

We experience any given Mexican film as a gestalt of story and form. When the script suffers, so, too, does the film; similarly, when the form suffers, so, too, does the story. A lack of coherence in the use of film devices and structure damages the film as a whole. Likewise, however good the director, a bad cinematographer, one lacking imagination and skill, can seriously harm the film; however good the director and the cinematographer, a bad editor can similarly wreak havoc.

Whereas these three entities play key roles in the making of any film, the screenwriter can be deeply involved in the process or completely separate from it. In either case, however, the script provides a constant reference for the director, cinematographer, and editor; even when they don't adhere to it, the script is there, and we can say, no, they did not follow the script but instead decided to do something different. For a case in point, consider the very public and angry breakup between screenwriter Guillermo Arriaga and director González Iñárritu over artistic differences and script interpretation, a team otherwise intricately entangled in the making of *Amores perros, 21 Grams,* and *Babel.*

Anatomies

While infinite in their combination, the devices, structures, and concepts key to a film's blueprint may be organized according to a sort of periodic table.

Screen Direction

In one of the ten vignettes that make up the omnibus film *Revolución* (2010), we can see director Rodrigo García's extensive use of screen direction. (In the United States, García is known for directing episodes of the HBO series

Six Feet Under and *In Treatment,* as well as the feature films *Things You Can Tell Just by Looking at Her* and *Mother and Child.*) Included in *Revolución* is García's short film *7th Street and Alvarado.* The film shows us how a careful use of movement within the shot and across sequences creates meaning and conflict. In one scene, pedestrians are going about their daily activities in a present-day Latino barrio of Los Angeles, moving mostly from screen left to screen right. Superimposed in the foreground appear exhausted men and women of the Mexican Revolution. They are walking systematically from the right to the left of the screen. Quite apart from other issues of time and space (the movement of the people and horses happens in its own space, floating in front of a present with its own spatial markers) and of the way an audience might create meaning from this juxtaposition, we can see how the blueprint works to create a tension between movement along the horizontal of the screen: conventionally, protagonists enter and move through the screen from left to right, while antagonists usually enter from the right and move toward the left. (Some argue that eyes move more comfortably from left to right for a variety of reasons, especially in countries where reading follows this directionality.)

In the careful orchestration of simultaneous movement and countermovement, García introduces two elements that, according to cinematographic convention and viewing expectation, should reflect some type of conflict between antagonist and protagonist. This doesn't happen here. García's two opposing movements—all in slow motion—create a sense of simultaneous, though discomfiting, flow. We are never told this, but we know and feel García's message: history lives with us, uncomfortably.

Frame Composition

To give the sense of distinct times to the activities of today's East Los Angeles denizens beneath the superimposed times of the early-twentieth-century revolutionaries and people weary from battle, García chooses distinct shapes (buildings, animals, people); slow pans; medium-long shots; natural lighting; and luscious blue, green, yellow, red, and brown colors (shot on rich color stock). He also slows the motion speed and creates counterdirectional movement that never collides. He uses a specific technique of movement direction to convey a message about history's inescapable presence in our lives and, as well, to elicit empathetic feelings (e.g., for the hardships of those who fought for freedoms enjoyed today) and an overall somber, sobering mood.

Other directors, such as Patricia Riggen, prefer to play it safer, using

Fig. 1. Revolución: 7th Street and Alvarado

framing composition (shape, lighting, color, motion) to make the viewing experience absolutely comfortable and comforting. We see this in her feature film *La misma luna/Under the Same Moon* (2007) and in her short film *Lindo y querido* (Beautiful and beloved), also in *Revolución*. In the latter film, concerning a dead father's repatriation to Mexico for burial, she uses conventional framing composition to convey the meaning of the story. The scenes shot in the United States depict a militaristic nationalism (U.S. flags, coffins with military jets, decals, and the like). Vibrant colors and traditional music fill the scenes in Mexico, depicting a community of people who share stories that value history and the many people who make history. It ends with a series of shots—a medium close-up of a daughter holding the dirt where her father is buried and then a pan out and fade—that show the community gathered together. "All we need is another revolution; that's what your grandfather would say," one octogenarian tells the daughter as the film fades out to its end.

Editing

Mexican filmmakers use editing either to hide a film's constructedness in representing, reframing, and reorganizing reality or to call attention to the constructedness of this (*re*)presentation of reality. In this respect, most directors resemble Patricia Riggen, who, as she does in her previously mentioned vignette and her *La misma luna*, uses conventions of editing to create the illusion of reality unfolding before our eyes. Others, such as Julián Hernández, use a self-reflexive montage approach in their editing. And a few, including Alfonso Cuarón and Fernando Sariñana, occasionally employ both techniques across their oeuvre. In all cases, however, editing involves purposefully constructing scenes by assembling shots in specific ways meant to guide viewers to the ideal audience's cognitive and emotive response.

This is not news. In 1926 Russian director Vsevolod Pudovkin identified editing as "one of the most significant instruments of effect possessed by the film technician and, therefore, by the scenarist also."[3] Given the clarity and precision of Pudovkin's observation, let me quote him at length here. The significance of editing, he continues, is that it "builds the scenes from separate pieces, of which each concentrates the attention of the spectator only on that element important to the action. The sequence of these pieces must not be uncontrolled, but must correspond to the natural transference of attention of an imaginary observer (who, in the end, is represented by the spectator)."[4] Conversely, he remarks, "If the editing be merely an uncontrolled combination of the various pieces, the spectator will understand (apprehend) nothing from it; but if it be co-orientated according to a definitely selected course of events or conceptual line, either agitated or calm, it will either excite or soothe the spectator."[5] For Pudovkin, then, careful editing is not simply splicing together shots but rather a tool the director uses for the "psychological guidance' of the spectator."[6]

Skilled Mexican filmmakers are intuitively aware that the art of cinema is the *art* of movement: (a) within the story frame there is movement in the form of shifts in states of mind and emotion, as well as physical action and motion speed and direction; and (b) at the level of the storytelling device and structure there is movement created by the edits, camera motion, and camera lensing. One of Pudovkin's contemporaries, Viktor Shklovsky, declared this, too, early in the history of film. A year before Pudovkin penned the words just quoted, Shklovsky wrote that "the primary raw material of cinema is not the filmed object but a certain method of filming it."[7] More recently, Colin McGinn has run home the foundational points made by Pudovkin and Shklovsky, stating that "movie art is largely the science of converting feeling into action, making movement the bearer of emotion."[8]

More specifically, Mexican filmmakers use editing (along with other elements I mention later) to convert feeling into action and make movement the bearer of emotion in ways that conform on a basic level to perceptual and psychological laws. Even the movement created by sharply juxtaposing images—the montage in Hernández, for instance, or even more radically that of the old-schooler Alejandro Jodorowsky—is usually not so radical as to be perceptually and psychologically intolerable and incomprehensible. If there were no sense to the montage—self-reflexive or not in aim—then we would simply lose interest; we would go elsewhere to fulfill our perceptual and psychological needs.

Fernando Eimbcke is a director who uses editing both to seamlessly present his storyworlds and to stretch time. We see this in his movie *Temporada de patos/Duck Season* (2004); his more behaviorist films, such as *Lake Tahoe* (2008); and his vignette *La bienvenida* (The welcoming) in *Revolución*. In the ten-minute vignette, for instance, which depicts twenty-four hours in the life of Armancio (Ansberto Flores López), a series of shots that average ten to twenty seconds separated by fades tells us nothing of his motivations but much about his life: after feeding his newborn, Armancio practices his tuba by a kerosene lamp. Fade in: daylight. He washes himself from a bucket of water and leaves the infant with a grandmother figure; dressed in a clean white shirt and black pants, he walks with tuba in hand to join the town's band. In all, the film's composition conveys the sense that he takes his tuba playing seriously.

Eimbcke's use of long takes, along with a series of well-timed fades, works to create a pace and rhythm that conveys the passage of time (day to night, then night to day, and then morning to afternoon). The pacing captures the tempo of life for the villagers of San Felipe Otlaltepec, and does so without sentimentality. The band awaits the arrival of some dignitaries. Cuts between shots of band members doing other things while waiting, such as reading the paper and combing their hair, are crafted with a precision of psychological guidance in mind. We sense the disappointment when the dignitaries fail to arrive, but they are not incensed by it. The camera, editing, lighting, and natural sounds convey a sense of a tempered response to the letdown. The cows moo, horses whinny, and Armancio continues to practice his tuba. Life goes on.

Carlos Reygadas uses editing to stretch and shrink time in his short film *Este es mi reino* (This is my kingdom), yet another segment of *Revolución*. The latter effect is especially pronounced in the construction of scenes that lead to the film's denouement. The quick succession of shots creates a mosaic effect that intensifies the action within the sequence. It creates frenetic energy and a sense of chaos. A few minutes into the film, Reygadas introduces a series of sudden jump cuts to depict kids jumping on a random wrecked car in a field, people burping, a man dedicating a poem to consciousness and ancestral roots, grown-ups throwing a bench at a car window, and a man peeing, among other actions. Reygadas introduces to these feverish sequences a cacophony of tuba and drum noises within the diegesis. Speaking in Spanish, a figure announces, "It's dangerous here. The police never come and never have been here"; at the same time, a woman declares in English, "They don't need disorder; they need *you* to tell *them*." But the audience already feels this. The images and sounds chosen convey a story wherein the countryside is anything but inert and knowable.

Of course, Reygadas's rather open-ended blueprint leaves many gaps to fill. This is a Reygadas trademark. All his filmic blueprints lack a sense of motivation on the part of the character (behaviorist), and his editing and other elements only very loosely guide the audience's meaning-making processes.

Mexican film directors are keenly aware of the way visual images can be cut to match one another or not. In the case of Reygadas's *Kingdom,* the film's effect of devolving into pandemonium is reinforced by images that do not match in terms of content, graphics, shape, motion, size, and color. The sounds of the tuba and drum function as an audio bridge that allows the audience to mentally glue together disparate images. That said, even this audio bridge is cacophonous. That is, Reygadas and similar directors (say, his disciple Amat Escalante) want to make audiences feel uncomfortable, even deeply uncomfortable.

For the most part, however, Reygadas and Escalante are exceptions. Most Mexican film directors (even of the art-house variety) use visual match cuts and audio bridges to create the illusion of action taking place seamlessly. These directors want us to derive our meaning and feeling from elsewhere in the blueprint, carefully controlling and directing matters to ensure that we do so.

Camera

Viewers typically do not notice a director's choice of medium (e.g., film vs. digital video), camera (e.g., 35 mm vs. 16 mm or Steadicam vs. handheld), camera movement (tracking and pan shots, say, or fixed vs. moving), and lens (conventional vs. wide-angle or telephoto). But these constitute important ingredients in directing audiences' meaning-making and feeling processes.

In his short film *Padre Nicolas Hung* (yet another segment of *Revolución*), Amat Escalante uses several kinds of camera movement and lensing to convey meaning in a story that has almost no dialogue. We do have a vague sense of the *because* that gives a vague indication of the plot: two children riding a donkey come across a priest hanging by his feet from a tree, with the burned carcass of a horse nearby. The boy tells the priest that "they" came to the farm and took all the grown-ups. The rest of the film's meaning is carried largely by the technical elements of the editing, camera movement, sound, and lensing. We get the deep sense of the characters' alienation and feelings of being lost and forsaken as the children and the priest travel through an arid landscape. The editing conveys shifts in time and place—they come across water and eventually a city—and the use of different lenses intensifies different moments of their journey. As they come close to dying from dehydration but continue to walk, Escalante uses a telephoto lens, its shallow depth of field compressing space; we see them walking toward us but seemingly not moving. Their motion is slowed to a near total stasis even though we know they are moving forward. Suspense is heightened. Will they make it, or will they die in the desert?

In the last series of shots, Escalante uses a wide-angle lens to speed up the motion within the frame. In this sequence, the priest is walking and the boy is carrying the little girl slumped on his back as they come to a freeway at the outskirts of a city. The wide-angle lens's depth of focus allows us to see simultaneously the outline of the city buildings, the children in the foreground, and the priest in the middle ground. Body language conveys how each character reacts to this moment. For the final shot, Escalante uses a long shot to show them walking into a McDonald's restaurant. The careful use of lens and mise-en-scène intensifies the experience of isolation and alienation: first, with the journey across the desert; and, second, with their diminutive status, a fragile state within a city of freeways and imperialist golden arches.

Lighting

Like all their peers, Mexican film directors know that lighting can convey meaning; its consistent use in a given film can help generate an overall mood. In *Padre Nicolas Hung,* Escalante operates as we might expect him to do. In the desert scenes he uses a wide aperture, allowing more light to enter the lens (overexposure) to intensify our sense of the brittle and dry landscape. The cinematographer Rodrigo Prieto (the director of photography, or DP, for González Iñárritu's films) used the technique of bleach bypass on the film negative to desaturate certain hues (e.g., in skin tones) and enhance other hues, such as reds and blues, to give *Amores perros* an imperfect look and (because light contrasts and shadows diminish) to compress foreground, middle ground, and background, adding to a sense of chaos and urgency. (He uses this technique in *21 Grams,* too, as well as in the story thread in *Babel* focused on Mexico.)

For *Sin nombre/Without a Name* (2009), Cary Fukunaga's DP, Adriano Goldman, chose to use just the lights found in working railroads; he used reflectors (bounce boards) to deflect and bounce the available light off objects and throw it toward the actors. Both Fukunaga and Goldman understand how light and shadow can intensify our sense of the anxiety and danger characters experience while awaiting the right moment to climb atop boxcars for an imperiled journey north to the United States. The move from a crane shot to a long shot on the ground, the foreboding sound of guards' whistles and the noise of the train's engine, and jolting movement—all intensify these emotions. These elements also mark this moment as pivotal in the story, for it is the beginning of Sayra's (Paulina Gaitan) dangerous journey through Mexico to the United States.

Locations

As I suggested with Escalante's short film, shot mostly in the desert, location, too, can convey meaning and emotion (short in duration) and mood (long in duration). And, although an audience might not know this, the choice of location is often so determinative of a film's meaning and mood that a director will sometimes create (via physical sets or special effects) an artificial location or find another natural location that better conveys the sense of place than the *actual* place does. The sequences in *Sin nombre* that the script and film identify as occurring in Honduras (Remedios) and Chiapas (Tapachula, southern Mexico) were actually shot in and around Mexico City. While cost and danger (Tapachula's train yard is infamously perilous) were motivations for filming in Mexico City, Fukunaga's location team did not find just any place to film. They worked to discover locations that would look like Remedios and Tapachula. (The final sequence is a crane shot of Sayra walking across a parking lot at a Sam's Club and Wal-Mart. This is portrayed as the United States in the film, but it was actually filmed in Mexico City.)

Location is one thing, but the objects and people within the location must cohere with it. Fukunaga had his professional Mexican actors work hard to learn the working-class accents of these regions. In this case we can see how the careful planning of location and elements associated with that location (whether genuine or ersatz), including the regional accent of characters, work together to take viewers to places they may never have been and pull them into a coherent story that leads them to invest emotionally in its characters and their journey.

Some directors, such as Alfonso Cuarón, use carefully chosen objects tied to a location to evoke an interface with other times and spaces. While *Children of Men* (2006) is set in the near future (2027), the objects Cuarón chooses to fill his locations—from homes of the wealthy to refugee camps—create a palimpsest of time and space: the audience is directed to overlay the locations in the film with those of Abu Ghraib, for instance.

Implied Director

The elements that make up a blueprint generate in us an image of a grand conductor, a master of ceremonies of film devices. These add up to our sense of an implied director's worldview.

In *Narration in the Fiction Film,* David Bordwell declares that we are well served by talking about film as "the organization of a set of cues for the construction of a story. To this we might add the useful concept of the implied director or implied creator."[9] The concept has prompted a great deal of debate, but I consider the implied director to be a useful notion. When we go to the movies, we do get a sense of an entity orchestrating all the parts to make the whole.

Of course we feel this presence to a greater or lesser degree. Many, though not all, of the bubblegum (sweet and easily chewed, but with no sustenance) and *refrito* (refried and rehashed) films I talk about later only weakly suggest the presence of an implied director—though the same can be said about some of those we might classify as art-house films. Nonetheless, many Mexican films evoke this presence powerfully. In Fukunaga's *Sin nombre,* for instance, we grow a strong sense of an intention behind the story's internal coherence and overall audiovisual aesthetic.

When we watch a Mexican film (or any film, for that matter), our minds give shape to this implied director, an entity who uses the devices of lighting, lenses, locations, and the like in ways that not only shape the story but convey a worldview, an evaluative stance regarding the world and its machinations. If the implied director takes shape in viewers' minds and does so in ways that are important to the viewing experience, then it *is* useful to take the phenomenon into account. Doing so does not require going to a Mexican filmmaker's biography; rather, we must assess how each blueprint generates this entity and what kind of worldview it projects. And this can lead to rather shocking and surprising results.

If we attend carefully to Guillermo del Toro's *Pan's Labyrinth,* we see that below the surface of its pagan, mystical, and mythologically informed fairy tale the blueprint itself indicates an implied director with a spiritualist worldview. It is not especially surprising that the implied director we build in our minds would end the film with the young, innocent Ofelia (Ivana Baquero), who is not totally of our world. Del Toro and his DP, Guillermo Navarro, use wide angles and lighting evocative of auras to present Ofelia in a Christ-like manner. The end comes. Ofelia does die on the human plane of existence but is resurrected as a queen of the underworld with light streaming from behind her. She passes across to an otherworldly spiritual realm, yet a realm as *material* as her everyday human reality. We grow a sense of an implied director who considers the solution to the violence and murder of the Spanish Civil War to be solved not by human hand but through a faith that life will be better in an ethereal otherworld. Location matters, of course. We build this worldview of the implied director "del Toro" because he locates *Pan's Labyrinth* in Spain during a particularly brutal moment in that nation's history. As all the ingredients of the blueprint begin to add up—location, lensing, lighting, choice of actors, historical moment, and so on—we develop a strong sense of the implied director's Jungian-Catholic spiritualist worldview. And as I'll detail at length later in the book, Alfonso Cuarón's filmic blueprint for *Children of Men* does not so much present a new worldview, as its art-house gloss might have us think, as it does an age-old tried and trite spiritualism.

In Reygadas's films *Japón* (2002), *Batalla en el cielo/Battle in Heaven* (2005), and *Luz silenciosa/Silent Light* (2008), and the short film *Kingdom,* the implied director, "Reygadas," denies the audience any sense of interiority to the characters. Reygadas has perfected a behaviorist cinema. He uses the camera only to show characters' actions without giving the audience any clue about the mind-set behind such actions. In *Japón,* for example, an unnamed, middle-aged protagonist (the nonprofessional actor Alejandro Ferretis) has, for no apparent reason, gerontophilic sex with his very aged landlady, Ascen (the nonprofessional Magdalena Flores). For no apparent reason, the villagers begin to take down her house stone by stone. In *Batalla en el cielo,* nothing explains why Ana (Anapola Mushkadiz), a wealthy young woman, would have sex with her overweight chauffeur, Marcos (Marcos Hernández), or why he suddenly kills her. And in the film *Luz silenciosa,* which follows the story of a Mennonite family—an isolated Germanic cultural and linguistic minority living in Chihuahua—and includes exceptionally long tracking shots (the opening one lasts five minutes, following as the night turns to morning), the audience has absolutely no idea why the father, Johan (Cornelio Wall Fehr), behaves as he does (e.g., his near totally mute or speechless affair with Marianne, played by Maria Pankratz) or why his wife, Esther (Miriam Toews), slips into a coma following a heart attack and then suddenly breathes life once again. The implied director here carefully controls the elements of the blueprint in ways that require a huge amount of filling in gaps—so much so that we can fill in almost any kind of meaning.

This gap-filling work might try the patience of a regular filmgoing crowd, but art-house and mainstream critics have applauded Reygadas's trademark style. Tatiana Lipkes considers his film *Japón* an "exploration of the lie hidden behind reality" (my translation).[10] José Teodoro considers *Batalla en el cielo* to be a "labyrinth of metaphors and confrontational imagery punctuated with incongruous sexual matches and cryptic rehearsals of Mexican social, political, and religious rituals."[11] And *Luz silenciosa* picked up five Golden Ariels (Mexico's equivalent of an Academy Award), including those for best director and best screenplay.

The degree and kind of work that a film's blueprint asks us to do lead us to create a mental image of an implied director. Some filmmakers, including Reygadas and Amat Escalante (among other world-cinema directors such as David Lynch, Werner Herzog, Andrei Tarkovsky, and Lars von Trier), create film blueprints with huge gaps to be filled, or not, as the viewer prefers. In the case of Reygadas, we can see how he prompts viewers to posit an implied director "Reygadas" with a behaviorist, blank-slate worldview.

The implied director concept as generated from the film-watching experience can reveal much about the way in which filmic blueprint elements function as more than cognitive and emotive guides for the audience. Specifically, it can reveal much about the unstated ideology of a film.

I don't want to throw intention out with the bathwater here. Echoing Marx's remarks about work, we can say that the intention behind the construction of a particular table to be a particular size, height, and so on is crucial for the outcome; it determines whether we end up with a round table, a square table, or what have you. And this sort of background intention is perhaps more important in cinema than in many other spheres. Cinema is such a complex activity, with so many involved, that it is difficult to pinpoint a single creator. You can attribute a film to an individual, calling it, say, "a film by Alfonso Cuarón" or "by del Toro," and so on, but these names are mere synecdoches for a collective entity: the implied director.

Whether the film is Mexican or something else, viewers see only the final product, and the general impression created by this final product and the resulting judgments are what generate the concept of the implied director or implied filmmaker. The implied director, then, is always present.

Toolbox in Action

When we view *De la calle/Streeters* (2001), we infer an implied director we likely call "Gerardo Tort," who orchestrates all the devices—jump cuts, bleached-out film stock, natural lighting and shadows, extradiegetic ominous and suspenseful music—to portray a coherent world of Mexico City's street kids. The implied director uses all the devices in the toolbox to unsentimentally bring the despair and destruction of contemporary youth to an assaultive immediacy. There is no attempt at embellishment and no infusion of pseudoreligious hope. The implied director creates a storyworld wherein rare exceptions exist: Rufino (Luis Fernando Peña) and Xóchitl (Maya Zapata), who imagine other ways of existing and who make plans to escape. They dream of leaving the sewers, alleys, and streets of Mexico City for Vera Cruz, where Rufino plans to work in the dockyards. The implied director uses all the previously mentioned tools to create compelling antagonists—more the rule than the exception, such as Rufino's supposed best friend, Cero (Armando Hernández). Through carefully choreographed acting, Hernández conveys a sociopathic psychology grown and directed toward the single purpose of survival. Stool pigeon to a corrupt cop (and rapist), Cero betrays his friends, Rufino and Xóchitl. Cero's cold-blooded actions lead to Xóchitl's rape and the murder of Rufino. In a present filled with hostility and violence, there is no future. There is no possibility of developing a causal or counterfactual system that would lead to their sense of possibility in the future. The careful writing of Cero's character and choreographing of body movement and facial expression convey powerfully the sense of his already living as dead in the world. Finally, Tort's careful choice of lighting, time of day (night), sound score, editing, camera angle, and actor expression and movement work together to intensify the ideal audience's experience of this tragic story. All this is achieved through a careful integration of form and story to create a film that holds at bay shallow, clichéd responses on the part of the ideal audience. It resists slips into the sentimentality so easily wrought in films about oppressed and exploited children.

Hecho a Mano . . .
Hecho por *Homo sapiens*

✾

While each is unique in his or her film-story expression, Mexican filmmakers are all feeling, thinking, and imagining human beings who share a deep and long evolutionary history with other filmmakers and audiences—human beings in our totality—the world over. We have learned to know ourselves as a single species, each one of whose members is endowed with more or less the same cognitive (intellectual and emotive) capacities, needing to satisfy the same basic (social, affective, intellectual, and biological) needs, and constantly seeking ways to realize new goals. As Alison Gopnik nicely sums it up, "Our ability to represent the causal structure of the world and the mind and to imagine and create possible new worlds and minds is one powerful engine of human change. But our ability to revise and transform those representations, to observe and experiment, and to learn from those observations and experiments gives us an even more powerful engine of change."[1]

Mexican filmmakers are human, and therefore they are biologically social and *socially biological* parts of nature. They are the biological part of nature that is capable of knowing and changing the world thanks to its social activity, and they are (inseparably) the social part of nature that develops its activity in a social, associative manner that, in turn, realizes changes in us as social and biological individuals and in our society, both in part and as a whole.

Indeed, it is now a quite well established fact that nature and nurture are distinct categories only at the epistemological level. At the ontological level they are part of one inseparable whole. This explains why there are so many biologically based cultural universals. For instance, while the specific everyday experiences of any given Mexican filmmaker might differ from another's, and the expression of those experiences might differ, too, both will feel pain, grief, happiness, anger, and sadness in neurobiologically the same way as do all the rest of us on the planet. For example, just because a macho man does not cry does not mean that he lacks the neurobiological capacity for sadness.

Mexican filmmakers share a cognitive and emotive architecture that pertains to the species as a whole. At the same time, because each filmmaker is an individual with his or her own unique set of experiences in the world, each will express this cognitive and emotive universal endowment in a unique way.

In infancy humans initiate a bodily exploratory learning that can, in a surprisingly short time, establish the foundations for that specifically human activity we identify as work: the transformation of image and imagination into something else, whether a drawing, a table, a novel, or a film. This ability rests on the development of several foundational capacities for planning and knowing causal and counterfactual links that exist within the natural and social worlds: once we recognize regularities in these worlds, we can make projections about what will happen, as in "A will be followed by B" (causality), and thus suppositions about what would have happened if things had been otherwise (counterfactuality), as in "If A had not happened, B would not have happened." As our abilities to formulate or perceive relations of causality emerge, we automatically come to possess the capacity to perceive and formulate counterfactual hypotheses, arguments, and thoughts.

These basic, innate mental mechanisms (causal, counterfactual, and probabilistic reasoning) firmly anchor our knowledge of the world. And, like people everywhere doing whatever sort of work, Mexican directors use them in making films. The aesthetic products that make up Mex-ciné are simply an extended, highly particularized formulation of counterfactuals and possibilities. They are stories representing chains of possible events, actions, and settings, which form the basis of all Mexican filmmakers' imagining and planning.

This use of causal, counterfactual, and probabilistic mechanisms in mapping and modifying our natural and social environments (the knowledge that a ball falls if dropped, say, or that a smile or a cry will change the action of another) comes to play centrally in a Mexican film director's sense of him- or herself as different from others and to ground his or her own capacities and abilities to make an object—a film—that adds something new to the world. While Mexican filmmakers share with the rest of humanity these evolved mechanisms and capacities for reason, emotion, imagination, perception, and the like, they choose to train this basic and shared equipment in directed ways, namely, for imagining, crafting, and realizing unique, idiosyncratic products we shuffle under the umbrella "Mexican film," or Mex-ciné.

This Mexican filmmaking activity is simply one of many manifestations of what we do as humans generally. Our survival and evolution as a species spring from our day-to-day social, cooperative work in our purposeful and productive transformation of nature (which is both us and not us), a nature that, in turn, transforms us. This work fundamentally involves our capacity to imagine, to have an image in our minds first and foremost before acting, before setting out to choose (or create) the tools we will need to express this image in material form.

In a capitalist socioeconomic planetary system, where the disparity between the haves and have-nots increases daily, work is turned into labor; that is, the creative and transformative powers of work become estranged, alienated, or barren. Work creates use-values (concrete, determinate products) and is qualitatively determined (an expenditure of human labor in a particular form and with a definite aim). But private ownership of the means of social production turns work into labor; it turns human, social creativity into profit for owners who hire and command workers and rule society. Labor creates exchange-value (the social relation between one commodity and any other commodity) and is measured only quantitatively (as the expenditure of simple human labor without consideration of skill or expertise acquired through training).

Treated as labor, the different kinds of activity resulting in different kinds of commodities are reduced to a single common denominator, their identity as human labor in general. As for value, it represents the social average time required to produce a specific commodity. Mexican filmmakers working in a global capitalist socioeconomic system one way or another face this absolute opposition between work and labor. (For more on these issues, see Karl Marx's *Capital*, especially his discussion of work in chapter 7 of volume 1.)

Yet Mexican filmmakers do work, not labor; they create something new in the world. Indeed, all that goes into making Mexican films—from the pen that drafts the script to the cameras, lenses, and lights that capture the shots—is simply a particularized manifestation of this uniquely universal human capacity. That is to say, at base, Mexican filmmakers are human. They are natural, biological beings who exist as social entities. They are part of nature, and through their social activity (filmmaking and otherwise) they reorganize everything and anything within nature to satisfy their natural, biological, and social needs. They metabolize the world out there in their reorganization of nature according to the laws (causal relations) operating in nature that we as a species began discovering and using to our advantage as early as the Paleolithic era, and perhaps before.

Our accumulated knowledge of the inner workings of nature and society allows Mexican filmmakers to make choices and use devices in creating their individual, idiosyncratic, and particularized blueprints. Throughout this practical (transformative and productive) experience, Mexican filmmakers perform their work, imagining how to reorganize the building blocks of reality, whether Mexico City (*Amores perros*), Tapachula (*Sin nombre*), Quintana Roo (*Sin dejar huella*), Acapulco (*Drama/Mex*), or the Oaxacan coast (*Y tu mamá también*), and then using the techniques available to film in idiosyncratic ways to tell stories that engage us and in some cases even ask us to look once again at reality from a new angle of perception, emotion, and cognition.

As social and biological subjects, then, Mexican filmmakers share with everyone else in the human species an evolution through self-generation, or *autopoiesis*. They are like all the rest of us, always already a part of nature, but a very peculiar one. Mexican filmmakers are both biological individuals and social creatures, born in a social environment where their senses and neurobiological equipment were trained and educated by parents, caregivers, extended family members, and others who attended to their needs in infancy and childhood. It is their Mexican social environment and existence (shaped first by family within a larger social tissue) that triggered and molded the functioning of all the faculties inscribed in their DNA, such as their capacities for thought, work, and language.

We are all protagonists in this odyssey. And Mexican filmmakers choose to create filmic narratives that mark interesting moments in this journey: blueprints of human attachment (social) and the physical (natural world) that allow the filmgoer to consider new possibilities and prepare for new ways of being in the world the future might demand.

In this odyssey, which begins even before we are born, the senses undergo an education. Like most animals on earth, we have eyes, but ours are part of a highly complex perceptual system that is part of an astronomically more complex organ, the human brain. In addition we are the only part of nature that studies and knows (some of) the laws governing nature as a whole. So we have eyes and brains and an increasingly precise knowledge of the functioning of that segment of nature that we call biology and optics. Thanks to this knowledge, we have, for instance, given our eyes new possibilities, new functions, and new aesthetic and other needs in the wake of the invention of ever more powerful instruments, such as wide-angle and telephoto lenses, not to speak of recent three-dimensional (3D) and CG technology.

Through our knowledge of nature—specifically, the part of nature studied by optics—we have given our eyes the capacity to see things far beyond that which biology itself allowed them. We have improved on biology.

Mexican filmmakers work to make (Greek, *poiein*) stories to move audiences to feel and think in specifically directed ways. And, as was already mentioned, they can use any number of devices and technologies, genres and styles, to tell a near-limitless number of stories, as many as the human imagination can serve up.

Like all of us, Mexican filmmakers, as they have lived their social lives, have learned to appreciate and reject all sorts of things, especially those most directly related to health, the preservation of their lives, the reproduction of the species, and the entertainment of individuals and groups. As a result they have also learned to ascribe a positive or a negative value to a series of things offered to the appreciation of their senses, which they accept or reject as beautiful or ugly, attractive or repulsive, tasty or disgusting.

Through their social practice and social transformation of nature, they have learned to appreciate and enjoy, rejecting or accepting a certain number of things and events that today we include under the umbrella of "aesthetics," conceived in a large, expansive way. This social activity we call aesthetics has its own forms of meaning and its own value orientations, ones distinct from other, more or less similar and related social practices, such as those known under the designations of "morality," "manners," "customs," "personal hygiene," "discriminating taste in food and wine," "fashion," "ceremony," and "ritual." In all these cases, what is attractive or repulsive, accepted or rejected, concerns seeing, tasting, smelling, hearing, and touching. Born and raised by families in Mexico, Mexican filmmakers acquire tastes that involve their total sensory system and its particularized education within a Mexican cultural, social, political, and historical context.

Director, Blueprint, and Audience Redux

Mexican filmmaking should enjoy total aesthetic freedom in artistic matters. The prevailing rule should be that there must be no (other) rule, nothing telling Mexican filmmakers what they should do or not do or how they should do it or not do it. Invention and creativity must take place without hindrance, without moral or political precepts.

What I identify as the aesthetic at work in Mex-ciné is at the same time a cognitive and emotional inclination or disposition and a specific social relation involving sensory systems and an embodied goal or intention. It is a special form of relating to our fellow humans through certain kinds of products of our work and a special form of relating to nature.

Any given Mexican film's recipe or blueprint—the particular way a sequenced presentation of images portrays and builds characterizations and plots—is a set of instructions the filmmaker established with a view toward the consumption of his or her work by audiences. Such blueprints are thus realizations of the intentions or goals sought by the filmmakers. They further bring to bear, of course, the cognitive and emotional attitudes and talents of the filmmakers and, at the receiving end, their audiences.

Earlier I briefly discussed how specific devices, structures, and concepts work in several filmic blueprints. To this I must more fully add the dimension of the mind/brain. This approach to Mexican films keeps centrally in mind that it is the director who disciplines his or her emotion and cognitive systems in the skillful creating of the blueprint (imagination plus the purposeful use of technique) to engage an ideal audience, which the director assumes shares basic sensory, emotive, and cognitive faculties. Such an approach, then, must include a sense of the way devices, tools, structures, and concepts interface with the mind/brain. Both making and viewing films involve capacities of the mind/brain, so that we must know a little about the operations of human minds/brains with respect to the creation and consumption of films if we are to determine whether a particular film adequately fulfills the intentions behind it.

As I already mentioned, we can and should use advances in other fields to understand Mexican films better. That said, I would like to offer a proviso. In the study of the brain, and more generally neural mechanisms and their functions in human beings, the research applies to real human beings. So when talking about neuroscience as applied to Mex-ciné, I am talking about the neurological mechanisms only of real filmmakers and audiences. Put simply, while we are not typically aware of the fact (unless, say, a mic boom accidentally falls into the frame, as sometimes happens), for most scenes, including even the most intimate lovemaking scenes, there are usually dozens of people in the room besides the director, the DP, lighting techs, and so on. From director to DP to actors, the scene is constructed by real people in such a way as to direct a real audience's perceptual, emotive, and cognitive systems, but the scene is always and for all eternity a fictional *construct*. The findings of neuroscience apply to these filmmakers (and audiences), but not to the fictional lovers.

So, while we experience any given Mexican film as a simulacrum of the real, it is carefully constructed to come off as such. Real people might play the roles of characters, but these entities are always and for all eternity ontologically *fictional*. As Kristin Thompson reminds us, "However much they may strike us as being like 'real people,' we can always trace that impression back to a set of specific, character-creating devices."[2]

We can learn a lot from advances in cognitive science and neurobiology about the way filmic blueprints are put together and to what end. Yadin Dudai's continued work in neurocinematics reveals, for instance, that "brief shots (less than a few seconds) with more than four visual items will not be effective because they contain superfluous visual information."[3] That is, the number of visual items that we can "chunk" (process as wholes) included in such shots would exceed the capacity of our "visuospatial sketchpad[s]."[4] If a filmmaker were to add information to such shots, he or she might consider using the audio channel, where "the phonological loop is not saturated."[5]

We can learn much from neuroscience and physics (especially optics and acoustics) about the complex function of perception, which involves many regions of the brain, but it is not the same thing to view a film of a car chase and to experience a car chase outside the theater, where I realize that I have to move (or even jump) out of the way to avoid being run over. Our perceptual experience at the movies is a fact-fiction copresence. You feel as if you should get out of the way but know that you do not really have to move. Here, too, we have, on the one hand, an actual object and, on the other, a representation of that object, namely, the filmic representation of the object. The perception of the object differs from the perception of an image of the object. No matter how mimetic the images are, they are not reality; they are *re*presentations of reality. This is our minds/brains making distinctions between our perception concerning reality and the perception concerning *an image of reality.*

A filmic image never gives us a straightforward perception. It is always a representation. Ira Konigsberg writes that "the images are an illusion and the viewing experience is . . . controlled."[6] A film is always a *selection*—and this even in the most mimetic, 3D images. Film narrative is a chunk of reality selected by the director, who reimagines and reorganizes it through the skillful use of device and structure. Directors decide what stories to tell and how to tell them, constantly choosing the fragments of reality that will appear onscreen because of the aesthetic choices they make. That is, they choose the images that will allow audiences to fill in the gaps both in the storytelling and among the images, namely, the illusory or fictional images they present. The choice of a deep focus or crane shot; of tracking or push-in/pull-out camera movement; of light or dark illumination; of circular, right-to-left, or left-to-right movement within the frame; of smash cuts, dissolves, or intercut editing techniques—all these in one way or another guide our attention in an

immediate and controlled manner and, taken as a whole, allow us to generate meaning from a film's compositional interrelationships. The pleasure this
produces is why we're willing to cough up the cash to see a film.

In *La zona* (2007) we see Rodrigo Plá's careful use of selecting in and selecting out information, as well as camera movement, to guide our attention
and generate meaning. The film opens with one take that follows the movement of Alejandro (Daniel Tovar) as he drives an SUV. The camera follows
the car as it slowly moves from right to left. The DP, Emiliano Villanueva,
then has the camera pan up to an aerial shot of a gated community and
follows a butterfly as it flies out of view (zapped, actually, by the electrified
perimeter fence), which seems to be that of a surveillance camera, leaving a
scene of concrete walls and barbed wire. At the film's end (eighty minutes
later), this sequence recurs, though without the extradiegetic sound. Now
the film includes only the diegetic sounds of birds, people moving boxes, and
a kid blowing a whistle. From inside the car, we see the butterfly cross the
windshield. Again the camera follows the car, but this time not in one take;
instead several shots show the car entering from the right and then moving across the screen to the left. As Alejandro leaves the gated community,
suddenly we see the car moving from left to right for the first time. To the
extent that the previously mentioned convention of reserving left-to-right
movement for protagonists is at work here, the car becomes a sort of moral
compass. As the car enters the cemetery where he will bury Miguel (Alan
Chávez), Alejandro enters the frame from left to right. The camera then
frames him carrying Miguel's body from the left to the right of the screen.

Mind the Blueprint

Blueprints provide the algorithms for the purposive use of devices, concepts,
and coherent structures to make something to be consumed and perhaps even
replicated postconsumption; blueprints show the components of a structure,
but they don't indicate the way and order in which the structure is to be made.
For film blueprints by or about Mexicans to work, they must contain relevant
instructions but omit information that the filmmaker assumes will be filled
in by his or her ideal audience. This implies a social relation wherein the filmmaker learns to create effective blueprints and the audiences learn to follow
them (and how, when, and where to fill in the gaps) within constraints specific to the motion-photographic storytelling medium of film. The blueprint
cues the audience to "grasp the narrative in certain ways," as David Bordwell

nicely sums up the matter in *Poetics of Cinema*.[7] This active, purposeful engagement with a film requires our constant use of induction, deduction, and abduction (inferring certain sorts of causes from effects) precisely because we have to follow choices made and paths taken according to options predetermined by the film's blueprint.

Keep in mind that even effective blueprints do not necessarily move all viewers in the same way. Bordwell states that "like all humans, filmmakers can't anticipate, let alone determine, all the effects that may arise from their endeavors," so that "the viewer has a freedom to seize upon certain cues and not others, pull them into a range of projects, and use the film in ways that couldn't be foreseen by the filmmakers."[8]

Determining how a blueprint can work differently for different audiences does not require much fieldwork in theaters. You can simply look at trailers for the same film targeting different audiences. Consider, for example, the U.S., Mexican, and European film trailers for *El crimen del padre Amaro*, which detect, distill, and reproduce entirely different meanings and moods. The U.S. trailer distills and reproduces only the sensations generated by witnessing a taboo romance; the shots selected establish Amaro (Gael García Bernal) as a priest (seen giving the holy sacrament of reconciliation, sitting in a confessional booth and saying "Tell me your sins"), who gives in to the temptation of the young and beautiful Amelia (seen disrobing and touching), as well as the tragic outcome: Ana Claudia Talancón as Amelia crying in deep anguish and the villagers throwing stones. The choral music ("Gloria" performed by the Mexfilm Orchestra and used as a leitmotiv in the film) functions as an extradiegetic audio bridge that glues together the disparate images. Drawn from a blueprint with a much wider scope, this distillation leads viewers to apprehend the film as concerning only two people and the test of their love and the love of God. In the Spanish (international) trailer, however, the distillation conveys a film that is hip (it uses an upbeat, pop-rock score as its extradiegetic audio bridge) and is about more than just two individuals. The images used include not only ones of Amaro, Amelia, and the church and its priests but also ones that convey corrupt political and religious institutions: narcotics traffic, the church, and building a hospital with laundered money. It ends with the biblical quotation "Let he who is without sin cast the first stone." This distillation apprehends the film in a certain way and, in turn, shows how it is supposed to guide the audience's manner of apprehending it: as a story that cuts through layers of our social tissue and in which all are involved. Same blueprint, different decodings, distillations, and reconstructions. The latter trailer, however, appears to more accurately reflect the blueprint and more successfully step into the shoes of the film's ideal audience.

Gap Filling

Mexican film blueprints cue audiences to fill in gaps of action, behavior, time, and place. Just as the map is not the territory, so, too, is the blueprint not the real world. This does not mean we leave the real world behind. As we encounter the blueprint, we cross-check with the real world (e.g., with natural laws) to fill gaps through the processes of abduction, deduction, and induction. And as the filmic blueprint unfolds, we continue to modify the way we fill in the gaps of characters, time, and place. Kristin Thompson proposes that films "evoke background constructions that relate to 1) our relevant knowledge of the real world, 2) aesthetic conventions, and 3) and the practical purposes for which the film is made."[9]

The more we watch the films of a director who uses similar techniques in all his or her films—the multiple films of Reygadas, for instance—the more we develop a competence in filling the gaps in that director's films. This describes the process by which critics ground their judgments when making remarks similar to the following one from Deleyto and Mar Azcona, who declare that González Iñárritu uses multiple protagonists and "temporal simultaneity" to challenge "the notion, so often championed in other genres, of an all-powerful individual whose actions can propel the world regardless of external circumstances."[10]

Neuroscience can be helpful here. A large number of researchers have considerably advanced our understanding of the way our perceptual and cognitive processes handle gaps: our literal blind spots—the visual scotoma caused by the optic nerve's attachment to the retina—and our visual perception of movement when viewing a rapid succession of stills, as with film. This research enriches our understanding of how we fill in this, say, gappiness of perception. We don't actually perceive all that we think we perceive—we have perceptual blind spots.

Brains not only fill in gaps but also slice the continuous into discrete "chunks" so as to store memories (and construct narratives: first this happened, and then that, replacing the pure continuity of the world with an inferred causal connectivity). That is, film editors do consciously what event segmentation does automatically. Jeffrey Zacks and his colleagues at Washington University, in Saint Louis, identify the brain mechanisms at work in our everyday, continuous "chunking" activities, the name they give to the process whereby the human brain chops the continuous into the episodic. "*Event segmentation*,"[11] as they call it, is the mental process that divides the flow of things into events and thus creates a unified sense of action. The process involves both short-term, working memory and cognitive schemas that allow us to anticipate and predict connections among events.

When they investigated event segmentation with respect to the film-viewing experience, Zacks and his colleagues discovered that the greater the coherence in the cuts between different shots (visual-aural field), the greater was the likelihood that the audience would agree on the interpretation of the film as a whole; and the greater the incoherence between the shots, the greater was the likelihood of different interpretations of the whole. To put it in a nutshell, audience interpretations are far less narrowly determined with big-gap films, such as those of Reygadas, than they are with films such as Augustín Díaz Yanes's more conventionally event segmented *Sólo queiro caminar/Walking Vengeance* (2009).

The brain's processes of filling in gaps and segmenting reality into events are put to different uses by different Mexican film directors. Some make cuts from one to another time or place in ways that radically change the information in the visual field, stretching working memory and all variety of other cognitive and perceptual operations. Others present things in a way that helps viewers comfortably construct the film as a seamless whole.

Perspective Function

Jens Eder identifies perspective generally as "the mental stance of sentient beings toward the objects of their external or internal environments. The perspective on objects of perception, thought, emotion, or volition is the specific realization of these processes of the mind."[12] In *Amores perros,* for instance, González Iñárritu tells the same event four times to play with this viewing-with-intentionality process. Of course this is a film, so he can place the ideal audience behind a lens that offers many different perspectives of the same event: the crash that holds together the three disparate stories that make up the film. Keep in mind that it is not only the camera lens, angle, and position that direct our attentional focus. Sound, lighting, and movement within the frame can also do this work. Sound, for example, is no mere accompaniment to the primacy of the visual. It can direct us to what is important and intensify the perspectival process. (J. K. Donnely, Jeff Smith, Susan Feagin, and Annabel Cohen, among others, offer interesting insights on sound in film.)

Each showing of the crash in this film aligns the audience with a dominant character's perspective. And as the film unfolds, the more we know of the character, the more the different perspectives of the crash take on meanings particular to the character dominant in that subplot, whether Octavio (Gael García Bernal), Valeria (Goya Toledo), or El Chivo (Emilio Echevarría).

The film opens with the first perspectival version of a car chase, one that focuses largely on the interior of Octavio's car and its hood. Octavio, along with his dog, Cofi, and his pal, Jorge (played by Humberto Busto), are being chased through the streets of Mexico City by a truck decorated with red and yellow flames. At this point the perspective is focused on those being chased. We don't know why they are being pursued, but we do know that Octavio is the important figure, the one to follow and the one we will follow in the subsequent flashback of his life: his love affair with his brother Ramiro's (Marco Pérez) wife, Susana (Vanessa Bauche); his fight with Cofi to make money to travel north to the United States with Susana; Cofi's getting shot at a dogfight; the chase; and Octavio's being stood up by Susana at the bus they were to take to travel north.

This first version situates the action (via a long shot) and then moves us to a perspective mostly inside the car (shot with a handheld camera), cutting back and forth between shots showing Jorge's efforts to contain Cofi's bleeding and ones of Octavio driving; these shots are occasionally mixed with over-the-shoulder and hood-mounted wide-angle shots that also show us the marauding truck in pursuit. The cuts between shots are frequent, averaging two to four seconds in length. The audience is offered a quick respite from the onslaught of images and sounds: Octavio and Jorge laugh nervously and uproariously when they think they have lost the truck. The vertiginous pace of the cuts continues. They run a red light. They crash. The scene then cuts to a bloodied woman pawing at a window, and a horn goes off. With this first perspective comes a worldview, that of Octavio's story: youthful, frenetic, and vital, as well as careless, selfish, and stupid.

The second perspectival version of this same crash takes place fifty-six minutes into the film. By now we know much about Octavio, his likes and dislikes, his actions and ambitions. We also know the reason for the chase. El Jarocho (Gustavo Sánchez Parra) shoots Cofi, leading Octavio to stab El Jarocho. When Octavio and Jorge jump in their car to flee, El Jarocho follows in his truck. With Octavio's background filled in and the motive for the chase established, we are now given a distilled version of the first sequence. Many of the same camera angles are used, but fewer of the shots are present. Also, the frenzied, anxious dialogue between Octavio and Jorge is somewhat muted;

Fig. 2. Amores perros: Octavio in the chase scene

it's as if we hear and see the whole thing once again from the perspective of someone standing behind a glass wall. An industrial techno soundtrack overlays the sequence this time, too, but we do not get a shot of the bloodied woman, Valeria. The perspective begins with Octavio and ends with Octavio. While this version offers a more controlled and focused perspective identified with and motivated by Octavio, González Iñárritu relies on our long-term memory's capacity to fill in the gap: that others are also victims of the crash.

The third perspectival version takes place shortly thereafter, at seventy-two minutes into the film. This is the crash experienced from Valeria's perspective. Valeria is driving with her dog, happy because her lover has left his wife. A catchy pop song, "Mi corazón," plays first at the extradiegetic level, then moves within the diegesis, playing on the radio. She tells her dog, Richie, to stop barking out the car window as she passes the figure we now know to be El Chivo, a disillusioned revolutionary turned homeless gun for hire. A medium close-up near or inside the car shows Valeria putting on lipstick as the signal turns green. There is a cut to a long shot of the car viewed from behind. The vehicle travels away from us into the background (i.e., vertically on the screen, a movement contrary to gravity and thus uncomfortable for viewers), where we see it (now diminutive relative to objects in the foreground) enter the intersection and another car traveling from screen right (the movement typical of antagonists entering a frame) smashing into it. The contrastive juxtaposition of the bubbly pop song with the movement of the cars (producing discomfort and a sense of antagonism) makes for a horrific moment. It also generates certain meanings: the path Valeria has chosen—to be with a man who has left his wife—will be not just difficult but tragic.

Fig. 3. Amores perros: Valeria in the crash scene

The fourth perspectival version takes place 116 minutes into the film. This version unspools from the perspective of El Chivo, who is hanging out with his many stray dogs while waiting to see who his next human target will be. As he follows his target, he pushes a cart (with a dog riding precariously on top), and then he looks to the right to see Valeria's dog barking from her car window. We hear Valeria ask, "What's the matter?," which acts as an audio bridge connecting us to the third version of the crash. A wide-angle shot shows El Chivo standing in front of a restaurant window, sizing up his next target and the car crash behind him.

A series of shots from a handheld camera and cuts lead us in and around the crash from a street-level view, one largely motivated by El Chivo's presence. We see the bloodied, mangled body of Jorge, as well as Octavio's, which is jammed behind the steering wheel. El Chivo pulls open the jammed door and helps himself to a wad of cash on the seat next to Octavio. Sirens are heard. An ambulance arrives. Then the camera cuts to a medium close-up of Valeria in her car. We hear her say, "Ayúdame," and see her bloodied hands and arms pushing frantically at a car window as she tries to get out. El Chivo picks up a limp Cofi from the street.

Not only do the quick cuts and blasts of sound intensify our experience of the crash, but the perspectival choices direct our inference of character type. In this last instance, we see that El Chivo is concerned primarily with grabbing the cash and saving Cofi, leaving others to help rescue the dead and torn.

In other films we see different uses of the camera to convey different perspectives, motivations, and even intimacies with the characters. Most of

Fig. 4. Amores perros: El Chivo in the crash scene

Sin nombre is filmed with a steady handheld camera. While the filming includes occasional crane shots, as well as the use of telephoto and wide-angle lenses, most of it is proximate. We experience this as an intensification of our intimacy and empathic connection with Sayra and Caspar. In *Matando Cabos* (2004; Killing Cabos), Alejandro Lozano uses techniques of intercutting, split screens, and the like to intensify simultaneous action, as well as a variety of storytelling devices that give idiosyncratic shape to the tales characters tell to other characters. The techniques used include the following.

- Slow motion: Lozano uses this technique in a scene where Javier "Jaque" (Tony Dalton) tells Mudo (Kristoff Raczyñski) a story about the big mob boss, Oscar Cabos.
- Unreliable narration: After Oscar Cabos (Pedro Armendáriz Jr.) is knocked unconscious in a toilet stall, he relates in voice-over how he can hear Jaque and Mudo in an adjacent stall and recounts the events that led him to being knocked out. As he narrates, the statements he makes do not match the visuals presented. "I know that I walked in on him kissing my daughter," he says, yet the film shows an image of Jaque naked in bed with the daughter. The unreliable narration underscores Cabos's megalomania: when things do not work the way he wants, he simply does not process it.
- Voice-over: Cabos's janitor presents his own tale in voice-over. We learn how chance kept him a janitor and made Cabos a big mafioso. Lozano uses 16 mm film stock with light fluctuating around the frame's edges to convey this story. We experience a certain it-could-have-been nostalgia and sympathy for the janitor.

- Documentary style: When Jaque begins to recount the story of his friend, the wrestler Mascarita (Joaquín Cosío), the style of the editing, lensing, and lighting shifts to that of a documentary. We are privy to interviews with friends and family, shots of Mascarita wrestling with goats, and his rise to fame from bouncer to famous wrestler. The style then shifts again, this time to that of a 1950s-style wrestling film, for a sequence that shows Mascarita being accosted by women and aliens with stun guns. The implied message: Mascarita is a cardboard cutout.

Matando Cabos thus uses a variety of styles to tell its stories, all of which clearly identify the personality and worldview of the particular teller.

Perspective orients us to the way we interface with a given character, whether in a serious or comic register. It can direct us toward insight into a character's worldview and portend action to come. The careful directing of perspective plays an important part in the viewer's process of building "a comprehensive *system of imaginative relations to characters*."[13] It can offer insight into their interests and motives. It works generally to influence our engagement with and appraisal of characters.

To sum up, the careful use of perspective in film can trigger emotion responses on multiple levels. Jens Eder specifies four levels of emotion that may be elicited in various ways.

1. Visual and aural techniques can produce "perceptual affects and rapidly changing moods."
2. Storyworld events can create conflicting, unstable, and changing "diegetic emotions" that influence viewer appraisal and empathic processes.
3. We ask questions and infer meanings generated by themes and character actions, goals, and outcomes that can lead to our emotional investment in the film.
4. Various forms of engagement with the film are intensified by "communicative emotions." We sense this when we ask of the implied director whether the film cultivated amoral intentions, whether our reactions are adequate, and how the implied director's moral landscape does or does match our own.[14]

Anticipation Function

In addition to serving the previously discussed functions, editing, camera movement and lens, sound, and lighting work together to trigger feelings of anticipation, anxiety, and the like. By carefully arranging these elements in the filmic blueprint, a director can trigger short-term expectations and long-term anticipations. Continuity editing, for example, is a mainstay in making sure that any long-term anticipations elicited take place without disruption. As Patrick Colm Hogan notes, "The relations between experience and very short-term expectations can have significant emotional consequences."[15] Hogan further comments, "[T]he manipulation of discontinuities, [and] thus the controlled disruption of short-term anticipations, can significantly contribute to the emotional impact of film."[16]

The most common "discontinuity-producing" disruptions come in the form of jump cuts (two sequential shots from slightly different perspectives) and smash cuts (abrupt shifts from one scene to another) and in juxtaposing nonmatching shots, disrupting match cuts (two matched images separated by a single shot), and sidestepping the 180-degree rule (whereby the camera stays to one side of an imaginary line that connects characters or objects); collectively these techniques form what Sergei Eisenstein called montage, or editing to condense space-time and information. (In addition several Mexican filmmakers, such as González Iñárritu, use the audio smash as another way to create discontinuity and a bang.) All these effects trigger and intensify present emotions and anticipated emotions.

When a filmmaker decides to use techniques that run counter to the conventions of motion and perspectival position, viewers experience discontinuity. As Hogan points out, this "can impede the trajectory suddenly in an unprojectable way (i.e., in a way we could not have projected beforehand) or it can advance the trajectory suddenly in an unprojectable way."[17] That is, the techniques disrupt but do not altogether stop our gap-filling work. We still create bridges that glue together disparate images. We may feel lost in the most dizzying of films, but our brains will do the work of creating coherence and balance. This undermines our "egocentric navigational control system, under cerebellar and basal ganglia control" in favor of "the well-known allocentric spatial relation system, under hippocampal and neocortical control."[18]

Mexican filmmakers generally tend not to violate the conventions of continuity editing, such as matching cuts and the 180-degree rule. But they also play with these conventions to achieve powerful emotional results. Of course, once these disruptions become formulaic, they will no longer work as ruptures. They will no longer elicit new perspectives or emotive and cognitive engagements with story content. Once we learn to expect some particular disruption, Reygadas and similar directors can no longer use it to surprise us.

Sound and Image Function

The careful use of sound and image can prompt powerful emotional responses. The ominous low buzzing sound and black screen that briefly precede the first car chase sequence in *Amores perros* can provoke significant anxiety. The convergence of the image of the big truck and its low, guttural muffler noise as it chases Octavio and Jorge can similarly generate anxious reactions.

But the convergence of sound and image can also have the opposite effect. In *Children of Men,* the congruence of sound and image works to send chills down an ideal viewer's back when extradiegetic harmonious choral music conjoins with an image of Kee giving birth to a baby, the savior of humanity. (For more on the interaction of sound and image, both polarization and congruence, see the work of Jeff Smith.)[19] Indeed, neuroscience has demonstrated that pleasant music not only causes listeners to feel tingles but also increases blood flow in the insula, the orbitofrontal cortex, the ventral medial prefrontal cortex, and the ventral striatum, all of which are regions of the brain involved in reward and emotion. The baby-birth sequence in *Children of Men* comes just after one filled with sounds of gunshots and people screaming and shouting. The quieting lull in the film's audiovisual pace aims to bring viewers down again before hitting their limbic systems even harder and more powerfully with the following sequence.

Beyond producing emotion by emphasizing images, a score can play a vital role in creating a film's mood. For instance, the Lynn Fainchtein score for *Amores perros* (she also scored Naranjo's *Voy a explotar* [I'm going to explode]) works alongside poignant visuals to trigger intense emotions of fear, anger, and grief, while Gustavo Santaolalla's compositions for the Andean *charango* and *ronroco* (stringed instruments) work to bridge the peak emotions and infuse *Amores perros* with a pervasive melancholic mood. (Larry Rohter provides useful information about the Argentinean Gustavo Santaolalla's compositions in a *New York Times* article dated August 15, 2008.)

Music can also provide an important series of memory markers for film audiences. That is, a particular soundtrack or set of composed sounds can attach to the presence and movements of characters. Music is a particularly effective way to lodge a particular scene in a viewer's memory. Many people often pay little attention to the music when watching a film, but directors can choose to work closely with their sound designers to create noticeable music leitmotivs.

In *Amar te duele* Sariñana and his sound designer use music as a way to distinguish the presence of the *nacos* (a pejorative term used to describe working-class Mexicans), such as Ulises, and the *fresas* (the wealthy elite), such as Mariana (Ximena Sariñana) and Renata (Martha Higareda). Music here works to emphasize what the film already achieves: dividing different groups of young people in artificial and destructive ways.

Carlos Carrera strategically uses the music score to throw a seamless web around the themes presented in *El crimen del Padre Amaro*. At the film's close, for instance, the camera pans out, and the sound of the choir inside the church changes to a more polished classical choral sound heard in the film's extradiegetic auditory channel. This choral music bridges the narrative with the film credits. A minute or so into the credits, however, the choral music fades out, to be replaced with the *narcocorrido* "Corrido del Padre Amaro," performed by los Cardenales de Nuevo León. The soundscape reinforces the film's message: the tragedy rests not only on the shoulders of Amaro, who seduces a young girl and indirectly causes her death by coercing her to have an abortion, but also on a corrupt and decrepit social tissue wherein the church, the state, and a drug economy all nest together.

In *Sin nombre* Cary Joji Fukunaga worked closely with music supervisor Lynn Fainchtein, along with the film scorer Marcelo Zarvos, to produce music that subtly marks the flow of consciousness for various characters and their physical movements across borders. When the film opens and we see the character Sayra and her family cross from Guatemala to Mexico, the music shifts from a soundscape representative of Guatemala to sounds characteristic of southern Mexico. More generally the dominant extradiegetic sounds in this film accumulate and direct the emotions of the ideal audience in the general direction of sadness, anger, fear, not happiness, calm, or comfort.

Music is extremely effective in generating quick emotional responses. As Isabelle Peretz and John Sloboda remark, "[L]ess than a quarter of a second of music is sufficient to elicit reliable emotional judgments. Extremely fast-acting processes are typically observed in response to biologically important stimuli. The fact that short musical extracts can arouse emotional responses similarly in every human being with rapid onset and with little awareness qualifies such experiences as *reflexes*."[20] More precisely, these peak emotions work in an accumulative sort of way to orient our so-called limbic system, or emotion center. Fukunaga and similar filmmakers carefully construct series of emotion tracers—a music score carefully calibrated along with the visuals— that accrete and move us toward an apprehension and deeply felt sense of the film's mood.

This mood is what we experience when we finish watching a film. We usually do not recall specific instances of emotions felt at any particular point.

Fig. 5. Sin nombre: Sayra and her family cross the river from Guatemala to Mexico

What we tend to recall immediately after watching a film is a general sensation of, say, discomfort and sadness. In a way what we remember is having seen a tragedy and not a comedy, for example. What we recall helps us identify the genre of the work we have seen. We may also experience a general appreciation of a film, an *evaluation*. I liked Fukunaga's film: it is powerful, technically accomplished, suspenseful, and unsentimental.

Indeed, the U.S. and British ad campaigns used different film trailers for *Sin nombre,* ones that selected different scenes and peak emotions. The result is that the two trailers establish two different mood expectations: the U.S. trailer misses the film's mark in its inaccurate reconstruction (or paraphrasing) of the filmic blueprint as sentimentally melodramatic; and the British trailer strips down and accurately reconstructs the blueprint in paraphrased form as serious and deeply tragic. The British trailer indicates that its creators worked harder than did their U.S. counterparts in uncovering the blueprint's kernel events and corresponding peak emotions to accurately move filmgoers toward apprehending and feeling the mood and genre the filmmakers intended. As the film unfolds, its score and other ingredients trigger an ever-increasing series of negative emotions, installing the filmgoer more and more in its tragic mood. From the minute the film begins, we experience a series of structured and directed emotion cues that create the mood, which in turn leads us to identify the genre as tragedy.

As with all things filmic, however, we need to keep in mind that these emotions are produced in an "as if" way. Indeed, the research on sounds and images that trigger subcortical flight, fright, and fight responses indicates that in many situations an appraisal mechanism kicks in before higher-level cognitive systems can render the judgments that may redirect or reinforce this automatic response. Even before the neocortex tells us that we are watching a representation of a car chase in Mexico City, the research suggests, some processing occurs in a subregion of the limbic system (specifically, the cingulate gyrus) that is at least partially responsible for determining emotional response. That is, the limbic system includes a subregion generating appraisals that are then more fully processed in the neocortex. This undermines any sharp distinction between emotion and cognition, for appraisal occurs in brain structures associated with both functions. The limbic system is, among other things, parsing and classifying real versus unreal.

Let me underscore here that fact is fact. Fiction is fiction—even in the most convincing and compelling of sound-image arrangements. That is, emotions brought on via film (or in the reading of literature or comic books, apprehending art, and the like) are real emotions; they bear some significant difference from emotions produced by real-world events—*in their behavioral upshots.*

Moral Function

Morality is an aspect of human behavior. In the real world, we choose to act ethically or not. With film, however, directors and audiences *ascribe* ethical values to characters and their actions. But, again, the technical means of characterization in film can, as Carl Plantinga argues, have "a marked persuasive appeal for many audiences by encouraging emotionally striking ways of thinking about, feeling for, and valuing persons, both fictional and real."[21] Such valuing activities include those involving moral values. And moral stances, moral evaluations, moral positions, and ethical behavior—all kinds of issues concerning ethics—are crucial to our experience of Mexican films.

To illustrate the point more fully, let me attend to the way two films construct (whether well or not so well) their protagonists and those characters' ethical systems. In making *Sólo quiero caminar,* director and screenwriter Augustín Díaz Yanes decided to make his protagonist a Mexican gangster's right-hand man, a fellow who kills on command. Díaz Yanes decided that this evildoer, Gabriel, would be played by an attractive, charismatic actor, and so he cast Diego Luna. Why? To create a source of conflict in the audience, placing viewers in the difficult position of condoning Gabriel's bad behavior. The filmmaker's choices about acting and events, as well as the use of various devices and structures, allow Díaz Yanes to elicit specifically directed emotions in the viewers, in this case, both attraction and revulsion, emotions *for and against* the character(s).

Fig. 6. Solo quiero caminar: opening shot of Gabriel

As both screenwriter and director, Díaz Yanes makes the sovereign deci-sion to create the character of Gabriel, whose actions are triggered by an emotion system tied to an ultimately contradictory ethical system that leads to his death. He opens the film using a tilted shot and low-to-high camera angle that frames Luna as Gabriel, immediately planting the seed that Ga-briel sees and acts a little differently than the rest of us do.

Soon after this prefacing shot, we learn that Gabriel feels deeply for his mother, who was beaten to death by his father. So, despite his mercenary ethics, the film introduces an internal coherence, allowing us to believe that he could fall in love with his boss's nemesis, Aurora (Ariadna Gil), whatever the cost. Yet there is no place for attachment, love, or protection for those (especially women) outside the gang, and so his emotion and attachment to Aurora lead to actions that defy the gang's code of loyalty.

In *Biutiful* (2010) González Iñárritu, who is both the director and a cow-riter, casts the ruggedly handsome and charismatic actor Javier Bardem in the role of the protagonist, Uxbal, a terminal cancer victim and father of two who nonetheless exploits undocumented women and children trying to survive in Spain. Díaz Yanes's Gabriel is coherent through and through, even in his altering loyalties; the tensions and contradictions in Uxbal's ethical system, however, make González Iñárritu's blueprint less coherent.

Bardem's acting is charismatic (and won him a best actor award at Cannes) and his physical look attractive, but the script's inconsistencies make it difficult for the audience to engage with him. Uxbal is both a do-gooder and an exploiter, a victim and a savior, but without any internal coherence of action, emotion, or code of conduct that would allow us to understand how these stick together in one character. He erupts with anger seemingly for no reason, suddenly becomes the caregiver to an abusive wife, earns a living as a calculating and exploitive handler of undocumented émigrés who nonetheless attends to their comforts (e.g., by installing a propane heater in the cell where they sleep at night), turns on a dime as a distressed martyr, and decides to entrust the care of his children to an undocumented émigré woman and not, say, to his more economically stable brother.

Yet the film blueprint never gives us any explanation. We never know why Uxbal would make the irrational choice to leave his children with someone in such a precarious socioeconomic position, or why he does any of his other actions. The story lacks the *because;* it lacks plot. We do not believe in Uxbal's problems, what he is doing, or the story itself. Rather, the contradictions of action (which Díaz Yanes overcomes by providing Gabriel's backstory) are flimsily held together by a syncretic New Age religious blanket (part Buddhist, part Christian) that González Iñárritu throws over the film to justify all incoherencies of character and event.

A given director's decisions about texturing a given character's emotion and codes of behavior constitute central and powerful means for engaging film audiences. When they are well made, we are firmly engaged.

The vehicle for reaching audiences, for conveying these moral judgments, is the emotional charge, the emotional power of persuasion carried by the film's images. That is, a successful film must do more than merely elicit moral judgments; it must power those judgments with emotional impact. The emotional impact is produced by the specific rhetorical means the filmmaker employs, the persuasive devices he or she uses. When filmmakers carefully choose effective rhetorical devices, the impact can be not only strong but also enduring, persisting even after viewers leave the theater.

We judge films from a double point of view: that of the characters' actions and that of the filmic blueprint. Thus, viewers may reject a film blueprint not because of resistance to or repulsion at its moral landscape but simply because, say, the film does not cohere or requires them to fill in too many gaps. The blueprint triggers evaluative thoughts and responses in the audience as a result of both character action and internal aesthetic coherence. Anne Bartsch identifies the latter as our experience of "metaemotions," the appraisal of the devices that make up the blueprint's aesthetic as "either pleasant and fascinating, or stressful and aversive."[22] At this level our metaemotional response is one that evaluates the coherence of the elements (or lack of it) that together make up the blueprint. These elements include script, acting, camera perspective, lighting, color pallet, music, and sound design.

Significantly, ideal audiences differ from real ones. We can decode the blueprint of a film by Díaz Yanes, González Iñárritu, or any other Mexican filmmaker to determine how it seeks to trigger an ideal audience response, but this ideal audience is rather limited in its outlook. Actual audience members carry their own moral concerns and ethical beliefs. They may not fill in the gaps as González Iñárritu expected them to when he crafted his blueprint. They may become angry and repulsed, not because the blueprint was designed to elicit those emotions but because the character's actions just don't add up. They may reject a film such as Reygadas's *Batalla en el cielo* because of a prudish sexual sensibility, for that film opens with a long close-up of a light-skinned blond woman performing fellatio on a dark-skinned, overweight Mexican man. (We later learn that this is Ana, played by Anapola Muskadiz, and her army general father's driver, Marcos, played by Marcos Hernandez.)

Finally, when it comes to ethics in Mexican films, we must keep in mind that real-life ethics differ radically from ethics in fictional realms. There is a difference between the cinematic moral landscape and that of everyday reality. Diego Luna and Javier Bardem do not (as far as we know) go home after a day's work on the set and kill or exploit people. The moral traits of Bardem have nothing to do with those of his character. The screenwriter and director are responsible for ascribing moral traits to fictional characters, and, as with other tasks, this can be done well or not. There is no identity equivalence between actors and real-world ethics, on the one hand, and characters and their ethical systems, on the other; the latter is limited to, among other such things, the myriad of storyworlds constructed and presented in Mexican films.

Emotional Body Language Function

Acting is a composite, a complex array of carefully choreographed actions—that is, movements based on intentions. In this sense an actor like Javier Bardem, who possesses extraordinary acting skills, can make even a poorly constructed film marginally palatable. This careful choreography of action and movement can trigger emotions in audiences. That is, the narrative blueprints of Mexican (and other) films tell stories using motion in all facets, especially the motion of the actors' bodies within the frame.

The human face provides many of our most subtle and complex cues for emotional responses. The face and its expressions help us identify a person as a threat or an ally, for instance. As Patrick Colm Hogan writes, "[W]e not only construe and recognize faces with great ease, we also experience congruent or complementary emotions when we see someone's face. Thus we may feel sorrow on seeing someone weep, and fear on seeing someone angry."[23] Carl Plantinga points out that body movement functions are an important communication system between film and audience, noting that "through variable framing and point-of-view structures, a film can display the parts of the actor's body that are the most emotionally communicative."[24]

Scientific research confirms the centrality of facial gesture and body movement generally in our appraisal of and engagement with people, nonhuman animals, and their simulacra in our everyday activities. Within the so-called limbic system, which is largely responsible for emotion, the amygdala has been identified as a key area. It is, for example, responsible for decoding sights, sounds, smells, and touch signals and determining their "affective relevance," as well as for initiating "adaptive behaviors via its connections to the motor systems."[25] Moreover, the amygdala orchestrates two emotional circuits in response to emotional body language (EBL), that is, bodily movements that convey emotion: the automatic, reflexlike subcortical circuit responsible for fight/flight responses and a controlled cortical circuit subtending recognition and deliberation, which tells us, say, that we need not run from a firing gun or try to save undocumented émigrés when these occur only in a film. As Beatrice de Gelder and her colleagues have determined, "[I]n higher organisms, both systems cooperate in decoding EBL signals and monitoring behavior following an emotional signal provided by EBL."[26]

These two circuits are connected to certain executive functions that allow us to be aware of our bodies in time and space, our bodily states, and to decide whether to act. The same circuits fire when watching a film that uses EBL in a pronounced way. This can guide, trigger, or intensify our emotion toward and knowledge of the characters. In *Cumbia Callera* (2007; Cumbia of the street), René Villarreal chooses to tell a modern-day Cinderella story, one of lost and found Converse sneakers that lead to the careful negotiation of a love triangle, almost entirely through the characters' body language. There is virtually no dialogue throughout its ninety-four minutes. Instead, Villarreal tells the story through a careful integration of diegetic and extradiegetic music (the *cumbia*, a Colombian dance form) along with the choreography of the beautiful bodies of Fernanda García Castañeda as "La Cori," Oliver Cantú Lozano as "El Neto," and Andul Zambrano as "El Güipirí." Not a word is spoken, yet we feel intensely for the characters, who have no moral or ideological obstacles to their free and creative explorations of themselves, their bodies, and the world they inhabit.

In *Ana y Daniel* (2009), Michael Franco chooses to use dialogue only to punctuate long sequences showing the characters' movements, especially movements that incorporate EBL. Franco's choice effectively leads audiences to feel and think deeply about the profound trauma experienced by the young siblings Ana (Marimar Vega) and Daniel (Dario Yazbek Bernal, the half brother of Gael García Bernal) after they are brutalized and forced to have sex with one another by exploitive, underworld Internet pornographers. Franco chooses to elide the rape, making the sequences that follow, when Ana and Daniel try to resume a normal life, all the more powerful. Ana's rage, sadness, and disgust are conveyed in her body language. Ana is older than her brother (in her late teens or early twenties) and more mature. Her body movements show her learning how to push her feelings aside and move on with her life. Daniel's slumped body and nonplussed facial expression contrast sharply. The trauma has radically curtailed the teenage boy's explorations of his own body and his girlfriend's, leaving him unable to pursue this in a healthy, natural way. He no longer knows what to do with his body; at one point he begins to caress his girlfriend affectionately but ends up nearly strangling her. Franco includes another scene that is at once powerfully disturbing and entirely persuasive. Through a series of jump cuts and freeze frames the audience follows Daniel as he enters Ana's bedroom at night, turns on her bedside light, wakes her, and undoes his pants. The sequence ends with a shot of Ana on her tummy, naked. Franco leaves us to infer the events, but his cinematography and editing, as well as the characters' body movements, lead the viewer to experience their tragedy to a disturbing, nearly nauseating degree.

For viewers of *Sólo queiro caminar,* the previously mentioned subcortical and cortical circuits work to decode the EBL signals of Luna as Gabriel. More generally they operate to determine whether to run when Gabriel fires his gun right at us. In this case the cortical system overrides the subcortical one, and we do not run away. But the independence of the two systems is important, for in evolutionary terms it has played an important role in the species' survival and "guarantees that an alerting event signaled in the subcortical pathway elicits a rapid reflex-like reaction in the absence of detailed stimulus processing and is not systematically overruled by concurrently available positive information."[27] And while the body is less expressive than the face, it is in one way less ambiguous, for it provides "the emotion as well as the associated action."[28] That is, a facial expression may indicate fright, but the body not only indicates the emotion but also executes the action connected to the emotion, thus creating a "less ambiguous signal and a more direct call for attention in the observer."[29] It's one thing to see someone who looks scared and quite another to see someone fleeing in panic.

Mexican filmmakers most likely are not familiar with the relevant science, but they recognize and fully exploit the way our facial expressions and body postures and movements convey emotion. In so doing they strengthen and solidify the audience's empathic engagement with a film's characters and their investment in the film as a whole.

The pivotal events that launch the plot at the beginning of *Sin nombre* are indicated largely by the careful direction of the facial expressions and movements of Edgar Flores, the nonprofessional actor who plays the protagonist, Caspar. In the first we see Caspar's body and face suddenly fill with a tangle of emotions: frustration, anger, sadness. Caspar has just heard that his patron, Lil' Mago (played by Tonocha Huerta Meijia), who leads the Tapachula cell of the Mara Salvatrucha street gang, has killed his beloved, Martha Marlene (Diana García). Without much ado, Lil' Mago tells Caspar to find himself another woman. In a medium shot that frames Caspar in the foreground, his back turned to Lil' Mago, we see the emotion move from his shoulders up into his twisted and contorted face. No words are spoken, no cries of anguish and anger are heard, and yet Caspar's body and face convey all this to the audience. Lil' Mago's obliviousness to the depth of Caspar's despair is important, but, whereas the audience is privy to this information, Lil' Mago is not. Thus, the moment might not appear significant to Lil' Mago, but the anguish and anger felt here will later erupt when Caspar kills him—an event that sends Caspar north and seals his tragic fate.

In this sense the scene just described is pivotal on a purely emotional level and absolutely central to the coherence of character necessary if the audience is to understand the action that follows. Not long thereafter, Caspar is on top of a rolling train, acting as Lil' Mago's henchman as the two men mug and terrorize people, such as Sayra and her family, who are risking their lives to travel north to the United States for work. When Lil' Mago holds a gun to Sayra's head, the camera pulls back, and we see Caspar's body fill with strength and anger flood his face as he brings his machete down on Lil' Mago.

In a matter of seconds the camera shows us both a body and a face upset but passive and then turning to overwhelming rage and a will to act. Again, without any words spoken, we see Caspar transform in body and mind from follower to leader, becoming someone who will now move forward in the world of independent mind and agency. He knows, however, that the gang's "blood-in, blood-out" code means his actions will lead to his death. His body crumples, he drops to his knees, and his head falls heavily forward and down. His body movement tells all: he has just signed his death warrant.

Other directors, such as Carlos Reygadas, Julián Hernández, Fernando Eimbcke, and Gerardo Naranjo, use emotional body language to solidify and strengthen audience engagement and signal plot turns. Perhaps this is not so

Fig. 7. Sin nombre: Caspar kills Lil' Mago

surprising. With the exception of Reygadas, who focuses on adult subjects, these directors deal mostly with preteens and teens, young subjects who seem more inclined to show feeling in gesture and facial expression than by speech. Naranjo's *Drama/Mex* (2006) follows the ups and downs of several teens, some at the beginning of that age and others older and about to pass into adulthood. In the 105 minutes that the film takes to tell the story, only a few words are spoken, but the director's careful orchestration of body movement and facial composition allows the characters unambiguously to convey their deep feelings: shame and sadness, anger and frustration, love and dejection, repulsion and affection.

Naranjo and his DP, Tobias Datum (who was the cinematographer for *How the Garcia Girls Spent Their Summer*), open *Drama/Mex* with a medium shot of a young woman (who we later learn is Fernanda, played by Diana García) sitting alone at a restaurant table. She twice utters the insult "hijo de puta" (son of a bitch), the second time with more intensity, conviction, and movement, a forward thrust while rehearsing the insult. In a series of cuts viewers see Fernanda biting her nails and knitting her brow as well as leaning back and forth over the table. Punctuating these anxious, anguished movements and looks are movements and facial expressions that convey a pensive, calm interiority. We are only a minute or so into the film, and we already know much about this character. Her body betrays deep anxiety and disquiet. Her facial expressions reveal a more practiced calm. After washing his hands and coiffing himself in the bathroom, the handsome boyfriend arrives; we later learn this is the deadbeat Chano, played by Emilio Valdés. We quickly discover that he stole money from her father. When Fernanda gets up and leaves, Datum's handheld camera follows her. Although she looks back, she continues on, but the not so angry look on her face when she sneaks the

Fig. 8. Sin nombre: Caspar after killing Lil' Mago

backward glance reveals a young woman in conflict: Fernanda knows she must get rid of the guy but nevertheless feels affection for him.

Time and Space Function

Mexican filmmakers can choose a variety of ways to manipulate time and space in their films. Of course Mexican directors did not invent this device. Manipulations of space and time appear at the foundations of filmmaking, and directors who execute them with skill and an eye to style and unity of affect are legion. Films that rely on this include, among many others, D. W. Griffith's 1916 classic *Intolerance;* Max Ophuls's *La Ronde* (1950), an adaptation of *Reigen,* by the Austrian playwright Arthur Schitzler; Anthony Mann's Western *Winchester '73* (1950); Michael Todd's 1956 adaptation of Jules Verne's *Around the World in 80 Days,* starring David Niven and Cantinflas; Francis Ford Coppola's sequel *The Godfather, Part 2* (1974); Quentin Tarantino's *Reservoir Dogs* (1992) and *Pulp Fiction* (1994); Spike Lee's *Malcolm X* (1992); and Pedro Almodóvar's *Bad Education* (2004). Nonetheless, it is worth noting that Mexican directors fully exploit the manipulation of time and space. For instance, as previously discussed, González Iñárritu offers four versions of the same crash as the main scaffolding to support the story of *Amores perros.* He also deploys a slight temporospatial discontinuity in the presentation of the three main story lines of *Babel,* asking the ideal audience to fill in gaps among the times and spaces of three countries: Japan, Morocco, and Mexico.

Others, including Hernández, Eimbcke, Escalante, Reygadas, and virtually all the others not previously mentioned, stretch out time and expand the sense of space with their choices of lenses, camera angles and tracking, and composition and editing, among other considerations. Stephen Prince writes that "the projective geometry of successive camera positions creat[es] a screen geography whose coordinates we can readily analogize with our own visual experience."[30] For instance, Reygadas asks his audiences to *feel* the passage of time by using shots that average between ten and twenty seconds, which produces an especially intense feeling of time for today's viewers, who are accustomed to shots lasting three to five seconds. Similarly, Eimbcke's use of dissolves make us acutely aware that time has passed. As was already mentioned, Díaz Yanes and his DP choose to open *Sólo quiero caminar* with a horizontally tilted shot (or Dutch angle) of Gabriel pointing his gun down at someone we infer to be lying on the ground, where he summarily shoots. Not only does this prologue-like opening (the titles roll only after this opening shot) establish his character as one who does not quite fit into the mob world, but it identifies an implied director who controls the construction of the time and space of the story. The framing and construction of Gabriel in space immediately cues us to conceive of the character as the *central* protagonist, yet one with an *eccentric* worldview.

Directors manipulate time and space to create narrative rhythm and engage audience interest, as well as to intensify the conflict and resolution that characters undergo within their social and physical environments. In crafting these manipulations, they also decide which spaces and times to elide in ways that will guide viewers (whether loosely or rigidly) in filling the spaces thus created in the storyworld.

Emotion Function

In *Understanding Indian Movies* Hogan goes so far as to declare that "the main purposes of literary art is to communicate emotion,"[31] rendering secondary the communication of themes, ideas, and worldviews. I have been mentioning emotions continually when discussing how film blueprints work, from emotions represented to empathy for character and from emotional body movement response to feelings about the construction of the blueprint as a whole. All these considerations have shown the importance of the mechanisms whereby elements that make up the film blueprint trigger emotions. Emotion and affect form a central part of the viewing experience.

Mexican filmmakers aim to create blueprints that trigger two sorts of processes for emotional response, "low road" and "high road." Low-road emotions are automatic reflex emotions elicited when changes in our environment trigger direct pathways from sensory cortex to amygdala; examples include anger, disgust, excitement, and joy. We can clearly see the expression of low-road emotions in the raw with infants who have yet to develop executive cognitive fictions that could control and balance these reflex emotions. Unlike the low-road emotions (reflex responses to changes in the environment), high-road emotions are more cognitively evaluative in nature; they can arise after the fact with hindsight or rest on considered beliefs about something. Such emotions include, for example, grief and the so-called self-evaluative emotions of shame and guilt. They can include our emotional response, say, of shame or guilt at seeing a photograph. The low- and high-road emotion systems work both separately and together. Indeed, even our low-road emotions include a rather crude belief system: our reflex response when we *think* we saw something move, for instance.

Emotions are what philosophers call intentional states: they are always about something in the world. And they are always evaluative in the sense that they express a relation of self to that something (even if that something is yourself). Advances in the neurosciences today indicate that a handful of emotions (anger, surprise, etc.) are reflexlike responses to perceptual cues; other emotions (guilt, shame, etc.) necessarily involve higher-order cognitions in their production. In fact, the research indicates that the two sorts of responses involve different neural pathways. But they are all so-called intentional states; they are about things in the world, including one's own self. They express a relation between elements in the world and the self as subject.

Emotions, then, are forms of awareness of the self and the world and of the interactions among human beings and between humans and the rest of the world. Whatever the role bodily experience and subjective feeling might play in them, emotions are also interpersonal and social. They form one of the foundations of the connectivity between people and of the general architecture of society. They work as both a social glue and a social tool.

Many human emotions evolved as social tools to foster the multifarious and omnipresent cooperation that we have developed and constantly improved while incessantly working to transform both nature and ourselves in order to survive and multiply individually, as groups, and as a species. They are social tools that allow us to communicate and signal our feelings. In this respect having an emotion may be important, but so, too, is the ability to express emotions and understand such expressions in others.

Emotions themselves are extremely varied and complex. Some have an obviously positive valence, such as those that are soothing and indispensable for parental bonding, child care, child rearing, and teaching. Many emotions encourage altruistic behavior, and others foster often unproductive and harmful actions. Many so-called negative emotions trigger aggressive behavior that can cause harm and death (even genocide), yet they may also serve a defensive function that might be to further life-saving goals or purposes.

In making a film blueprint, the filmmaker guides the ebb and flow of both sorts of emotions. Carl Plantinga identifies these as "art emotions" because they are triggered not by messy, everyday encounters and actions but rather by the carefully constructed blueprint.[32] We sigh with relief, jump from our seats, and tear up—but always as directed by the "hypercoherent, exaggerated, and wildly distorted" blueprint.[33] For Hogan the film blueprint more generally operates by generating "emotion-laden sensitivity to opportunities and threats. Any disruptions of anticipation—including those caused by violations of continuity editing—are likely to have emotional effects to spur attention to causes. Attention to causes is, in turn, likely to foster thematic inference and the reconstrual of story elements."[34] And for Jens Eder, the film blueprint moves us across an emotion system landscape made up of a series of "complex episodes through the interaction of stimulus-representations, memory content, motivational tendencies, and mechanisms of control."[35] For Eder, then, the triggers of audience emotion involve "actions, motives and conflicts, the totality of the properties of the represented objects, and [extend] even beyond these."[36]

This control of our emotions is most commonly seen and experienced as character driven; that is, it stems from our engagement with a character's success or failure in overcoming obstacles to his or her goals. All this engagement, however, always happens in an "as-if" way. As Plantinga succinctly points out, "When spectators empathize with a character, they may or may not feel something similar to what she or he experiences . . . but it is rarely the same affect, and it is always tempered by the implicit awareness of the institutions of fiction and the viewing situation. The implicit knowledge of mainstream film conventions, including the probably happy ending, also assures viewers that their sympathy will typically result in psychic rewards."[37]

Emotion and cognition are never far apart in our film-viewing experience. For example, we experience emotions when evaluating the film itself or its blueprint. We may like or dislike a film not because of a character's action or an implied director's worldview but because the ingredients that make up the film do not cohere. This evaluation emotion, like that of our character-driven emotion, is in response to an *invented reality*—a new creation and addition to the existing world.

This coupling of emotion and cognition happens on a more basic level, too. When a film's plot falls apart or characters act in ways that are internally incoherent, given the film's logic, we stop investing emotionally.

And just as the logic system of a film influences our emotional investment, so, too, can a preexisting affect or mood influence how we interpret
and assign meaning to the story. We have all had the experience of walking
into a film in a bad mood. If the film's emotion system is uplifting, our mood
may prevent us from engaging the film as the blueprint requires and thus
lead us to misunderstand it. Both episodic emotions and enduring moods are
commonly viewed as helping determine epistemic salience; you notice what
you care about, and a given mood can lead you to emphasize certain elements about others. Seth Duncan and Lisa Feldman Barrett remark of their
research on the functioning of core affect that "what people literally see in the
world around them may in part be determined by their core affective state."[38]
This is a quick reminder that the viewing of Mexican films is done by flesh
and blood audiences who may or may not be in the mood to step into the
shoes of the ideal audience and who, therefore, will likely misread the sign-
posts, gap-filling cues, and emotion triggers presented by the film blueprint.

The mechanisms at work in our experience of basic, as well as more evaluative, emotions are the same across cultures—our shared evolution as a species guarantees this. Hogan writes that "our memories are structured in the
same ways, our cognitive processes are virtually identical, our emotional pro-
pensities differ only marginally."[39] And no matter where on the planet we are,
we all feel the real pain of torture and mutilation. That said, the expression of
some emotions may differ according to accident of birth in time (history) and
location (culture). Being born in Mexico, say, may lead someone to express
grief more outwardly than would a Japanese man of similar age, education,
and so on.

Directors can create blueprints that embrace or flatten distinctions between certain emotions and their expression. In some cases doing so might
result in rather prejudiced stories. (I'll mention a few later.) And a blueprint's
specific approach for triggering emotions can tell us much about the ideal
audience a director has in mind. We all feel joy and suffering, for example, but
films based on the melodramatic blueprint form tend to make an ideal audience feel them in particularly constrained, shallow, and stereotypical ways.

Laughter Function

Some contemporary Mexican film blueprints aim not only to make us feel
good but to giggle and laugh. Sometimes this has a deeper purpose, as in
films in which the laughing is closely tied to critique; Luis Estrada's *La ley
de Herodes* (1999) exemplifies this strategy. And there is laughing almost for

laughing's sake. Consider the bumbling, foolish actions that dominate films such as *7 mujeres, 1 homosexual y Carlos* (2004), or *Ladrón que roba a ladrón* (2007), among many others. Still other films, such as Carlos Cuarón's *Rudo y Cursi* (2008), aim to turn on smiles and giggles in relating rambunctious modern-day morality tales. In each such film we can see the director's "will to style" in the dominant use of what we might think of as humorous stimulus-delivery devices, that is, devices the directors use to variously distill, arrange, and deliver incongruous movements or beliefs, bringing them all together in the viewers' minds. (I use the term *will to style* here and elsewhere as a shorthand way to identify the degree of the presence of willfulness in the director's use of technique, imagination, and responsibility to subject matter.)

Laughter within film is carefully orchestrated, but so, too, is laughter as a result of the filmgoing experience. Directors can provoke it as a reflection of joy and mirth but also of debasement and humiliation. And, again, it can be used to stimulate thought about serious social, economic, and political problems.

The distillation, design, and delivery devices used to make viewers laugh run from the simple to the complex. Furthermore, films that provoke laughter by bringing together incongruous beliefs, for instance, may rest heavily on specific and idiosyncratic beliefs. An audience outside Mexico City, for instance, might not pick up on the incongruities of folk belief, say, because they are not familiar with the common doxa of the locale.

The humor blueprint can also be quite simple. People the world over share similar responses to incongruous movements, and the misreading of minds to comic effect is also a worldwide phenomenon. We see much of both in Mexican films that promise and produce laughter in all sorts of audiences.

Research in the cognitive and evolutionary biological sciences suggests that laughter has both a biological and a social dimension. Like other of our evolved mental faculties, our capacity to laugh helps promote the survival of the species. All humans, whatever their surrounding culture, typically have what has been called a "laughter-coordinating center" (located in the brain's dorsal upper pons, part of the brain stem that connects the cerebral cortex to the medulla oblongata), which coordinates the systems involved in laughter when, for instance, we are tickled by another person or, for instance, in response to incongruous or unexpected and recognizably safe stimuli.

Matthew Gervais and David Sloan Wilson argue that "incongruity and unexpectedness" cross-culturally undergird all "formal laughter-evoking humor,"[40] although this "perceived inconsistency between one's current and past experiences" must be formally framed by contexts of safety and play.[41] Rituals of laughter, they claim, offer an "alternate type of intelligibility, that is, a meaningful interpretation of some stimulus or event that is different from that which was initially assumed."[42]

In *Inside Jokes,* Mathew M. Hurley, Daniel C. Dennett, and Reginald B. Adams Jr. consider tickling to be a "swift and involuntary alternation between perceptions of attack and friendly touch. As this happens in a first-person, present-moment, sensory mental space based on reality, the experience does not require the cognitive tools that are necessary to elaborate a theory of mind or fictional mental spaces."[43] Moreover, they add, this attack/friendly touch response likely springs from an evolved false alarm signal sent to the group, indicating that the perceived threat is actually nonthreatening. This coast-is-clear signal, which indicates to the group *not* to be anxious, most likely broadened in meaning to communicate "detection of a resolution to an incongruity."[44] Our pleasure experienced in the laughter and its contagion seem to support this position.

Laughter involves a socially important distinction. Laughing *with* acts as a social glue that harmonizes the biological and behavioral state of a group. We can readily see how laughing with others who are laughing as an expression of happiness can and does bond a proximate social circle. In this sense, of course, laughter is an *adaptation:* its contagious function attracts the goodwill of parents and others in their world. This kind of laughter can also move us in an aesthetic way: we enjoy and are moved by the movement, expression, and sounds of a laughing child just as we would be moved by music, painting, or a well-made, fun, and funny Mexican film. Our engagement with representations of *laughing with,* then, whether the context be listening to a funny story or joke or watching a funny film, appears to be a nice by-product of the coast-is-clear or false-alarm signal following a perceived threat to the group. Laughing *at,* however, always involves an element of exclusion and further entrenches in- and out-group dynamics.

The difference between spontaneous and artificial laughter constitutes another important distinction (the former is known as "Duchenne laugher," the latter as "non-Duchenne laughter"). As we grow from infancy into childhood and beyond, we acquire and constantly fine-tune a capacity to differentiate these two kinds of laughter, a capacity that involves memory, models of others' minds, and mirror neurons, among other things. We constantly infer the mental states and intentions that we believe yield others' laughter in any given context, and children must constantly test such inferences when developing the ability to do this.

Andrea Samson and her research team have obtained results suggesting that we process all incongruity, including that found in humor, using the brain's left hemisphere, which is generally responsible for analysis, abstraction, and logical thinking.[45] Using fMRI to measure blood flow to the brain, they found activation in this hemisphere not just when subjects were presented with incongruities to resolve but also when they viewed various sorts of humorous nonverbal cartoons. More generally, this hemisphere predominates when we work out the humor in situations involving wordplay, semantic eccentricity, or misattributions of mental states to others. That is, the perception of humor and its consequent laughter result from the resolution of an incongruity performed via the same processes involved in general problem-solving activities, from our quick detection of logical flaws or the conflict between different domains of belief and our swift mental work in resolving them.

We fill in gaps and build conceptual schemas, or "mental spaces," by inferring from available data. That is, we use induction, abduction, and deduction to generate beliefs about how things work now and how they will work in the future. Hurley, Dennett, and Adams propose that humor is triggered by the "detection of a false belief in a mental spaces. Since we each can be expected to have tried to optimize our use of our inferential capacities to create these mental spaces, every such false anticipation reveals something about the limits of our useful knowledge about the domain involved."[46] So when we laugh, we "*unintentionally* reveal something of strategic interest about [our] knowledge."[47] When we do not laugh or find something funny, then, perhaps this is because we do not find that matter to be of strategic interest. Consequently, Mexican directors who aim to amuse a wide range of demographically and culturally diverse viewers will do well to build blueprints that rest on "highly accessible knowledge stores,"[48] that is, beliefs that a variety of people will find to be strategically interesting.

So there is raw humor, found in the wild, and the carefully distilled and directed humor found in film, which is experienced in an "as-if" way." As Hurley, Dennett, and Adams remark, artfulness of presentation in design, delivery, and timing can make something funnier in the retelling than in the direct experience thereof. Why? At least in part because, they explain, all the "distracting features" are bracketed, and only the "distilled comic essence" is transmitted."[49] At the same time, the retelling or reshowing can fail if the distillation, delivery, and timing are off. For example, if the material is delivered too quickly for the key elements to enter mental space, viewers may fail to grasp the incongruity; conversely, slow delivery increases the chance that "some conflicting piece of information will bring the key belief into epistemic doubt."[50]

Like any good joke or persuasive speech, a funny Mexican film needs to lead viewers at just the right speed and just long enough for them to acquire incongruent information without allowing other, secondary information (whether visual or auditory) the time to interfere with the primary information. The blueprint Carlos Cuarón uses for *Rudo y Cursi* (2008) is that of a humorous film, but this blueprint requires the viewer to laugh at, not with, the main characters, Beto, or "El Rudo" (Diego Luna), and his step-brother, Tato Verdusco, or "Cursi" (Gael García Bernal), who were born and raised in the Cihuatlán Valle of Jalisco and work as young men at a banana plantation. Initially, though, things may seem otherwise. The film opens with light, melodic *bajo sexto* music and a playful mock-epic voice-over narration. This not only establishes the lightheartedness of the film's tone but lays the groundwork for the humor and laughter to follow. Both Luna and García Bernal exaggerate their body movements and facial gestures to intensify incongruities, such as smiling while hopping around in pain or grimacing while experiencing pleasure. And Cursi projects an incongruous sense of himself as a talented singer. He's terrible, and everyone knows this but him. The script also includes lots of puns and dirty jokes. All this is aimed to make the ideal audience laugh with the characters.

As the film progresses, however, laughing at begins to dominate. When Rudo and Cursi travel to Mexico City, the implied director's worldview becomes apparent: their loud jokes and exaggerated movements portray country bumpkins cut off from and totally ignorant of the way things and people work in the world. We are supposed to *laugh at* their behavior, which depicts them not simply as the proverbial hapless schlemiels slipping on banana peels but as ignoramuses who have never seen Cup o' Noodles containers and possess preternaturally bad taste in furniture (gold embossed), cars (bling-bling rims), art (velvet Jesus posters), and clothes (electric blue tasseled charro suits). Cuarón's ideal audience is not a Rudo or a Cursi in the sense of real workers (whether on banana plantations or elsewhere), who know quite well how the world and its objects work, Cup o' Noodles included. The blueprint constructs an image of an implied director and ideal audience who laugh at Rudo and Cursi, and it betrays a deep prejudice against workers of the world generally.

Reality Effect Function

Neuroscience and cognitive science have made clearly important advances. But real minds and the worlds they construct categorically differ from fictional minds and the storyworlds in which they occur. Research on the brain's social circuitry can help us understand what goes on when people interact with one another and how they calibrate, judge, and evaluate emotions, as well as how they respond to them. And this research does enrich our understanding of the operations whereby real minds create and consume fiction.

Nonetheless, the science remains ancillary to the object of the study: in this case, Mexican films themselves. Herbert Lindenberger nicely articulates how advances in the brain sciences can enrich, but not replace, our objects of study: "We may come to know more about how we perceive, process, and enjoy art than we suspected before [and what] we learn from science may well affect the methods we choose to exercise our interpretive and evaluative skills,"[51] but that's all. We can increase our knowledge about the functions of the human brain and how it generates perceptions, emotions, and thoughts, but this knowledge may never lead us to knowing, say, the exact recipe for making the perfect Mexican film. As Plantinga remarks, "Films invite spectators to see, hear, and experience their created 'worlds' in particular ways, but these ways of experiencing are not necessarily those of any particular person or body."[52]

The experience of viewing Mexican films involves multiple brain processes in various systems, subtending both emotion and cognition, as well as blueprints that elicit a coherent sense of a built storyworld, yet the fictional is not the real; the map is not the territory. As Plantinga reminds us, "Movies often appeal to viewers not because they reflect experience, but because they idealize and exaggerate it. Movies are hypercoherent; they streamline reality, including in their narratives only what is needed to generated their desired effect."[53]

U.S.-Mexico Crossings, Trends, and Backdrops

Many twenty-first-century films by or about Mexicans are bound up with stories that one way or another cross the border between Mexico and the United States. In some cases, the film's story line plots the actions and develops the characterizations of individuals who cross the border. In other cases, a Mexican film achieves "crossover" success, with distribution and consumption in both countries. And in still other cases, Mexican directors or actors cross the border to work for Hollywood titans.

Character Crossings

A large number of Mexican films exemplify the first category. A few Mexican-directed and Mexican-cast films are set in the United States. Examples include Amat Escalante's *Los bastardos/The Bastards* (2009), a Spanish-language film about a day laborer turned hired gun; Juan Daniel Zavaleta's *El evangelista* (2006), a day-in-the-life tale about a Bible-quoting hit man who lives in Chicago; and Joe Menendez's comedic crime film *Ladrón que roba a ladrón/To Rob a Thief* (2007), set somewhere in Southern California. Most such Mexican films, however, cross into the United States but are not set there exclusively. They typically represent the material reality of people forced by dire economic necessity to make the difficult and dangerous crossing.

A few films, however, depict well-heeled characters who cross seeking spiritual self-awakening and other nonmaterial goals. In *40 días/40 Days* (2009), the director, Juan Carlos Martín (and his screenwriter, Pablo Soler Frost), tracks one day in the lives of three angst-ridden middle-class Mexican characters who drive a Mercedes convertible from Mexico City through northern Mexico and into the United States. As they travel across arid wastelands, bleak industrial landscapes, a Navajo reservation, and cities that include post-Katrina New Orleans, they drink, get high, recite poetry, and pause to contemplate life and death. For instance the character Ecuador (Luisa Saenz) takes a cue from a dragonfly smashed against the Mercedes' windshield to wax poetic on her difficult childhood: her parents abandoned her at tennis summer camp. Likewise inspired, the gay character, El Pato (Andrés Almeida), reads lines from his fiction, expressing his feelings of "hollowness" and asserting that "fear becomes him."

Making sure the audience fully understands that the characters have undertaken this crossing to find enlightenment (and showing it all with a straight face), Martín chooses to break up the straightforward realism with random sequences filtered through the subjective, grainy, overexposed viewpoint of a handheld video camera operated by Andrés (Hector Arredondo). Other elements further reinforce the spiritual worldview: an overexposed quality to the film that gives it a sprinkle of golden luminescence; a folk-inspired score reminiscent of Simon and Garfunkel, which punctuates the extradiegetic soundscape; and chapter breaks with titles such as "*muerte*" (death), "*paisaje*" (landscape), and "*alma*" (soul). Martín ends the film with a priest appearing as a deus ex machina to comfort Ecuador after Andrés's mysterious and sudden death.

When Juan Carlos Martín's characters cross the border for some ready-made McSpiritual salvation, the journey from Mexico seems to be as easy as picking up an order at a drive-though restaurant. We can see another borderland spirituality at play in *Santitos/Little Saints* (1999). In this film, which is an adaptation of María Amparo Escandón's novel (Amparo Escandón is also the screenwriter), director Alejandro Springall follows the journey of the pious protagonist, Esperanza (Dolores Heredia), and her quest to find her daughter; Esperanza does not believe that her daughter died of a tonsillectomy gone wrong and so begins to follow a trail of saintly visions that appear willy-nilly (the first appears on her oven's glass door, for instance), one that takes her from Vera Cruz (True Cross) to Tijuana and then across the border to Los Angeles. While she ends up empty-handed after crisscrossing the border, she returns to Vera Cruz having found her heart (she falls for a *luchador,* or masked wrestler, named Angel of Justice, played by Alberto Estrella); enlightened, she is now ready to get on with her life.

The crossing as *only* a spiritual journey (middle-class bohemian, *santito*-syncretic, or otherwise) seen in *40 Days* and *Santitos* is one extreme of the materialist–spiritual divide that informs today's Mexican border-crossing films. Others offer more of a middle ground, blending the spiritual with the socioeconomic. In *La tragedia de Macario/*The tragedy of Macario (2005), for instance, the director, Pablo Véliz, includes a strong spiritual current (e.g., the protagonist Macario's visions of a corrido-singing Virgin of Guadalupe) alongside a docudrama-styled realism that depicts the material conditions of those trying to scratch out a living in a small Mexican town. Although the camera-narrator closely follows Macario's plight and horrific journey (in a train boxcar) across the border, Véliz sugarcoats the climactic tragedy, when Marcario and others in the boxcar die from asphyxiation, by ending the film with a vision of the Virgin of Guadalupe singing a corrido about the event, which actually happened in Victoria, Texas.

In *La misma luna,* Patrica Riggen (director) and Ligiah Villalobos (screenwriter) show how bleak economic prospects in Mexico separate a mother, Rosario (Kate del Castillo), from her child, Carlitos (Adrián Alonso, the popular wide-eyed child actor who appears in Gustavo Loza's *Al otro lado* and Issa López's *Casi divas*). Rosario leaves Carlitos to find work in the United States but ends up exploited as a maid working for an upper-middle-class Anglo. Carlitos's repeated visions of a particular street corner and phone booth in Los Angeles, along with memories of hearing his mother's voice as she told stories, leads him in and out of danger as he crosses the border and travels to the American city. Against all odds—and the audiences' measures of the possible—Rosario and Carlitos miraculously find one another at this mystically foreseen Los Angeles street corner. By establishing this psychic thread between mother and son, Riggen can tie up all the film's frayed ends, so that when the titles roll, the audience knows to keep the faith. No matter the economic hardship, exploitation, and human tragedy, all will end happily ever after.

Other Mexican directors use different forms of the mystical as a deus ex machina plot device. For instance, in one thread of Gustavo Loza's three-part film *Al otro lado/To the Other Side* (2004), we follow the day-in-the-life story of the young Prisciliano Martínez (played by Adrián Alonso), who lives in Mexico City; the other two threads follow stories of children trying to cross borders from Cuba to the United States and from Morocco into Spain. Martínez so desperately misses his father, Rafael (Ignacio Guadalupe), who left to find work in the United States, that he builds a makeshift raft to cross a nearby lake in the belief that he will find Rafael on the other side. Loza nicely captures the strength of will of children and how their minds collect and confuse adult conversation and information into a mishmash: Rafael imagines and then builds his raft, sets out across the lake, and then sinks and drowns. Loza's sensitive and realistic portrait of the young Rafael's sensibility,

Fig. 9. La misma luna: Rosario

however, is overwhelmed by a heavy-handed emphasis on the myth of La Llorona, which has been threaded into the plot (in the legend, she drowns her children to be with her lover, and her lamentations are now sometimes heard near lakes); it is her weepy calling, and not the child's misdirected imagination, that leads to the tragic end.

Yet some Mexican filmmakers incorporate the otherworldly in their border-crossing films for stricter reasons of style. In *Buscando a Leti/In Search of Leti* (2007), for example, Dalia Tapia (both director and screenwriter) in- cludes just enough Catholicism to create a realistic portrait of a family living in the city of Zacatecas; with the parents in Chicago making money to send to Mexico, it is left to the grandparents to raise the seven children. Indeed, Catholicism supports and feeds the racism of the grandmother, Agustina (Carmen Cenko), who favors the light-skinned and blond (*güera*) grandchild over the darker ("like those Tarazcan Indians") protagonist, Leti (Tatiana Tein Tapia); the Abrahamic (or Manichean) dichotomy of light versus dark as good versus evil plays into the grandmother's racist and elitist ideology. Ironically, as the casting and script inform us, the grandmother is as dark-complexioned as Leti.

Of course the otherworldly is not the only device used to move plots or give dimension to character in contemporary border-crossing Mexican films. The U.S.-Mexico border itself can function as an initiating device for stories that take place almost entirely in Mexico. *Buscando a Leti*, for instance, begins with the mother, María (Antonia Rivera), writing a letter to her husband, Juan (Gilberto Lozano), who lives and works in Chicago. Decisions are made for María to leave Mexico and join Juan; we do not see the journey, but not until María is in Chicago does the story of Leti and her siblings in Zacatecas unfold. María Novaro's film *Sin dejar huella/Without a Trace* (2000) (also released as *Leaving No Trace*) begins with Ana (played by the Spanish actress Aitana Sánchez-Gijón) on the Mexican side of the El Paso/Juárez border about to be caught by *la Migra* (the U.S. Immigration and Naturalization Services, or INS).

After the opening sequence, which establishes Ana's character and her traffic in fake Mayan relics for U.S. markets, Novaro cuts to a sequence that establishes the character Aurelia (Tiaré Scanda), a single mother and *maquiladora* (factory) worker who wants more than she gets in her current life, one filled with macho violence and exploitation. She sits at the edge of the Rio Grande, contemplating the possibility not of crossing into the United States but of finding a better life somewhere else in Mexico. That is, Novaro uses the border merely as an impetus for change. Ana hitches a ride with Aurelia, and their journey to the Yucatan and emancipation begins.

Salvador Aguirre's *De ida y vuelta/Back and Forth* (2000) (also released as *To and Fro*) begins with the homecoming of Filiberto, or "Fili" (Gerardo Taracena), the bastard son of a recently deceased *hacendado* (landowner) who has been living in the United States. Fili arrives in a fancy new pickup truck, smiling larger than life with the air of having made it. The real story, however, quickly unfolds. The audience discovers that he has recrossed the border not to bring riches back home to woo his sweetheart, Soledad (Tiaré Scanda, who appears in *Sin dejar huella* as well), but rather for survival—to find work. He borrowed the truck to return home with the hope of finding a job at the deceased father's ranch, now under the draconian rule of the legitimate son.

Fili also discovers that Soledad has married his childhood friend, Luis (Ricardo Esquerra), who is one of the farmers victimized by the new *hacendado* (Fili's half brother), who seeks to control all the local sources of water, and when the legal system fails to expropriate the lands, he sends in his gun-toting henchmen to violently dispossess the families of their lands. The outcome: Luis and Soledad meet a tragic end. The border acts as an initiating device, leading to a story that harshly depicts the reality of the exploitation and oppression of farmers as they seek to find work both in rural Mexico and in the United States.

With few exceptions, such as Novaro's *Sin dejar huella,* Riggen's *La misma luna,* and Springall's *Santitos,* crossings of the U.S.-Mexico border make for stories that include or culminate in tragedy. For instance, one of the three plot threads that make up Alejandro González Iñárritu's *Babel* (2006) follows the story of a Mexican nanny, Amelia (Adriana Barraza), and her nephew, Santiago (Gael García Bernal), who cross into Mexico with the two children in her care to attend celebrations for the wedding of her son, Luis. The journey to Mexico proceeds without incident, but the trip back (one undertaken by two Mexicans with two blond children in the backseat) ends in catastrophe: they cross illegally and very dramatically into the United States; the children nearly die in the desert; and Amelia is jailed and deported back to Mexico.

Director Crossings

It is not only plots and characters that cross the border; directors, cinematographers, and actors do so as well. While not risking their lives wading through rapid river currents, crawling through rat-infested sewers, or trekking across deserts, a handful of high-profile and well-heeled Mexicans working in the film industry have worked or studied in the United States for a variety of reasons, including economic ones.

Some directors come to the United States for education and training, as did Fernando Sariñana, who studied at UCLA's film school. Antonio Serrano crossed a different border when he went to Britain to train in the dramatic arts, after which he returned to the Mexican film industry, making films such as the popular *Sexo, pudor y lágrimas/Sex, Shame, and Tears* (1999), as well as working in the telenovela industry. When making telenovelas, his camera crosses the border into the United States to shoot sequences that are supposed to be set in Mexico, as he did for his 2007 high-production telenovela biopic miniseries *Como ama una mujer* (How a woman loves) (Alex Cox was the director for the second unit). This series follows the rise of singer and actress Sophia Márquez (Leinor Varela), a character inspired by the life and songs of Jennifer Lopez. Serrano uses some aerial shots and sweeping pans to let the audience know this takes place in Mexico City, but the high-gloss shots of specific living and work locations are all filmed in the United States. Sophia Márquez does not live and work in even a represented Mexico City. She lives and works absolutely and totally in a fairy tale Mexico City.

The much media-hyped and marketed "Three Amigos" consists of Alfonso Cuarón, Guillermo del Toro, and Alejandro González Iñárritu. Like many contemporary directors in Mexico, these men began careers in television (advertising and shows) and then moved into feature-length filmmaking. With their respective art-house and mainstream breakout successes, each has crossed over to Hollywood; some of them even live much of the year in the United States.

Arguably the first out of the gate, Cuarón proved himself a good return on the money with the runaway success of the Yuppie-themed romantic comedy

Sólo con tu pareja (1991; Only with your partner), set in Mexico City. With backing variously from Warner Brothers, Fox Studios, Columbia Pictures, and Universal Studio, Cuarón went on to make *The Little Princess* (1995), *Great Expectations* (1998), *Harry Potter and the Prisoner of Azkaban* (2004), and *Children of Men* (2006), which cost $88 million to make (films by Mexican directors typically get $1–2 million in funding). Along the way, and during a time when Hollywood was looking to independents to bring vitality back to a waning industry, Cuarón made *Y tu mamá también / And Your Mom Too* (2001); the film found acclaim in both the art-house and mainstream spheres and was distributed by Fox.

Del Toro successfully deployed his eye for the horrific and baroque and his special effects wizardry in his 1991 film *Cronos*. His ability to deftly blend the horror and science-fiction genres into a riveting coming-of-age story made him yet another good bet for Hollywood. In 1997 he made the successful science-fiction film *Mimic;* in 2002 he intensified the gothic-horror look of the vampire franchise with the second installment of *Blade;* and in the twenty-first century he lassoed a big-budget comic-book franchise, serving up *Hellboy* (2004) and *Hellboy II* (2008) to more than healthy-sized international audiences. During this period del Toro managed to make two successful films set in Spain, *Devil's Backbone* (2001) and *Pan's Labyrinth* (2006); both received multinational funding and backing from Hollywood studios (Sony and Time-Warner, respectively).

The last to come into the fold was Alejandro González Iñárritu. For his breakout film, the hip and kinetic *Amores perros*, González Iñárritu received the bulk of his funding from Altavista, although his privately funded production company, Zeta Films, and others also contributed substantially (14 percent came from sources such as media mogul Carlos Slim Helú); the film's total budget reached $2.4 million. *Amores perros* caught the eye of a young, educated, middle-class audience in Mexico City and the attention of Hollywood. Released in March 2001, by July it had grossed $5 million in the United States and $20 million worldwide. It also largely launched the crossover career of Gael García Bernal. González Iñárritu next made *21 Grams* (2003), set in Memphis and boasting an all-star cast, including Sean Penn, Robin Wright Penn, and Benicio del Toro. After that, he dipped into Paramount Pictures' deep pockets to make *Babel* (2006). While arguably the last to arrive, it seemed written in the cards that González Iñárritu would end up steering the helm of this trio of filmmakers. He had been developing his big public persona long before as Mexico City's most popular disc jockey, then as creative director of publicity for the Mexican media behemoth Televisa.

Mexican directors are not the only ones drawn to the heat of the U.S. film industry. The cinematographer Rodrigo Prieto worked behind the camera on Iñárritu's *Amores perros, 21 Grams,* and *Babel,* as well as Ang Lee's *Brokeback Mountain* (2005). Rodrigo García (the DP for several of María Novaro's films, including *Lola* [1989] and *Danzón* [1991]) has shot episodes for the HBO shows *In Treatment* (2008), *Six Feet Under* (2001–5), and *The Sopranos* (2004); García has tried his hand at directing feature films, including *Things You Can Tell Just by Looking at Her* (2000), *Mother and Child* (2009), and *Albert Nobbs* (2011). Guillermo Navarro worked on several del Toro films, including *The Devil's Backbone, Pan's Labyrinth, Hellboy,* and *Hellboy II;* he also shot Mark A. Z. Dippé's *Spawn* (1997) and Robert Rodriguez's *Spy Kids* (2001). The DP for Cuarón's *Y tu mamá también* and *Children of Men,* along with Alfonso Arau's *Like Water for Chocolate* (1989), Emmanuel Lubezki has also worked on Tim Burton's *Sleepy Hollow* (1999), Michael Mann's *Ali* (2001), Brad Silberling's *Series of Unfortunate Incidents* (2004), Terence Malick's *New World* (2005), and the Coen Brothers' *Burn after Reading* (2008), among other projects. And this is just a few of the Mexican cinematographers who have made the crossing.

Actor Crossings

From María Félix, Anthony (Rudolfo Oaxaca) Quinn, Raquel Torres, Ramón Navarro, Ricardo Montalban, Gilbert Roland, and Dolores Del Río to Gael García Bernal, Salma Hayek, and Demían Bichir, Mexican actors and actresses have crossed the border in a steady flow. In *Heroes, Lovers, and Others,* Clara E. Rodríguez sums up this history.

> The early period was very likely the most generous of times for Latinos in film; many Latinos appeared in these early films, and they appealed to a wide audience. The climate warmed in the forties, when the screen image of Latinos improved, though it remained limited. The most barren of times occurred during the cold war era. The sixties and seventies were the worst of times, in terms of the quality of Latino characterizations, and the eighties represented the greatest contrast in the treatment of Latinos. The present is—relatively speaking, at least—the best of times for Latinos in film.[1]

In *Tex[t]-Mex* William Nericcio identifies the psychic rips, scars, and hallucinations that beset Latina actors crossing over, such as the "Mexican Spitfire" Lupe Veles (María Guadalupe Vélez de Villalobos) and Rita Hayworth (Margarita Carmen Dolores Cansino, who plucked her brows and radically refigured herself at the request of Columbia Pictures mogul Harry Cohn). Nericcio makes visible Hayworth's deep alienation, which eventually led to her soaked-in-alcohol decline as her "waking world became less and less tethered to material, concrete realities."[2]

Several contemporary Mexican actors of Middle Eastern origin have crossed over (media mogul Carlos Slim Helú shares this origin); the group includes Salma Hayek and Demián Bichir, as well as Demián's parents and his brothers, Bruno and Odiseo, all of whom participate in the theater and film industry. Hayek and Bichir moved from careers in telenovelas to Mexican feature films, and then on to U.S. films and television shows. From *Teresa* (1989) Salma Hayek went on to star in several action films set in Mexico but made in the United States, such as Robert Rodriguez's *Desperado* (1995) and *From Dusk till Dawn* (1996) and Barry Sonnenfeld's *Wild Wild West* (1999); she also acted in goofball comedies, such as Andy Tennant's *Fools Rush In* (1997) and the telenovela-style television series *Ugly Betty* (which she produced). Demián Bichir started his career at age fourteen in Televisa's telenovela *Rina* (1977) and, after starring in other telenovelas throughout the 1980s, moved on to become a mainstay of the Mexican art-house and mainstream industry, appearing in Jorge Fons's controversial and critically acclaimed *Rojo amanacer* (1989), Carlos Carrera's *La vida conyugal/Married Life* (1993), and *Cilantro y perejil/Recipes to Stay Together* (1995), Fernando Sariñana's *Todo el poder/Gimme the Power* (1999), and Antonio Serrano's *Sexo, pudor y lágrimas* (1999), among others. Demián Bichir has recently crossed over, starring in Steven Soderbergh's two-part biopic *Che* (2008); the Showtime network television series *Weeds* (2008), where he plays the Tijuana mayor and drug kingpin Esteban Reyes; and the Chris Weitz film *A Better Life* (2011), where he plays an undocumented gardener trying to make ends meet while living in East Los Angeles.

We should not forget the crossover successes of the Mex-ciné poster boys: Diego Luna and Gael García Bernal. (Sergio de la Mora provides additional information on these two in *Cinemachismo*.) Like the Bichir brothers (Demián, Bruno, and Odiseo), Diego Luna and Gael García Bernal come from families well entrenched film and theater. Luna hails from parents who worked as set designers in both theater and film, and García Bernal from actors in and directors of films. They, too, began acting at a young age in telenovelas, with Luna starring alongside García Bernal in *El abuelo y yo* (1992). Playing the central protagonists in the hip, daring, and politically interrogative *Y tu mamá también*—the embodiment of *buena onda* (good time) films— launched Luna and García Bernal across all sorts of borders. (The Mexican media uses *buena onda* as a shorthand term to characterize the wave of vital, cutting-edge Mexican films being made in the new millennium.) They have appeared regularly in international art-house films, as well as mainstream productions made and set in the United States: Gregory Jacobs's *Criminal*, the 2004 remake of Fabián Bielinsky's Argentinean *Nueve reinas*, Pedro Almodóvar's *Bad Education* (2004), Michael Gondry's *Science of Sleep* (2006), Harmony Korine's *Mister Lonely* (2007), Lukas Moodysson's *Mammoth* (2009), and Matt Piedmonts *Casa de Mi Padre* (2012), among others.

The crossover, however, is not unidirectional, moving only south to north. Many Mexican actors work in other nations' film industries, including those of Argentina, Colombia, Chile, and Brazil. For example, Damián Alcazár appears in Sebastián Cordero's *Crónicas* (2004), a film backed by del Toro and Cuarón and set in Ecuador; Demián Bichir stars in Juan Carlos Valdivia's *American Visa* (2005), set in Bolivia; and Bárbara Mori is the central protagonist of Claudio Dabed's *Pretendiendo* (2006), which takes place in Chile. Of course, like many people, actors will go where there's work, and production companies are themselves becoming increasingly multinational. Money from Portugal, Denmark, France, Germany, and the United States funded Bille August's 1993 film adaptation of Isabel Allende's novel *La casa de los espíritus/House of the Spirits;* the film included an international cast. Portuguese and Danish production companies funded Mike Newell's 2007 adaptation of Gabriel García Márquez's *El amor en los tiempos del cólera/Love in the Time of Cholera*, another film that starred actors from across the globe, including Javier Bardem.

With casting and money moving across borders, it is becoming increasingly difficult to talk about a national cinema. As A. O. Scott observes in a *New York Times* article published on January 21, 2007, "The boundaries separating national cinemas are more porous than ever."[3] For a case in point, Scott points to González Iñárritu's *Babel*, which was released by Paramount Vantage (a division of Paramount Pictures owned by the multinational corporation Viacom) with English subtitles that translate the dialogue in Spanish, Berber (Tamazight), and Japanese. Mexican films do not exist outside global capitalism, which Scott calls "the universal idiom of movie production and consumption."[4]

U.S. Crossings

The Mexican film plots, actors, directors, and cinematographers crossing the border to *el Norte* constitute a mere speck of sand if you compare this with the massive movement of Hollywood films constantly crossing into Mexico for the purpose of either exhibition or production. This ominously looming U.S. presence forms a backdrop to today's Mexican filmmaking.

The crossings are both representational and material. Above all, U.S. directors have for some time been going to Mexico to exploit the cheap labor there and the dollar's strength against the peso.

But U.S. directors have been drawn to Mexico since the early days of filmmaking. During the early twentieth century, some filmmakers traveled to border towns in Texas to film events in the Mexican Revolution. As Zuzana M. Pick carefully documents, they guaranteed their profits by using heavy-handed depictions of the revolution that were sure to include acts of heroism and romance. Later in the century, Sergei Eisenstein (in the 1930s) and the U.S.-trained director Fernando de Fuentes (1930s through the early 1950s), among others, would give Mexico and its inhabitants—especially rural ones—a pastoral, idealized makeover. As Pick remarks generally of this era, "spectatorship and image making are irrevocably tied to *mexicanidad*—a powerful trope designating at once a search for authenticity and a fashioning of an identity capable of accommodating the multiple, even conflicting features that make up the national imaginary."[5]

Again Mexico's cheap, exploitable labor pool has attracted quite a few U.S. directors. When making *Titanic* (1997), James Cameron went to Baja California for Mexican laborers who would build a full-scale replica of the eponymous ship. For *Fat Man and Little Boy* (1989), Roland Joffé had a replica of Los Alamos built in Durango, Mexico. Mexico's jungles and lax environmental policies helped John McTiernan cut production costs to a minimum in the filming of *Predator* (1987) and *Medicine Man* (1992). David Lynch cut costs by using Mexico's studios and landscapes to bring to silver-screen life his 1984 adaptation of *Dune*. Similarly, Paul Verhoven found Mexico's landscapes to be appropriately otherworldly for depicting life on Mars in his science-fiction thriller *Total Recall* (1990).

Many an Anglo actor, too, has crossed the border either literally or figuratively. Many Anglos in "brownface" line the streets and take siestas under trees in Fred Niblo's *Mark of Zorro* (1920) and many 1950s and 1960s Westerns, including Paul Landres and Lambert Hillyer's early 1950s television show *The Cisco Kid*, John Sturges's *Magnificent Seven* (1960), and Sam Pekinpah's *Wild Bunch* (1969). In Elia Kazan's *Viva Zapata* (1952), Marlon Brando appears in brownface, playing the role of the revolutionary Emiliano Zapata, and, as Steinbeck requested in the screenplay, Zapata's love interest, "Soldadera" (played by the Mexican born actress known as "Margo"), is depicted as a rural woman-girl "with a kind of savage animal beauty."[6] The Austro-Hungarian American Jewish actor Paul Muni plays Johnnie Ramirez in Archie Mayo's social-realist drama *Bordertown* (1935), and a brownfaced Charlton Heston steps into the shoes of the suave Mexican ambassador, Miguel "Mike" Vargas, in Orson Welles's *Touch of Evil* (1958). There are, of course, countless other examples.

Just as U.S. directors cross the border for Mexico's cheaper labor, so, too, does the border motivate action as an element in a plot, for "characters are driven to cross it," as Charles Ramírez Berg succinctly sums it up.[7] We've come to expect this of Westerns—those mentioned previously as well as Pekinpah's 1970s exploitation-influenced *Bring Me the Head of Alfredo Garcia* (1974) and Billy Bob Thornton's *All the Pretty Horses* (2000). In this last film, for instance, we follow the bildungsroman story of an Anglo cowboy, John Grady Cole (Matt Damon), as he crosses into Mexico to tame mustangs of a certain Mexican hybrid breed, much as he tames Mexican señorita Alejandra (played by the Spaniard Penelope Cruz). As he domesticates the wild Other (whether horse or woman), he learns of his own capabilities in the world and empowers himself.

Mexico appears as a plot device in a variety of genres and styles. Some films use Mexico to formulate a critique of the United States; Mexico serves this purpose for Ron Kovic (Tom Cruise) in Oliver Stone's *Born on the Fourth of July* (1989) and also for Charlie Smith (Jack Nicholson) in Tony Richardson's social-realist film *The Border* (1981). In the latter work, Smith gradually opens his eyes to the corruption in the United States, with its excessive materialism (manifested by Smith's neighbors, his Anglo wife, and fellow border patrol agents) versus the integrity and humanity of Mexico (figured by María [Elpidia Carrillo], with whom he forms an attachment and who lives along the Rio Grande). For Camilla Fojas, *The Border* is simply a gussied-up Western; much like yesteryear's cowboy, the border patrol officer functions as the "incarnation of U.S. moral values [and] of a serious and exemplary devotion and duty to the nation and its peoples."[8] Moreover, Fojas argues, while Richardson invests Charlie with a richer than usual emotional and moral mindscape, blame for his own corruption ultimately attaches to his hysterically greedy wife, so that in the end the film holds him up as the archetypal white savior to the "humble and victimized Mexican woman."[9]

Travel to Mexico works as plot device in many Hollywood screwball comedies and dramatic tragedies. Gore Verbinski's comedy *The Mexican* (2001) opens with Jerry Wellbach's (Brad Pitt) romantic relationship with Samantha (Julia Roberts) in shambles; the ensuing events are set in motion when the Mafia forces Jerry to travel to Mexico to recover a stolen gun for "El Jefe." As the film unfolds, we see a Mexico filled to the brim with gangsters and hoodlums (both straight and queer), sombrero-wearing farmers, wizened old people, mystical cemeteries, mysteriously crowing roosters, and random mariachi bands. As his journey through Mexico comes to a close, Wellbach becomes a more considerate person and caring boyfriend.

Several other films portray Mexico as redemptive. Tony Scott's *Man on Fire* (2004) does not present Mexicans as wizened or lazy, as *The Mexican* does, but it uses the country as the chaotic, violent, and irrational backdrop that allows the protagonist to find redemption. When the story begins, the audience meets the washed-up former military officer and CIA agent John Creasy (Denzel Washington). By its end Creasy has found his humanity once again, even giving his life to save the (supposedly) mixed-race Anglo-Mexican Pita (Dakota Fanning), the daughter of a wealthy industrialist, Sammy (Marc Anthony). Pita is kidnapped, and a series of screw-ups by the Mexican police chief (played by Italian actor Giancarlo Giannini, who speaks Spanish with an Italian accent) puts Creasy at center stage to save the day. Along the way the audience meets a series of irrational Mexican characters, including the father, Sammy; for example, he prays to the Virgin of Guadalupe to save his factory, exemplifying this irrationality.

Notably, *Man on Fire* goes to great lengths to depict Mexico City with a certain realistic coherence: the film includes aerial shots of the city, as well as shots that follow its densely packed people going to and from work and sequences that show Creasy driving Pita from Las Lomas, where she lives in her fortress, to her school near the Zócalo. On a second glance, however, the blueprint reveals its many incoherent gaps—slips that reveal a filmmaker who has not done enough homework. For instance, people who live in wealthy neighborhoods such as Las Lomas do not take their children to schools in the center of Mexico City, much less have their children taught by nuns, who in Mexico are mostly illiterate. Members of Mexico City's haute bourgeoisie tend to keep to their fortified neighborhoods. Travel, when it occurs, is undertaken for business reasons.

Redemption figures prominently in U.S. films that cross into Mexico. David Ayer's *Harsh Times* (2005) offers yet another tale of redemption for a down-and-out former soldier. This time the story follows Jim Luther Davis (Christian Bale), who suffers from post–traumatic stress disorder caused by a recent special ops mission in the Middle East but finds his peace in Mexico, whose bucolic landscape provides him with the comforts of home cooking and the affectionate arms of his love interest, Marta (Tammy Trull). Marta enchants Jim with her sage-sounding folkloric riddles. A couple of Tecate beer cans in hand, Jim tells his buddy, Mike Alonzo (Freddy Rodriguez), that Marta is "untouched" and "of the earth."

Like their Mex-ciné counterparts, Hollywood story lines that travel south of the border can take a spiritual tack. For instance, Darren Aronofsky's film *The Fountain* (2006) offers yet another unreeling of Anglo fantasy make-believe. In the three parallel stories, Hugh Jackman plays three different protagonists: a modern-day oncologist, Tommy; a superhumanly fit Spanish conquistador, Tomas Creo, who is attacked by a marauding Mayan high priest covered in tattoos and wielding a dagger; and a Buddhist-like figure, Tom, who inhabits an outer-galactic biosphere. Not one to shortchange the details, Aronofsky spent part of his budget's more than $30 million to capture an "authentic Mayan feel" by transporting Mayans to Montreal to work as extras. The film's end tells it all: images of the three stories are juxtaposed in quick succession as Tom reaches some sort of nirvanic bliss, sitting in the lotus position and enveloped in white light as he ascends into the universe from his New Age biospheric spacecraft.

In contemporary big-production cinema (Hollywood or otherwise), Mexico is all too often portrayed in terms of a fundamental stereotypic opposition: peace versus violence. Mel Gibson's *Apocalypto* (2006) depicts pre-Columbian Mayan life as one of either peace and harmony or chaos and bloodshed. Gibson's filmmaking here is lazy and irresponsible, collapsing a century and a half of Mayan history into a day without showing or even vaguely indicating that the Maya had an extraordinary civilization built on an extremely sophisticated and advanced agricultural irrigation system capable of feeding hundreds of thousands of families. The film's final message echoes the tried and true formula of European imperialism: the white man (Spanish conquistadores) arrives to save the primitive Other (the Maya) from destroying one another. And this association with primitive violence persists: when three Anglo college kids wander across the border in Zev Berman's *Borderland* (2009), they fall victim to a gang of bloodthirsty satanic drug smugglers; it seems Berman's idea of Mexicans today matches that of Gibson's uninformed, childish, and sadistic imagination.

Scholars, including Mary Beltrán, Camilla Fojas, Clara E. Rodríguez, William Nericcio, Charles Ramírez Berg, and Isabel Molina-Guzman, have carefully considered the negative representation of Mexicans and Latinos manufactured by the U.S. film industry. In *Magical Reels* John King comments on early-twentieth-century U.S. films that created greaser/bandit stereotypes. He writes, "The North Americans created a vision of the Revolution and of an 'other'—the Mexican people."[10] Such early films were, he informs us, "a blend of popular southern literature (dime novels, the Western) and the daily press and newsreel reporting of the Revolution."[11] For King, the stereotypes worked as an ideological tool to further solidify U.S. expansionism.

Clara E. Rodríguez follows the historical shift from exotic and hyper-erotic to dirty, degenerate, and drug addicted. For instance, Rodríguez writes, "The relatively old fifties stereotypes of Latin lover and Latina bombshell would become more intensely 'other'—more alien, exoticized, eroticized, and violent—beginning in the sixties, intensifying in the seventies and continuing into the eighties."[12] Others excavate the Latino figure in contemporary popular cultural iconography. Katarzyna Marciniak considers the representation of "aliens" in a variety of narrative fictions, including depictions of undocumented immigrants in Gregory Nava's *El Norte* and the Mexicans literalized as "foreigner-aliens" and "substandard others" in Sonnenfeld's *Men in Black*.[13] In *Latino Images in Film*, Charles Ramírez Berg reads Schwarzenegger's flesh-over-metal Terminator and the Replicants in *Blade Runner* as futuristic *bandoleros*.

This inglorious, larger-than-life silver-screen canvas casts just as wide a shadow over Mexico and its filmmaking industry. Mexican filmmakers must imagine and create within and against this representational (and material) history.

Contexts, Critiques, Distribution, Exhibition, and Obstacles

✄

Twenty-first-century Mexican films have been identified by media pundits, scholars, and their directors themselves as part of the vital, vibrant *buena onda* (roughly, "new vibe") Mexican cinema that, in the words of Alfonso Cuarón, is "reclaiming its part in the world."[1] Many take *Amores perros* and *Y tu mamá también* to be the films that best embody this *buena onda* worldview.

For instance, Jethro Soutar considers how the contemporary look, action, language, and sociopolitical concerns of the characters in *Amores perros* appeal to a "demographic of the cinemagoing public" comprising "the young and the educated."[2] He adds that *Y tu mamá también* "lit up screens with its depiction of the lost generation of Mexico's youth while providing social commentary on the country to boot."[3] For Carlos Reygadas, this *buena onda* cinema grows from and appeals to a population he identifies as the "crisis-generation" filmmakers and audiences.[4] In the search for new forms to shape new, contemporary stories, Mexican film directors, according to Ann Marie Stock, began to "look beyond the confines of strict geopolitical parameters."[5]

Through their production company, Canana Films (2003), Gael García Bernal and Diego Luna have been helping to churn out films that capture this new vibe spirit. These projects include Gerardo Naranjo's *Drama/Mex*, Díaz Yanes's *Sólo quiero caminar* and *Revolución*, Laura Amelia Guzmán and Israel Cárdenas's *Cochochi* (2008), and Jorge Hernandez Aldana's psychologically cryptic *El Búfalo de la noche/The Night Buffalo* (2007), an adaptation of Guillermo Arriaga's novel of the same name.

I already mentioned how Naranjo uses characters' body language in *Drama/Mex* to elicit emotion in the audience. He triggers emotion and conveys mood with a minimum of dialogue and employs long, grainy shots (Su-

per 16 film blown up to 35 mm) to convey the young characters' deep disaffec-
tion with themselves, others, and the world. Naranjo creates a blueprint that
amplifies the inert and hollow nature of youth today. When making *El búfalo
de la noche,* Hernandez Aldana (a Venezuelan-born director who used to create television ads) chose filmic devices (e.g., overexposed lighting with a gray-
blue tint reminiscent of hospitals), a kaleidoscopic time structure, sounds
(Omar Rodríguez-López's bass-heavy techno and electronica tracks), and
plot (a love triangle and a suicide) to create a cool, emotionally guarded story
about several young, beautiful twenty-somethings who lack direction and
meaning in a dead and deadening world. The blueprint elides information
about the lives of the characters and their motivations, leaving many big questions unanswered. Why does Gregorio (Gabriel González) kill himself? Why
is Manuel (Diego Luna) crazy over—and even willing to die for—Gregorio's
ex-girlfriend, Tania (Liz Gallardo)? The blueprint seeks to pull in a young,
middle-class audience (e.g., via the casting of attractive young actors and the
use of nonmainstream dance music) yet to keep viewers at a distant remove
from the lives and world of this crisis generation. No answers are given. All
involved remain estranged from themselves and others. We feel nothing.

While identified as technically innovative, new, and representative of
today's crisis generation, the directors themselves clearly recognize that the
techniques they use and stories they tell build on and extend what has been
done before. Cuarón, del Toro, María Novaro, Francisco Athié, José Buil,
Carlos Carrera, Dana Rotberg, and Marisa Sistach all trained under such
veterans as Arturo Ripstein Sr., Pedro Armendáriz, and Felipe Cazals, among
others at the Centro de Capacitación Cinematográfica and the Centro de
Estudios Cinematográficos. In addition, Laura Podalsky has identified how
Amores perros and *Y tu mamá también* share "thematic preoccupations and
stylistic tendencies with U.S. films like *Rebel Without a Cause.*"[6]

Nonetheless, while these directors share significant common ground with
such U.S. forebears in terms of theme and stylistic choices, Podalsky reveals
how they enlarge and complicate the filmic terrain. For Podalsky Mexican
films tend to register "a decentered subjectivity typical of living in 'industrial-
izing' countries whose place in a globalizing world is particularly uncertain."[7]
Furthermore, she argues that even if the two traditions share, say, themes
of disaffected youth, Mexican cinema privileges working- and underclass
representations and indicts "societies riddled by mundane acts of violence,
exploitation, and emotional brutality."[8] Twenty-first-century Mexican film
directors make new the experience of films, but they do so by standing on the
shoulders of those who have come before, Mexican or otherwise.

Time and Place Contexts

Matters of time (history) and place (geographic region) importantly inflect the kinds of blueprints Mexican filmmakers create. For instance, if we do not understand the history of the PRI (Institutional Revolutionary Party) and the PAN (National Action Party) administrations in Mexico, we will not fully understand Luis Estrada's *La ley de Herodes* as social satire aimed at political critique. The ideal audience needs this information, but the film does not provide it. We need to know this information if we are to experience the full range of thoughts and feelings the blueprint is designed to convey. Yet some filmmakers choose to make blueprints that abstract time and place. In the thread of *Babel* set in Mexico, González Iñárritu includes a scene showing the bloody and violent decapitation of a chicken during a wedding reception, although this is filtered through the perspective of a young Anglo boy from the United States. Even though Mexican wedding receptions do not include slaughtering chickens, the ideal audience is supposed to feel the horror of the moment as seen from the Anglo boy's outsider point of view.

The more information we have about the particular film industry (e.g., its traditions, genres, and distribution practices) and applicable historical context (e.g., relevant political and social issues), the more we are likely to step into the ideal audience's shoes. Of course, González Iñárritu is assuming an ideal audience that will not have this storehouse of knowledge; again, Mexicans do not decapitate chickens at wedding receptions. Those of us who know this to be the case will, of course, reject this scene—and if enough of these out-of-time and out-of-place scenes accumulate, as they do in *Babel*, we may well reject the entire film.

This sort of knowledge of time and place opens us to interesting and fruitful film comparisons. For instance, Luis Buñuel's *Los olvidados/The Young and the Damned* (1952) offers a compelling baseline for comparisons and contrasts to the times and spaces represented in other, more contemporary films set in Mexico City. Given that Buñuel has been identified as a "perverse elder statesman for the subsequent generations of Mexperimentalists,"[9] it is not surprising that we find a thread of influence running from him to contemporary filmmakers such as Gerardo Tort. Like *Los olvidados*, Tort's 2001 film *De la calle/Streeters*, an adaptation of Jesús González Dávila's play, portrays the plight of poor children living in Mexico City. While the thematic focus is the same, however, the contrasts are remarkable. Buñuel's camera follows the story of poor children living a tragic and fragile existence, but *within families*, albeit poor ones. Buñuel captures a growing Mexico City, which, although freeways are being built, still includes room for growing vegetables and keeping chickens and cows. The children are able to eat, grow, and even trust adults in this early 1950s Mexico City, a place that has yet to rip apart at its socioeconomic seams.

While poverty, violence, and tragedy are the backbone to Buñuel's film, the tragic death of it character, Pablo, is intensified precisely because this Mexico City exists before capitalism has destroyed its social tissue. There is still a glimmer of hope for Buñuel's *olvidados* (forgotten ones).

This point stands out when we see Tort's *De la calle*, where poor children are depicted as homeless, victimized by police, and forced to live in the sewers of an early-twenty-first-century Mexico City. We see how, in the fifty years that have passed since Buñuel's forgotten ones, capitalism's transformation of material reality has led to the near total abandonment and obliteration of Mexico City's street children. In tracing the course of capitalism from the production of necessary goods (foods, clothes, etc.) to the production of useless (personal betterment commodities) and even destructive goods (weapons of war), Eli Zaretsky identifies the general trend toward creating a hollow emptiness in people, where everyday life is experienced as "formless, with no common core, in inexplicable disarray."[10] This is the trend we see and feel when watching first Buñuel's and then Tort's representation of children in Mexico City.

There's a glimmer of hope in Buñuel's 1950s that has been completely extinguished for Tort's *olvidados*. In Buñuel's film the disfranchised still enjoy a sliver of possibility for life; by the early-twenty-first century, the fate of the forgotten ones has been sealed.

For this reason Tort chooses to begin and end the film with a Ferris wheel, a circular image that intensifies the ideal audience's sense that the impoverished lack any possibility of escape from exploitation and oppression. When Rufino tries to escape, his supposed best friend, Cero, stabs him to death at the foot of the Ferris wheel. The shapes and lines shown here suggest Rufino's failed attempt to find a new trajectory for himself and his love interest, Xóchitl, a line away from the Ferris wheel of this circular and tragic life.

Socioeconomic and Political Contexts

Other sorts of contexts matter, too. In material terms, the political and economic contexts in which a Mexican filmmaker operates can determine the possible means for the work done in expressing and realizing ideas, images, and stories.

This influence can take the form of public- or private-sector funds that establish the bounds within which a filmmaker can navigate. As the previously cited remark from Carl J. Mora indicates, NAFTA trade and tax policies made it difficult for Mexican filmmakers to secure public funding, nearly wiping out the film industry altogether in the 1980s and 1990s. Also, with a noose around IMCINE, which had traditionally secured protective measures for Mexican filmmakers, Mexican directors who manage to make films encounter a crushing avalanche of U.S. films competing for space at the theaters. Very few screens are available in Mexico for Mexican films.

At the same time, private multinational sources of funding can impose all sorts of direct and indirect controls and censoring mechanisms that straitjacket a filmmaker's work. For instance, Televisa and its subsidiary, Televicine, have bought up the rights to distribute many of Mexico's films in order to control their release, either delaying or completely preventing it, so as to increase profits from the exhibition of their own *comedias* and *comedia románticas.*

Political contexts matter significantly in the making of Mexican films. Nonunion films have been banned in Mexico since the 1920s, when the PRI became the nation's official governing party, yet if trade unions do exist, they must be officially recognized by the government. With unions in the state's control, film-industry workers lacked any authentically independent representation. If a director tried to make a film criticizing the administration—or worse, the sitting president—the administration would simply kill the film by having the union's leader organize a strike at just the right moment.

This sort of thing has occurred several times. When Luis Estrada failed to secure public funds for the distribution of *La ley de Herodes,* he found the money elsewhere. Curiously, however, the copies of his film were lost on their way to the theaters. In another case, the Presidential Military Guard and the Carlos Salinas de Gortari administration tried to bury Jorge Fons's *Rojo amanecer* (1989), a film that tells of the brutal mass murder (estimates of the dead run to six hundred) and rape of students, workers, and civilians by the judicial police and military in the 1968 "Tlatelolco Massacre." While massive pressure from the film industry and the public forced the Salinas de Gortari administration to give the film a limited screening in Mexico, Fons continued to face insurmountable obstacles in its international distribution.

Francisco Vargas Quevedo's *El violín* (2006) is a more recent example of a film that met such a fate. Based on the true story of the farmer Carlos Prieto, the film is a no-holds-barred portrayal of today's Mexican military, which condones the rape and killing of innocent people. It is a rich, unsentimental portrait of farmers and their struggles to survive in a country with a long history of policy making that seeks their obliteration.

By the time Vargas Quevedo had finished the film and begun the process of securing its distribution, the final policies of NAFTA were in play, driving up the price of basic grains a hundredfold. The story of this film's difficulties reflects the administration's anticipation of uprisings around the country in response to this increase. In the name of clamping down on the drug cartels, the Felipe Calderón administration had already been securing the countryside with the kind of military outposts the film depicts; the military was given carte blanche to squash any actual or presumed revolts.

In January 2008, the signatories to NAFTA began to fully enforce the last section of the treaty, which caused a sharp increase in the cost of basic staples, such as rice and beans, a development that wreaked havoc on the lives of people who earn less than a dollar a day. In anticipation of the powder keg about to explode in the countryside, President Calderón mobilized the military against the people, all in the name of cracking down on the narcotics trade. (As reported in the *New York Times* on August 3, 2010, Guillermo Valdés Castellanos, Mexico's director of national security and investigation, or Cisen, estimated the "drug-related" death toll since Calderón took office to be upward of twenty-eight thousand.)[11]

Like Estrada's *La ley de Herodes, El violín* nearly died on the postproduction-room floor as a result of backdoor dealings. Quevedo had to dig into his own pockets for distribution—and even then the film was exhibited at only a handful of theaters in Mexico City. In spite of all this, the film has enjoyed a rich life among distributors and buyers of pirate copies.

Political Critique

Many a media pundit applauded the shift in power when the PAN beat the PRI in 2000, predicting that it would liberate the industry and open the gates for films critical of the government. Some filmmakers chose to critique the government fairly directly, while others took a more indirect angle. In this respect, some blueprints are more successful, others less so.

Genre conventions are often used to soften sociopolitical critiques leveled at contemporary government administrations. We see this clearly with Luis Estrada's choice of comedic satire in *La ley de Herodes;* by setting the action in a vague and distant time (roughly the 1940s) and an unidentified place (somewhere in northern Mexico), he softens the blow directed toward the PRI administration as it was losing power to the PAN in 1999. Similarly, Estrada sets his social satire *Un mundo maravilloso* (2006; A wonderful world) in a never-never land. He opens with turning pages in a book of fairy tales and a sweet, melodic voice-over: "Once upon a time in a not too distant future in a marvelous country . . ." A page with a painted castle becomes animated and then morphs into a straightforward realist shot of a Davos-like economic forum filled with wealthy capitalists celebrating a speech on laissez-faire capitalism as the cure-all for the world's ailments. Then we follow the rags-to-riches story of Juan Pérez (Damián Alcázar), which is meant to critique the PRI, the PAN, and global capitalism generally. Estrada ends the film on a bittersweet note: Juan miraculously achieves the suburban middle-class dream (through a deus ex machina plot maneuver), with his friends from the barrio happily in tow. Estrada lobs a critique at the government but ultimately endorses an individualist, free-market solution to today's corruption, exploitation, and oppression.

Jorge Ramírez Suárez uses the conventions of the political thriller to frame his critique of the government in *Conejo en la luna/Rabbit on the Moon* (2004). The director principally employs suspense to propel the story of a graphic designer named Antonio (Bruno Bichir) as he descends into the greedy and murderous world of Mexico City's politicians, judges, and police. The tradition of the suspense thriller, which typically takes the audience into the underbelly of corruption, provides a palatable frame; the film focuses less on a corrupt government per se and more on a loose canon and lone rotten apple—the politician Nicolas López (Álvaro Guerrero), identified as a sadist and gay—as the source of all the corruption and social ills generally.

The director Fernando Sariñana chooses the dark comedic mode to shape his social critique in *Todo el poder* (1999; Gimme the power). While the ideal audience is meant to feel good at recognizing the implicit criticism of the Mexican government that lies beneath the surface of the comic action, Sariñana ultimately plays it safe, identifying the source of the corruption in a series of individuals (a judge, a petty police official, and a government functionary) and not the executive branch and its chief.

These film blueprints, which Estrada, Ramírez Suárez, and Sariñana ostensibly created to provide political critiques, aim to lead the films' ideal audiences to feel pleasure and a sense of accomplishment in sleuthing out not a transnational web of corruption but corruption as a result of a lone, loose, and perverse individual. Not that the films should be judged otherwise, but it might be difficult for people who know better—who open their doors to an everyday material reality filled with suffering and dying at the hands of a senile and corrupt capitalist system—to invest in films that proclaim themselves to be antiestablishment in such a shortsighted way.

Distribution

Whether they make social satires, political thrillers, or hard-hitting, sociopolitically aware, realist dramas, Mexican filmmakers generally find it difficult not only to secure funds but also to distribute and exhibit their works. The big squeeze on IMCINE and other sources of public funding has prompted an increased reliance on private sources of funding, such as Televisa or Carlos Slim Helú's Estudio Mexico Films. However Mexican filmmakers choose to fund their films, though, they still face huge expenses for distribution and exhibition. As Roy Armes explains of non-Hollywood cinema generally.

> The producer is forced to cede rights in his film to the distributor, since he needs a distribution guarantee to raise the risk capital. The distributor does not, however, need to yield these rights in turn to the exhibitor, since the latter needs only a regular flow of assorted films on short-term hire. Power in the film industry therefore resides in the distribution company, which as a purely financial organization, can be located anywhere in the world: it is an intermediary stage not bound geographically to either the studios where the films are produced or the cinemas where they are exhibited.[12]

It is not surprising, then, that U.S.-owned distribution companies predominating in Mexico are not willing to let others in on the action. They want control over the distribution of Mexican films in Mexico and everywhere else.

Nevertheless, Mexico does have its own production and distribution companies, including Altavista, Galavisión, Univisión, and TVAzteca, among others. With state support waning and a young, middle-class demographic coming to prominence, the production company Altavista was born from the coupling of a large event management company (Corporación Interamericana de Entretenimiento, or CIE) and Sinca Inbursa. Altavista is one of the main sources of funding for Mexican films, especially those targeting young, middle-class Mexican audiences. For example, Altavista largely bankrolled *Amores perros,* covering 86 percent of the budget, and NuVision poured over a million dollars into the marketing ($70,000 is typical for a Mexican film) and put it on 220 screens when it opened. As a result, 270,000 Mexican filmgoers went to see it the opening weekend. As Soutar writes, "It would go on to be the biggest box-office draw of the year and finished up grossing U.S.$8.8 million in Mexico, making it then the second-most successful domestic film ever (after *Sexo, Pudor y Lágrimas/Sex, Shame, and Tears*)."[13]

Such production and distribution companies are generally not interested in art-house, independent Mexican films. With a majority of Mexicans having developed a taste for Hollywood blockbusters, all but a few local distribution companies in Mexico are hostile to Mexican films. The Mexican production company Decine, for instance, decided to release *Al otro lado* at the same time as *Batman Begins* and *Madagascar*. Rather than seeing this as an opportunity to promote *Al otro lado*, Decine gave the film only a two-week run before wiping it from the screens. Eugenio Polgovsky's 2008 film on the conditions of child labor in rural Mexico, *Los herederos/The Inheritors*, made money at the Mexican box office, yet by its second week Cinemex exhibitors had relegated it to 11:00 a.m. screening slots, where it quickly lost audiences and its marketing steam. Laura Amelia Guzmán and Israel Cárdenas's *Cochochi* (2007) met an even worse fate. It ran for only two days before disappearing from the cinemas altogether.

To secure a solid place in filmmaking, Mexico would have to create, as Roy Armes remarks, "a secure domestic distribution base with well-developed exhibition circuits. Without this, the possibility of a profitable return on investment in film production does not exist. But the very existence of such a base means that the country is more than ever vulnerable to imports from abroad, unless—like present-day India—it can produce on its own the many hundreds of films needed each year to feed such exhibition outlets."[14] But this is not what has happened, for NAFTA paved the way for U.S. distributors to control everything. It is Warner Brothers, Universal, Sony, Fox, and other similar corporations that decide what the public does and does not see. There are more than four thousand screens in Mexico, yet when *El violín* was ready for distribution, only twenty copies were made. The huge spread of *Shrek 3* across Mexico easily suffocated *El violín*'s limited-run showings. In fact Mexican films are often marketed and distributed only during the months of seasonal drops in audience attendance.

Ironically, even though filmmaker Alfredo Joskowicz remarks that Mexican theaters show fewer than 10 percent of locally produced films, he celebrates the positive side effects of NAFTA, specifically, "the proliferation of the American-style" multiplex theater with "improved screening facilities and improved technical specifications."[15] For Joskowicz, this development ushered in a "new freedom of choice" for Mexican audiences.[16]

Once a film is distributed, most of every dollar it makes goes to the distributor. So even if the film is a blockbuster in Mexico, by the time the producer is repaid and the exhibitor takes its cut, nothing is left for the director. As a result, the average Mexican director is now lucky to make one film every twelve years. Before NAFTA Mexican directors were averaging a film every four years.[17]

While a long tradition of cultivating tastes for the Hollywood blockbuster certainly makes life difficult for most Mexican filmmakers, it seems to have helped some directors, including Sarañana and Antonio Serrano, find increased ticket sales. In 1999, when Serrano's film *Sexo, pudor y lágrimas* was released all over Mexico, it made a quick profit of $12.5 million. Fox's deep-pocket marketing campaign probably didn't hurt. The same happened with Sariñana's *Todo el poder,* which also turned a big profit for the distributor and producer. While the industry's marketing and distribution titans no doubt helped sell tickets, these films succeeded in part because their light content appealed to a middle-class Mexican audience willing to pay for two hours of fantasy wish fulfillment. Conversely, Columbia Tri-Star's decision to back and distribute Carlos Carrera's more controversial *El crimen del Padre Amaro* was arguably the decisive factor pushing its sales, not its crushing critique of corruption and criminal behavior in the Catholic Church; it exhibited at over 360 screens and turned another quick profit of $5.7 million. All this, however, pales in comparison with Paramount Pictures' decision to back González Iñárritu's *Babel,* a film that, according to Simeon Regel, generated $56 million in worldwide sales.

Exhibitors

In 1992 the Mexican film industry witnessed the deregulation of ticket prices. At the same time, Cinemark entered the exhibition market with its Cinemex theater chain in Mexico City. The Ramírez family followed quickly, introducing Cinépolis, a chain of theaters that would eventually spread to small towns and cities across Mexico and elsewhere in Latin America—and that would blatantly cater to an upper-middle-class Mexican audience.

A sort of "lifestyle cinema," Cinépolis publishes its own glossy magazine, advertising Armani handbags, Chanel shoes, and "world-class" spas and restaurants. The chain offers a range of theater experiences: for an extra fifty pesos beyond the regular hundred-peso ticket, you may enter a variety of different VIP screening rooms variously identified as the Sala del Movimiento, the Sala de la Imaginación, the Sala 3D, the Sala Inspiracional, the

Sala Interactiva, and the Sala de Música. For that elite experience—and yet another hundred pesos—it offers patrons experience of the VIP room called La Cúspide. This also includes entrance to a lounge area called *el lobby,* where patrons can spend more money purchasing a *comida japonesa,* cappuccino, dessert, or cocktail, all to be brought to them either in the lounge or during the film "poco a poco en un *mood* de confort y tranquilidad" (little by little in a mood of comfort and tranquility); once in the theater itself, they receive waiter service and cushy leather-clad recliner-style chairs to sit in while watching the film. Considering that around twenty million Mexicans are forced to live on five pesos a day (about fifty cents), a night out at the Cinépolis is more than extravagant.

Denizens of Cinépolis are not just the well-heeled with a taste for the Hollywood blockbuster or Mexico's teen-oriented bubblegum films. Press and commercial screenings for the seventh Morelia International Film Festival (October 3–11, 2009) were held, as Paul Julian Smith notes, in "the enviably modern Cinépolis Centro theaters, complete with stadium seating and digital projection."[18]

The Ramírez family empire continues to grow and turn big profits. By 2001 there were about two thousand Cinépolis screens in Mexico. Their presence in Mexico and other Latin American nations continues to increase, and the chain has now captured more than 45 percent of the exhibition market. (It has also made forays into Southern California and the Indian subcontinent.) The empire has moved into production, largely limiting itself to bubblegum films, such as Alejandro Gamboa's *El tigre de Santa Julia* (2002; The Tiger of Santa Julia) and *La primera noche* (2003; The First Night), as well as Eva Lopéz Sánchez's *La última y nos vamos* (2009; One more and we leave) and the animation *Otra película de huevos y un pollo* (2009; Another film about eggs and a chicken).

Trends

The rise in ticket prices in theater chains that increasingly monopolize exhibition accompanied a growing number of *refrito* films, movies with refried formulas that aim to please adult viewers by offering formulations of time, place, character, and event typical of soap operas. These *are* Mexican films, but they are made in ways that put them out of time and place. The dialogue is in Spanish and sometimes even in regionally identifiable Mexican Spanish. But these films artificially take anything Mexican out of Mexico. Movement between and within places, as well as the treatment of physical and psychological problems, has little to do with everyday life in Mexico.

Many such films are written or directed by those who have long track records working in telenovelas. The former telenovela screenwriter Issa López is the current darling of the directors making this fare, such as Sariñana with his *Niñas mal* (2007; Bad girls) and Gabriela Tagliavini with her *Ladies' Night* (2003). López also wrote the screenplay for her own directorial efforts, such as *Efectos secundarios* (2006; Side effects) and *Casi divas* (2008; Road to fame). And the producers fill up the mise-en-scènes with soap opera and pop stars to guarantee big dollar returns on their investments. For his film *El tigre de Santa Julia,* for example, a project backed by Televisa, Alejandro Gamboa cast the pop singer and telenovela star Irán Castillo as the love interest, Gloria; the film reduces the Mexican Revolution to the comedic antics of the character José de Jesús Negret, known as El Tigre (Miguel Rodarte). In Chava Cartas's film *Amor xtremo* (2006; Xtreme Love), we follow the ups and downs of two brothers as they drive, motorbikes in tow, from Mexico City to Las Vegas. As the film unfolds, the older brother, Patricio (Javier Acosta), comes to terms with the trauma of a motorbike accident (reliving the event in nightmares), and the younger brother, Sebastián (Aarón Díaz), is trying to live up to the older brother's Mexican reputation as a motorcyclist. While the story includes some moral conflict to chew on—whether the brothers should race for money or motorcycle parts—Cartas's camera is really more interested in showing us slow-motion shots of motorbikes flying through the air and the ripped abs of the telenovela star Aarón Díaz (known from Televisa's *Clase 406,* which aired in 2002–3).

Like many such films, *Amor xtremo* relies heavily not only on its telenovela stars, including Irán Castillo as Patricio's former love interest, Melisa, but also on pop culture icons such as the Latin Grammy–winning pop singer and actress Ximena Sariñana (who began her acting career in 1996, at age eleven, starring in the telenovela *Luz clarita*), who appears as Sebastián's love interest, Mariné. She also provides songs for the Mexican rock soundtrack (and for Sariñana's *Amar te duele*). (The Sariñana family appears to be cornering the market on Mexican bubblegum films. Fernando Sariñana produced *Amor xtremo;* his wife, Carolina Rivera, and his son, Carlos Sariñana, cowrote the screenplay; and his daughter, Ximena, stars in it.) As with the other films mentioned previously, the audience is not meant to ask questions. Did the father lose all his business to gambling and alcohol? How do the brothers manage to afford a brand new, extended-cab, four-wheel-drive truck, let alone the gas needed to fill its tank all the way to the border? How is it possible that the countryside from Mexico City to the border never changes and that the towns and gas stations they stop at all have a clean, strip-mall veneer? The blueprint demands that audiences set aside such worries and enjoy the ride.

Obstacles

Mexican directors have chosen to use the medium of film to tell stories, some of which reach far beyond the nation's borders. While Mexican directors may include Mexican cultural, historical, geographic, and linguistic details in their stories, they may choose to omit them, too. They can choose among any number of ways to tell stories that include Mexicanness, or *mexicanidad,* either abundantly or meagerly. In this sense just because a director is born Mexican does not mean that he or she has to use a specific technique or follow a prescribed set of plots, themes, and characterizations. Some directors might use the devices we recognize in *commedia all'italiana,* for instance, in their attempt to reach out and comment on a particular social and political climate, as happens with Sariñana's *Todo el poder* or Serrano's *Sexo, pudor y lágrimas.* Others might use a recognizable Italian neorealism, as Eimbcke does in *Temporada de patos,* where he tells the coming-of-age story of three fourteen-year-old kids spending the day at home on a Sunday afternoon, exploring the full limits of their sensory systems.

Filmmaking is an expensive way to tell stories, especially, though not only, because it requires a large number of people. Even a frugally budgeted film can cost surprisingly large amounts. *Temporada de patos* is shot in black and white, its cast comprises only a handful of pubescent kids, and its sets are almost entirely limited to one apartment building (the housing development in Mexico City known as Nonoalco Tlatelolco), yet it cost nearly one million dollars to make. The investment paid off. *Temporada de patos* picked up an Ariel in 2005, and much media attention at Cannes, and this success helped Eimbcke rather quickly secure funding for *Lake Tahoe* (2008); that film, which is set in the Yucatan and evokes the style of the director Jim Jarmusch, was distributed by Warner Brothers.

Money, then, is always an obstacle. Films cost a lot of money to make (far more than, say, it costs to make a novel or comic book), and filmmaking involves the work of many people who participate in conceiving, writing, shooting, casting, costuming, lighting, editing, and scoring, among other activities. Both making and then distributing a film require a big investment of time and money, constraints that Mexican filmmakers are constantly trying to overcome.

The sky is the limit in terms of stories told and how one can tell these stories. Nonetheless, filmmakers face constraints, not just economic but also technological (before the Steadicam was invented, some shots were much more difficult, if not impossible), social, and historical. All directors work in specific times and places, which shape the economic, technical, and social challenges they face. In *Poetics of Cinema* David Bordwell offers the example of a producer who limits a director's use of long shots because they require more labor in postproduction editing, but he adds, "It's not just that the film-maker's choices are *constrained;* they are also actively *constituted* in large part by socially structured factors of this sort."[19]

Within these constraints, of course, Mexican films do get made, some of them extraordinarily well. And once the films make it through all the distribution and exhibition hoops, the socially organized activity of filmmaking to a large extent develops a life of its own.

Within the economic, social, and political constraints—and, as I have briefly shown, these shift in time and place—Mexican filmmakers try to surmount the obstacles they encounter, looking everywhere to do so. This is what I mean by saying that Mex-ciné takes on a life of its own. Mex-ciné resembles a relay race, with one director passing the baton to the next and each trying to improve on the previous one. At another level, Mexican film as a unique (idiomatic) entity participates in a larger relay race, one involving film directors from all over the world. Its winners are those who consider all the options (story and technique) as open and for the taking, avoiding the formulaic, worn out, and trite. Its winners are those who understand that Mex-ciné shares with films made the world over technical and other aspirations but is ultimately expressive of its own idiom and following its own path of development. Its winners are those that uphold the prescriptive dictum: the art of filmmaking should be totally free.

Refrito and Buena Onda Films
Put to the Test

It is now time to show how systematic analysis can lead to critical evaluation of twenty-first-century films by or about Mexicans. I will unpack how the blueprints are put together and show how they aim to guide the senses, thoughts, and feelings of their ideal audiences. I will then show how these blueprints succeed or fail.

As I have already asserted, twenty-first-century Mexican films run the gamut from good to bad, success to failure. Some directors exert a will to style, leading to stable and coherent choices in visual and auditory devices, composition, plot, and character. Francisco Vargas exhibits this trait, which is visible in *El violín,* a film that unsentimentally engages with its ideal audience. Directors of bubblegum and *refrito* films, however, generally suffer a diminished will to style in making their filmic blueprints. As a result their films fail to cohere, stand outside any recognizable time and place, and rely on ready-made conventions and clichés to trigger only a rather limited set of emotions in their audiences. Whether set in Mexico City or the countryside, these films are made for ideal audiences seemingly reluctant to venture outside a certain "comfort zone," one that usually comprises magazines such as *Gente* or *¡Hola!*—Mexican equivalents of *People* and *Hello*—and extends to fairy tale telenovelas.

Refritos

El sueño del héroe

Arau's lazy application of the device of "magical realism" in *Zapata: El sueño del héroe* epitomizes the problems of the *refrito* film. Arau reduces the revolutionary struggle of hundreds of thousands, if not millions, to the vision quests and heroic acts of a Zapata born among Mayan ruins to the blessing of *curanderas* (healers) and sounds now stereotypically associated with mysticism (Andean flute music). The hackneyed film devices and sentimental visuals and sounds function as cure-alls for any and all unresolved problems and incoherences in the blueprint. The film relies on an ideal audience that will fall for its magical realist tricks and prepackaged exoticism. It asks that we evaluate it according to "special" standards, judging its quality by its identity politics: the commonly bad mestizo or the usually pure of heart, superstitious, and gullible campesino as the source of authentic rural ethnic culture ("local color"), for instance.

Cansada de besar sapos

A more contemporary example of the *refrito* blueprint is seen in Jorge Colón's *Cansada de besar sapos/Tired of Kissing Frogs* (2006). The film follows the story of an advertising agency worker, Martha (Ana Serradilla), and her adventures on the dating scene in Mexico City. She ends up falling for a café worker and aspiring theater actor, Javier (José María de Tavira). Colón's film incorporates a formulaic plot and a massive amount of product placement (Apple computers, Saab and Peugeot cars, and Hugo Boss outfits), but what makes it stand out is its depiction of Mexico City's inhabitants, all of whom seem to be of pure European descent; with the exception of the superintendent of Martha's apartment building and the man who delivers milk, all the characters are played by actors who could be French or Italian.

Colón's choices about filming almost make the location appear to be somewhere other than Mexico City. While a glimpse of the Torre Latinamericana identifies the locale as Mexico City, when shooting in the streets Colón's camera stays tipped up, so that we never see the city's massive traffic of people and cars. Martha's apartment is located in the downtown area near the Zócalo, which in actuality (whether day or night) is packed to near suffocation with folks from all walks of life, as well as street vendors hawking their wares. (Authorities have now expelled street vendors from the Zócalo and its environs, but they were present in the thousands when Colón shot his film.) While in reality the streets of Mexico City are more like those of Calcutta, Colón's camera cleans and Europeanizes the place in its fairy tale depiction of Mexican Yuppie life.

Fig. 10. Cansada de besar sapos: a view of the streets from Martha's apartment

Sexo, pudor y lágrimas

Like Colón, Antonio Serrano serves up what we might think of as an extended advertisement for Mexican Yuppie life. (Perhaps this should come as little surprise, given that he is also the director of telenovelas such as *Teresa* [1989] and *Nada personal* [1999].) Serrano sets *Sexo, pudor y lágrimas* in and around two adjacent apartment buildings in the area of Mexico City known as Polanco, a very wealthy and traditionally Jewish bourgeois enclave near the Bosque de Chapultepec.

This story follows the lives of several friends. With the exception of Tomás (Demián Bichir) and Andrea (Cecilia Suárez), both of whom have blonde hair, the characters are played by soap-opera stars: Susana Zabaleta as Ana (who appeared in the telenovela *Cadenas de amargura*, among many others), Jorge Salinas as Miguel (a heartthrob telenovela star who similarly appeared in *Cadenas de amargura*, among many others), and Mónica Dionne (an actress in the Telemundo telenovela *Madre Luna*) as María. As with *Cansada de besar sapos*, the only actors with dark complexions and non-European features play the workers: the furniture deliverymen and the maid.

The film never provides any information about how the central characters make their livings and manage to sustain their lifestyle; they seem to live and breathe a middle-class lifestyle without having to work. Basic elements of the plot should constantly puzzle viewers. Tomás arrives after having traveled around Europe, and a viewer may reasonably want to know how he was able to travel there in the first place. How do any of the characters earn money? Instead of getting answers, we are thrown some risqué comedic moments, as when Tomás sits naked on a couch.

Fig. 11. Sexo, pudor y lágrimas: the deliveryman

Fig. 12. Sexo, pudor y lágrimas: Tomás on the couch

As does Colón's in *Cansada de besar sapos,* Serrano's camera provides a limited notion of place. Except during the film's beginning and end, which feature shots of the streets and apartment buildings that situate the action, the camera focuses exclusively on the characters inside the apartments.

Finally, to wrap up some very loose ends, Serrano throws us the out-of-the-blue suicide of Tomás. He throws himself down the building's elevator shaft, and all the fractured relationships are magically glued back together.

Whether you like the film or not, you cannot fault Serrano much here. His ambition is *not* to make a film that is distant from the telenovela. His ideal audience is, in fact, the same audience, one that will not ask too many questions about the lives of its characters within a larger sense of historical time and geographic space.

Todo el poder

Some Mexican films do seem to reflect a director's ambition to be daring, vital, and experimental, yet they still end up being little more than *refritos* or gussied-up telenovelas. Sariñana's blockbuster *Todo el poder* is one such film.

The film follows the story of Gabriel (Demián Bichir), a divorced journalist who lives in Mexico City and has been variously mugged (five times), kidnapped, and carjacked. Along the way we discover that the police and government are directly tied to the underworld, which orchestrates all the kidnappings, muggings, and car thefts. In this Sariñana accurately reflects the reality of everyday life in today's Mexico City, yet he betrays this authenticity by turning the plot into a fairy tale. First, Sariñana filters the events through the point of view of a protagonist, Gabriel, who, though unemployed, somehow manages to afford to live in an expensive apartment and socialize with Mexico City's haute bourgeoisie. Adding to this incoherence is Sariñana's anachronistic portrayal of the concierge at Gabriel's building; concierges (as well as children playing in the streets) have been little seen in Mexico City during the last forty years.

The characterization of the love interest, Sofía (Cecilia Suárez), does not help. Just off the unemployment line, she is trying to sell insurance policies (Gabriel would be her first) yet lives in an extraordinary loft apartment with a wardrobe Imelda Marcos would envy.

Sariñana serves up a fairy tale guy with a fairy tale lover. The loose-fitting personalities that hang off such incoherent characterizations make it all the more difficult for a non-telenovela-watching audience to invest, either emotionally or cognitively, in the story's representation of the serious everyday problems that plague Mexico City's denizens.

The protagonist's movement in the city adds to the making of Sariñana's fairy tale. Gabriel lives in a phantom Mexico City. This is odd, given that *Todo el poder* opens with an aerial pan that begins in the southern part of the city (recognizable structures of the university appear), travels across the city (showing several readily recognizable architectural and topological features, including the Torre Latinamericano; the World Trade Center Mexico City; and Maximilian's legacy, the Avenida Reforma), and then sweeps down to a street filled with people packed elbow to elbow, going in and out of the Calzada de Tlalpan subway station. Those familiar with the city will rec-

Fig. 13. Todo el poder: Gabriel with his concierge

ognize other places, such as Tlalpan and the well-heeled neighborhood of Chimalistac.

However, we soon realize that these shots simply establish atmosphere. Sariñana's Mexico City resembles Serrano's and Colón's: its ghost-town-like streets allow Gabriel to park his car in front of his apartment building any time he wants, and he can drive through this Mexico City and its main avenue, Paseo de la Reforma, without hitting any traffic. The real Mexico City is always packed with cars, and those who own expensive cars keep them parked in courtyards behind guarded doors and gates. In the film's Mexico City, however, Gabriel can move effortlessly from his neighborhood to a contraband storage facility in the middle of nowhere, where he can sleuth out underworld activity. The filmic blueprint asks the filmgoer to suspend more than disbelief in confronting its gaping holes.

The telenovela is at least honest about its ambitions, or lack thereof, unabashedly using stock figures that lack depth and complexity and abstracting characters from any specificity of time and place. The difference between *Todo el poder* and a telenovela is that the latter does not aspire to be more. *Todo el poder* does aspire to be more—specifically, to be a sociopolitical critique—yet it relies on soap-opera techniques. In this way it seeks to appeal to the tastes and social-climbing ambitions of the Mexican middle class, people who are afraid of being kidnapped and mugged but don't want this problem to be treated as anything other than a fairy tale. *Todo el poder* thus uses soap-opera techniques while presenting itself as more sophisticated than a soap opera.

Something similar happens with other Mex-ciné themes and preoccupations. For example, while films based on the theme of urban and rural dislocation may be as diverse as required by historic and geographic circumstances, as well as by the imaginative needs and creative purposes of their directors, *Todo el poder* and other *refrito* films offer flattened depictions of place and time, as well as characterization. In the last instance, the filmgoer will not invest in the emotional ups and downs of the characters, not because they are Yuppies but because they exist out of time and place and lack motivation and (compelling) interior states of mind. After a one-night stand that ends badly in Nicolás Echevarría's *Vivir mata/Life Kills* (2002), the audience never knows why the protagonists, Silvia (Susana Zabaleta, who also appears in *Sexo, pudor y lagrimas*) and Diego (Daniel Giménez Cacho), would go to the ends of the earth (in this case the Cabeza de Juarez in Mexico City) to declare their eternal love for each other. Echevarría includes splashes of indie/alternative/talk-radio broadcasts that wax poetic on the chaos of the megalopolis, as well as surreal dream sequences (a cow and a refrigerator in an aquarium), but these elements fail to infuse much complexity. In *El segundo airé/A Second Chance*, Sariñana's use of "artsy" flashbacks (e.g., black-and-white still photographs that visually come alive) to days when the middle-aged and tired Moisés (Jesús Ochoa) and Julia (Lisa Owen) were full of youthful passion and left-identified rebellion does little to inject interest in their failing relationship and washed-up lives.

Buena Onda

According to media pundits and others, Alfonso Cuarón and González Iñárritu launched the *buena onda* film scene of the twenty-first century. An analysis of the way their blueprints are put together and the effects of that construction, however, may reveal a less than vital filmmaking enterprise.

Y tu mamá también

Alfonso Cuáron's *Y tu mamá también* tells the story of Tenoch, Julio, and Luisa as they travel from Mexico City to the Oaxacan coast. Highbrow media critics and academicians alike hailed their journey across Mexico's countryside and the various people they encounter (about whom a voice-over narrator provides details) as an incisive, subtle, social critique of class, gender, and race relations in Mexico. Nuala Finnegan, for instance, identifies the film as at once the "product of globalized culture industry" and a work stamped by the "local."[1]

Fig. 14. Y tu mamá también: Chuy and family with Tenoch, Julio, and Luisa

Undeniably, Cuarón's camera offers details we never see in *Todo el poder; Sexo, pudor y lágrimas;* or other such films. We see the interior of modest apartments (e.g., Julio's and Luisa's), as well the inside of Tenoch's grand gated house; we see the insides of country clubs, taverns, and hotel rooms; we see various landscapes. We are even privy to some rather personal moments: the beautifully shot scene of Julio and Tenoch masturbating together by a pool. One might expect this to add up to a film that reveals more than it conceals, that details more than it abstracts. Yet when all is said and done, its parts add up to a whole in only a contingent and loose way. There is an overwhelming sense that Cuarón's will to style is rather laissez-faire: let the series of unmotivated images do the work of connecting the dots.

Let me make this point clearer with some examples. The film describes how building hotels in the area destroys the peaceful existence that the fisherman Jesús "Chuy" Caranza (Silverio Palacios) enjoys with his wife, Mabel, and their children.

The voice-over narrator tells us that Chuy will soon be forced to work as a janitor in one of the hotels about to be built. For Finnegan this is an "explicit reference to the rapid modernizing of Mexico's tourist industry and the predatory impulses of the various local vested interests," one that "bears eloquent testimony to the perilous nature of life on the margins of modern Mexico."[2] Fishing as a means of economic self-sufficiency, however, provides anything but a marginal livelihood. And the destructive force ruining Chuy's self-sufficiency is not tourism as an abstract entity but rather the massive investment by foreign capitalists who are buying the land and the labor force needed to build monstrous buildings like the ones in Acapulco, Ixtapa, Cancún, or Puerto Vallarta, where they have ruined the countryside; it is massive penetration by capitalists, who need poor people to remain poor, and to keep them that way, by cutting them off from any means of achieving autonomy. Put simply, Chuy's boat allows him to make a living as a fisherman—enough to keep his family fed and clothed—but this is not good for capitalism. Capitalism benefits by having Chuy lose his boat and become dirt poor, leaving him desperate for any kind of work under any conditions.

But this is not the only information that the film leaves out. In this sense Finnegan's reading is not inaccurate; she is simply responding to an incomplete filmic blueprint. In Mexico, with the narcotics trade dirtying all levels of the government and state, real estate and hotel construction provide an important means of giving the economy a clean face. The film's voice-over mentions the massive development of the tourist trade, which is eating up the coasts of Mexico, but leaves out this key ingredient.

As the trio travels to the coast, the voice-over narrator tells filmgoers about the deaths of poor people. It mentions them by name and gives a certain amount of detail about their occupations and what they were doing when they died. But Cuarón does not include any larger context to explain why these deaths are so common and visible among the poor. This is another important omission, for the voice-over narrator fails to draw out the establishment's role in these deaths, which occur in bus accidents. People who use public transportation belong mostly to the working class or poor, for that is all they can afford. Insufficient regulation of public transportation has left the buses unsafe, but policy makers are rarely interested in improving public transportation—after all, they don't use it themselves. All the markers and crosses that the trio passes indicate deaths among people who must travel great distances to get to the hotels where they work or to reach the markets where they sell their goods, doing so in busses that are really just coffins on wheels.

On another occasion, the film shows the Mexican army pulling over cars at a roadblock. Finnegan identifies this as a "telling political comment" that reveals how the U.S. Drug Enforcement Agency has put pressure on the Mexican government to buckle down on the drug trade. However, the film presents this very much in passing as an inconvenience and even a joke: the three travelers laugh with relief at not getting caught smoking marijuana.

At no moment in the film is it mentioned that such use of the army is illegal. According to the Mexican constitution, the army is there to defend the country against an invading army and has a mission to protect against foreign armies. Nowhere in the constitution does it state that the armed forces can

Fig. 15. Y tu mamá también: Julio, Luisa, and Tenoch at a drug checkpoint

be assigned to police Mexican citizens. The voice-over fails to mention that over the past twenty years successive administrations have used the excuse of the so-called war on drugs as a justification for deploying the armed forces throughout Mexico as a repressive force used against farmers, the poorest, most exploited segment of the population. Cuarón's voice-over and camera inform us of many things but disclose very little.

Using the convention of the road trip to follow the characters and also to show a cross section of Mexico's peoples and landscapes, the film elicits expectations on three fronts. First, it prompts viewers to expect the use of a "changing landscape to externalize conflict and character."[3] Second, it leads them to expect the story to move from a "civilized" urban setting, where class and sexual taboos are upheld, to a "lawless frontier,"[4] where they dissolve. Third, it suggests that it will offer a fuller meaning to the lives of the poor, those unseen by Julio, Tenoch, and Luisa. It holds up its end of the bargain for points 1 and 2, but because there is no class outlook, it falls short on point 3. But perhaps others will disagree. After all, the film seems to satisfy its ideal audience's needs and expectations—that is, an audience hungry for film that rehashes ready-made liberal themes.

Perhaps most telling of Cuarón's laissez-faire approach to making blueprints is the time it takes to drive from Mexico City to the south-central portion of Mexico's Pacific coast. Even stopping a lot, this takes no more than ten hours, but in the film it takes several days. Of course Cuarón is free to stretch time to tell his story. Nonetheless, a Mexican audience would know that this would be a relatively short trip; a foreign audience might not. In the eyes of a Mexican audience, then, the story would be less realistic.

This aspect of the film's blueprint further identifies Cuarón's ideal audience: a left-leaning, non-Mexican audience (perhaps Cannes or Sundance festival attendees) who will not notice such careless oversights. This ideal audience will appreciate Cuarón's picturesque shots and sociopolitical critique, but in a very superficial way, much as one might appreciate a postcard from this part of the world. That is, Cuarón wants to make sure that the particular remains picturesque, artistic, and devoid of significance. It's as if we are seeing Mexico through the eyes of Tenoch, Julio, and Luisa traveling in the comfort of their car and with a limited appetite for a *real* knowledge of the country.

We can level the same critique at Alfonso's brother, Carlos Cuarón, who similarly turns to the Pacific coast in his directorial debut, *Rudo y Cursi,* which remains among the top five highest-grossing Mex-ciné films. The story follows a banana plantation laborer and foreman as he rises to fame playing soccer. While Carlos Cuarón, too, uses a third-person voice-over to fill in details otherwise not shown in the film, in this film the effect is more comedic: the narrator explains the history of soccer and punctuates the action with trite remarks about life's ups and downs. In yet another similarity, Carlos Cuarón infuses this film, too, with a vaguely leftist worldview, critiquing soccer as rife with greed and corruption that chew up and spit out the two stepbrothers, Beto and Tato. And yet Cuarón leans heavily on a capitalist fairy tale cherished among the poor everywhere: one day a professional recruiter—here it is the sports agent Batuta, or "Baton" (Guillermo Francella), but we could fill in the blank with any profession—will arrive in your town and discover you, and then you'll experience a meteoric rise out of the gutter (though if you win this lottery, your rough [*rudo*] and "corny" [*cursi*] ways will bring you back to the banana fields or wherever you began). Again, I'm surprised at how a film made with a lot of talented people and a large budget could contain the mistakes it does. As soon as the film begins, we see Beto, nicknamed "Rudo" (Diego Luna), telling a crass joke to his coworkers and his stepbrother, Tato, nicknamed "Cursi" (Gael García Bernal), who is carrying bananas. It's the end of a workday. Neither actor exhibits the posture or manners of someone working under the hot sun all day; both look, move, and act like healthy, young, and gym-groomed movie stars. At the end of the work day the audience sees a truck with workers drive down a dirt road. Rudo suddenly makes a hundred-meter sprint, as if he has been training for the Olympics; this is hardly a guy who has been doing hard labor all day and, indeed, all his life. Moreover—and we see something similar with González Iñárritu—Carlos Cuarón depicts these two "hicks" from the countryside as having a rather limited range of cognitive and emotive states: flip-flopping from dim-witted reactions (e.g., they do not know how to push the button on the key to turn off the alarm of an SUV) to jealous explosions (Cursi's tantrums at seeing his ex-girlfriend out with another man), hot-tempered outbursts (both fly off the handle at the drop of a hat), and deceitful actions (Rudo sneaking out of his house and away from his family at night to go to Mexico City to play soccer).

Babel

Might González Iñárritu's *Babel* also cater to a left-leaning, Cannes-attending international audience? Does it at once elicit a *feeling for* and *feeling through* the plight of the Other, as Laura Podalsky argues it does in "Migrant Feelings: Melodrama, *Babel,* and Affective Communities"? Or is it simply an art-house melodrama whereby an educated, left-leaning, middle-class audience can feel for the suffering of others but keep a safe remove?

Along with *Amores perros, 21 Grams,* and *Biutiful,* the film *Babel* focuses centrally on "the beauty of interpersonal relationships, the wonders of physical contact between human beings, and the power and fragility of human happiness."[5] *Babel* differs from González Iñárritu's earlier films, however, in that it is "interested [not] in simultaneity but in the networked nature of human life; therefore, the film crosscuts between the stories regardless of their chronology to emphasize the links between them. Had the stories been narrated in chronological order, the feeling of an intricate worldwide tapestry would not have been as powerful."[6]

Babel comprises twenty-four narrative blocks, or sequences. The film ostensibly concerns lapses in communication, misunderstandings, and the difficulties of translation between cultures. It is supposedly inspired by the biblical origin myth about diversity in languages and cultures (Gen. 11:1–9). Deleyto and Mar Azcona argue that technically (in terms of the editing, mise-en-scène, score, lensing choices, and so on) the film links the different narrative blocks to ultimately forge "connections between people where verbal exchanges could not reach, [so that] the lack of a common language becomes less of a barrier to communication."[7] The end, they argue, clearly reveals how words "cannot come close to the power of deeply felt human contact in those moments of physical and emotional communion."[8]

In addition, the film supposedly deals with the North African culture of Morocco, the North American cultures of the United States and Mexico, and the Asian culture of Japan. More accurately (despite the film's title and publi-

Fig. 16. Babel: Chieko in a car with her father

cized intentions), the film concerns parents and children and, more generally, adults and minors, or the "adult" behavior of "First World" people and the "childish" behavior of "Third World" people.

One story takes place in contemporary Tokyo and follows the characters Yasujiro (Kôji Yakusho), a well-to-do businessman, and his deaf teenage daughter, Chieko (Rinko Kikuchi, somewhat miscast, for she was then twenty-four years old). They are in crisis, both individually and in their relationship.

Chieko is obsessed with her mother's suicide. She entertains thoughts about committing suicide by jumping from her high-rise apartment (as her mother did, we are to infer) and is determined to lose her virginity before doing so.

As the film advances, the viewer discovers that the hunting gun used by Yasujiro is the same one used to shoot Susan Jones (Cate Blanchett) in Morocco. This leads to the second story, which revolves largely around the very poor boys, Ahmed and Yussef, who test the rifle's range by shooting at a tourist bus bearing the name Tours du Sud—the French *tours,* or "tower," possibly referring the ideal audience back to the film's title, (tower of) *Babel,* and its central theme of miscommunication. Yussef accidentally shoots Susan Jones, who is traveling in Morocco with her husband, Richard (Brad Pitt). In the third plotline, an undocumented Mexican nanny, Amelia (Adriana Barraza), is taking care of two children, Mike (Nathan Gamble) and Debbie (Elle Fanning) Jones, in San Diego. Deleyto and Mar Azcona consider the portrayal of the different geographic regions and their people to be "the closest one can

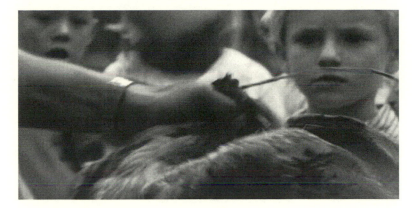

Fig. 17. Babel: decapitated chicken spurting blood

get to paradise in a movie about transnational stories, intercultural communication, and borders of various kinds."[9]

The third thread follows Amelia and her nephew, Santiago (Gael García Bernal), as they take Mike and Debbie across the border to the wedding of her son, Luis (Robert "Bernie" Esquivel), in Los Lobos. As they cross the border, images of Tijuana and the diegetic recording of "Cumbia sobre el río" indicate that they are in Mexico. The two-minute sequence is made up of sixty-four shots, conveying a maximum of frenetic energy and exhilaration.

The party starts early in the day and goes on until nearly dawn. As mentioned previously, moreover, Santiago kills a chicken as Mike and Debbie watch, using a swirling motion that severs the head from the body.

While driving back to San Diego, Santiago decides to take a route that passes through a more remote customs outpost located in Tecate. When he gets there, he is sarcastic and aggressive with the customs officers. Pissed off, he guns the car down a road and crosses the border followed by patrol cars.

Deep in the Sonora desert he tells Amelia to get out of the car with the kids and promises to return and pick them up as soon as he loses the patrol cars. Amelia walks in the barren sand and gets lost. Dehydrated and sunburned, she leaves the children under a tree while she looks for help. She walks in the burning desert with deep grief and a haggard look. Finally, Amelia stops a border patrol agent, and a helicopter is dispatched to look for the children. The children are found and safely returned home, but Amelia is arrested and deported to Mexico.

Deleyto and Mar Azcona argue that this demonstrates how borders

Fig. 18. Babel: Amelia carrying Debbie

protect some and victimize others. Moreover, they assert that the film "encourages us to expand our perspective on borders well beyond the lines of separation between countries and the spaces created around them and warns against a perspective that forgets that, beyond theoretical conceptualizations, borders continue to be specific geographical places where experiences like Amelia's take place every day."[10] Finally, they consider this film to join others by González Iñárritu in building "a cinematic style and a very personal yet culturally relevant worldview around the interstices between shots, between places, between nations, and between narrative and chronological instants."[11] They conclude, "Starting from a particular moment in the history of Mexican cinema, and from a particular place within Mexican culture, he has become the paragon of the contemporary filmmaker by appropriating and expanding the conventions of a new genre and constructing from the edges of the empire a new transnational citizenship and, in the process, a new object of cinematic fascination."[12]

Each story is simple and straightforward in itself. Individually and together, however, they are also rather light and largely irrelevant to one another. I summarized the stories to indicate how the film loosely fits together, but, in fact, the threads do not unfold in such a linear, straightforward way. González Iñárritu and his screenwriter, Guillermo Arriaga, have interwoven the events, offsetting them chronologically to some extent, as a means of catering to the sort of viewers who might attend an international film festival.

The film picked up prizes in both Europe and the United States, including the Golden Globe Award for Best Motion Picture. It had a total of seven

Academy Award nominations: best motion picture of the year, best performance by a supporting actress (Adriana Barraza and Rinko Kikuchi), achievement in directing (González Iñárritu), best original screenplay, achievement in film editing (Stephen Mirrione and Douglas Crise), and achievement in music written for motion pictures (Gustavo Santaolalla). As it turned out, *Babel* won only one Oscar—and this, much to González Iñárritu's dismay (even though in interviews he characterizes the score as a film's DNA), went to Gustavo Santaolalla.

Much went into orchestrating the mise-en-scène. Deleyto and Mar Azcona mention how the color red is used as a central motif that unifies the four different stories and three locations: "umber for Morocco, primary red for Mexico, and pink/magenta for Tokyo."[13] And, González Iñárritu has stated in various interviews that his film depicts our present plight in a globalized world. Yet the film's implied director comes off as a showy, rather phony, and ideologically reactionary director infatuated with Anglo film stars. The interrelations among the stories are artificial and do not depict or illuminate in any way the forces that unify our planet, namely, the capitalist system, which dominates through oppression and exploitation.

Brad Pitt, who two years earlier played the beautiful, golden-haired, and golden-bodied demigod Achilles in *Troy*, shaved from face to toes and displaying powerful muscles that helped conquer lands and peoples, appears here as Mr. Jones, a man wasted by age and grief, whose power lies only in money, the strings he can pull, and the help of the U.S. embassy. He parades his pain all the way to a country he does not know and will never know by traveling in a tour bus. Just as he finds himself in the north of Africa, he could have found himself in Vietnam or Argentina. It would make no difference, because wherever he is he remains in his economic and political imperialist bubble. He knows little about the world he inhabits but much about his purchasing power; with little regard for Amelia's plans to attend her son's wedding, he coerces her into looking after his children, an action that nearly costs Amelia and the children their lives.

Amelia has been his nanny for many years, yet her employer has apparently found neither the time nor the inclination to learn even a few words of Spanish. The audience is not told Mr. Jones's occupation. All the viewer knows is that he is wealthy, American, and blond, just as blond as his wife and his two very blond children. The audience may easily conclude that if acknowledged blond citizens of the United States have difficulties or problems, it is because nonblond people are mean or stupid, or both, like children. Amelia and Santiago, two adults, act as irrationally as do the adolescents

Chieko (Rinko Kikuchi), Ahmed (Said Tarchani), Yussef (Boubker Ait El Caid), and Zhora (Wahiba Sahmi), and all the mishaps are their doing.

All the other adults involved in the movement toward the denouements of the stories are seen as white or authority figures who make the right decisions and act in appropriate and rational ways. The actions thus judged appropriate include the following.

- Torturing an old man in order to find a rifle
- Shooting at an old man and his two adolescent boys
- Driving a bus away from a town that may be hiding terrorists, and thus stranding a wounded woman and her husband
- Operating on the stranded woman by sewing her wound without administering anesthesia or washing one's hands
- Ordering a Mexican nanny to postpone her son's wedding

With this world outlook, it is not surprising that the then governor of California, Arnold Schwarzenegger, appeared at a film ceremony so as to personally to hand a prize to González Iñárritu for *Babel,* a film that has earned, according to estimates, $49 million at the box office.

Surprisingly or not, given the previous list, González Iñárritu is known to be a very religious Christian. For example, he insisted that the shot of Brad Pitt carrying Cate Blanchett must resemble *La Pietà.* And at the beginning and the end of shooting in each location, he went through a blessing ritual with his crew and actors, asking them all to shout "Abba Eli" (Father, the highest).

In interviews González Iñárritu talks of himself as a very careful craftsman who oversees every single detail and is in complete control of all that goes on in front of the camera, including, of course, the choice of actors. González Iñárritu had Adriana Barraza gain thirty-five pounds for her role as Amelia. One must suppose that in his mind a Mexican nanny must be fat and ugly to have the real Mexican look. His insistence that Barraza carry Elle Fanning just right led him to spend two days filming in the desert, although he knew that Barraza has a long history of heart problems.

The implied director "González Iñárritu" thus begins to appear egocentric, macho, spiritual, and reactionary. This is an implied director who is ready to carry the very macho and very Mexican myth of the stoic *mamá* to extremes, one who makes many mistakes in continuity and the facts behind his representations of Mexico and Mexicans.

Often the director of photography, editor, or screenwriter (or the many others who help make a film) can help prevent a director from taking wrong

Fig. 19. Babel: Richard carrying a wounded Susan

turns. That is, the many subdirectors involved in making a film can help realize a good result despite a director's ego. As Emmanuel Lubezki remarks in an interview with Lisa Hirsch in the March 9, 2006, issue of *Daily Variety,* the DP's job is to help directors "translate their ideas and their emotions into film."[14] For whatever reason, this appears not to have happened with González Iñárritu's *Babel* or apparently with *Amores perros,* a "tridramatic soap opera" that was successful only because of its Vicente-Fox-style "technomarketing," according to the noted Mexican critic Jorge Ayala Blanco.[15]

Children of Men

In Alfonso Cuarón's dystopian *Children of Men* (2006), set in the United Kingdom of 2027, we see yet another global move by a Mexican filmmaker. Cuarón, however, chooses to represent trauma at both the individual and the collective levels. Theo Faron (Clive Owen) suffers from more than just the trauma of his child's untimely death in an unidentified flu pandemic.

Faron's stooped, lethargic demeanor and affection for the whiskey flask mirror the emotional body movement of all the other people filling the film's backdrop. Cuarón seeks to show a world governed by greed and a divide-and-conquer mentality that has been brought to its final precipice: there is no future because humans can no longer reproduce. The result, as Cuarón's camera shows it, is torpor, estrangement, and malaise for Britain's "citizens," such as Theo, and trauma and desperation for Britain's caged and tortured noncitizens, or "fugees."

Fig. 20. Children of Men: a London street in 2027

Fig. 21. Children of Men: Theo passes caged fugees

Does Cuarón succeed in making a film that portrays how the visceral and real capitalist divide-and-conquer stratagem pits one human against another in this xenophobic snowballing toward self-destruction? In the world Theo inhabits, official state policy includes the inhumane treatment of racially marked Others, such as Roma Gypsies and Jamaican or North African émigrés, among many others, caging these fugees and then carting them to city-sized deportation centers on the fringes of the country. Does Cuarón's use of technique (form), as well as plot, characterization, and mise-en-scène (content), succeed at conveying this sense of malaise and trauma as projected into the future?

Fig. 22. Children of Men: Jasper Palmer talking to Theo

Further, does Cuarón do a good job at parlaying the film's various manifestations of individually experienced malaise and trauma onto a massively collective scale? Does the cast of characters allow us to cognitively and emotively assemble parts into wholes, sewing into a coherent fabric the jaded journalist, Theo, who awakens to life; the pot-smoking hippie recluse, Jasper Palmer (Michael Caine), a former political cartoonist whose laughter is lined with remorse; and Jasper's ex-journalist, wheelchair-bound, catatonic wife, who serves as a constant reminder of his and the world's failure? Those who rebel, under the banner of the Fishes, seemingly fighting for justice, include Theo's estranged ex-wife, Julian Taylor (Julianne Moore), as well as the ambitious (and murderous) Luke (Chiwetel Ejiofor) and Patric (Charlie Hunnam).

Indeed, a closer look at how Cuarón's recipe aims to move its (ideal) audience cognitively and emotionally reveals an implicit reactionary worldview. The film asks that the audience leave rationality at the door and take leaps of faith, accepting that the plot and characterizations work coherently and that the world will be a better place.

In making the film's recipe, or blueprint, Cuarón unquestionably intended the audience to consider the consequences of the present day as shaped by chaos and barbarism. From the moment the film begins, when Cuarón's camera identifies the dyspeptic Theo as its focus, and then follows with a choreographed bomb explosion that disrupts his morning coffee ritual, the blueprint asks that the audience identify with Theo, specifically with his gradual awakening from complacency to active social awareness and concern.

Fig. 23. Children of Men: Theo as a bomb explodes

Cuarón's recipe asks the audience to follow and feel along with Theo as he comes into a compassionate consciousness, and so we travel with him through an aged and aging world (no new birth has occurred in eighteen years), where sharp lines divide the rich from the poor. As Theo carries out a cash-paying mission to deliver a young woman, Kee (Clare-Hope Ashitey), to a country-side safe house, he passes roadside cages filled with desperate fugees guarded by troops of "Homeland Security" soldiers; barbed-wired fences, barricades, and stone walls that keep the rich safe and comfortable; petrified and charred cow corpses lying upside down in country fields; abandoned playgrounds and schools; and war-torn fugee detention and deportation centers the size of small cities. In the episodic form of the picaresque, the film follows Theo as he encounters different people high and low on the food chain, including his cousin Nigel (Danny Huston), the well-to-do minister of culture, living without a care high above those who despair.

We meet the individuals who make up the rebel band of Fishes as well; we come into contact with the young Kee, a woman of Ghanaian origin, who, as it turns out to Theo's surprise, carries in her womb the "key" to saving humanity. We meet Miriam (Pam Ferris), a New Age midwife given to prac-ticing tai chi and wearing eco-friendly clothes. And we meet those lower on the pecking order, including Marichka, a Roma Gypsy, and Syd, a Cockney Homeland Security guard.

The recipe of the film is designed to make the audience increasingly feel for Theo as he overcomes obstacles to safeguard Kee's passage to the coast, intensifying the viewer's connection by throwing in near-death misses, such as an escape from the murderous Fishes, an attack by marauding British sol-

Fig. 24. Children of Men: Theo visiting his cousin Nigel

diers wielding firearms, and assaults from a hodgepodge of noncitizen Others in a war-torn Bexhill deportation ghetto.

In making his recipe, Cuarón intended the viewer to feel triumph, first, with Theo's dexterous midwifery and the sight of the newborn, and later in his final hour: rowing a small boat, Theo takes Kee and the newborn though an underground tunnel (graffitied with primitive icons reminiscent of ancient pictographs) to safety, a buoy somewhere in the English Channel where she is to meet members of the Human Project. Before they arrive in their ship, *Tomorrow,* Theo is fully redeemed: no longer the hardened individual we meet at the beginning, he shows Kee how to comfort the newborn and then dies in a pool of blood. The *Tomorrow* arrives, and the credits roll.

The film's recipe is designed to take the audience along with Theo on his journey, which ends in the triumph of good over evil and awakens him fully to a bleeding-heart compassion; we are meant to share Theo's deep feelings for, as Cuarón states in the film's production notes, "human experiences" that lead us to "the social and political."

As much as is possible, given the complex multiple authorship of the film (reflected in a long list of credits, from producer to director of photography to costume designer and music score composer), *Children of Men* has Cuarón's intention all over it. Cuarón is the director, editor, and top-billed screenwriter (the writing credits also identify Timothy J. Sexton along with a number of others, including Clive Owen, who contributed edits on the set). Along with his tried-and-true cinematographer, Emmanuel Lubezki (also the DP for the mystical and primitivist *Apocalypto* and *New World*), Cuarón, as he informs us in the director's commentary, wants to drive home this unity of vision to his

Fig. 25. Children of Men: the arrival of the ship Tomorrow

ideal audience (media pundits) by going for various sorts of counterintuitive cinematic derring-do.

To give it that Cannes Festival, auteuresque je ne sais quoi, Cuarón uses a deep-focus long shot when audiences probably expect a medium close-up shot. He rigged a special camera and modified a car (making a bubble out of the front windshield, for instance) to offer us a 360-degree tracking shot of Theo, Julian, Miriam, Kee, and Luke inside a moving car as it travels along a country road and is ambushed. Cuarón gives a strong and steady nod to Orson Welles (specifically, to the single-take sequence that opens *Touch of Evil*), Robert Altman (*The Player*), and Martin Scorsese (*Goodfellas*) with his single-take handheld-camera shot (complete with blood-splattered lens) of Theo dodging bullets and bloodied corpses in search of a kidnapped Kee. He shuns convention, offering little to no backstory for his central figures—or the reason for this world's blight. He carefully orchestrates his mise-en-scène to make this United Kingdom of 2027 look much like it does today. There's no stuffing the mise-en-scène with otherworldly gadgets, modes of transport, and outlandish sartorial styles. Instead Cuarón gives his 1960s-era baby-boomer audience a nudge-nudge wink-wink with mise-en-scènes chock-full of that earlier time's iconographic countercultural references: Pink Floyd, Bob Dylan, the Rolling Stones, and John Lennon, for instance.

Whether or not Cuarón's techniques and mise-en-scène choices are innovative, they do little for the film as such. A quick example suffices: the apparently single-take 360-degree tracking shot inside the car, heralded by Cuarón and critics alike as a great cinematic innovation, actually ends up taking the air out of what could have been a rather intensely felt moment. The long take, along with the goofy inclusion of Theo and Julian blowing a Ping-Pong ball back and forth, deflates our emotional response. And whereas enormous effort was expended to create the technology that allowed this shot, when they are ambushed by a marauding gang of thugs, there is a certain laziness in continuity. For example, the sound of the motorcycle used by one of the attackers is too high-pitched for the size of its engine.

In truth, this 360-degree single-take tracking shot is not a technical and directorial feat but the result of digitally splicing shots. In "Of Steadicams and Skycams," Tom Huntington mentions in passing that "filmmakers can also cheat by digitally stitching together several shots to make them look like a single take, as the makers of *Children of Men* did to create an epic tracking shot through a battleground."[16]

So a shot that is supposed to trigger our awe at its technical wizardry and a film sequence that is supposed to move us from comfort (inside the car) to horror (hooligans screaming like banshees) likely leave us feeling nonplussed, if not even a little embarrassed for Cuarón. Is the playful to-and-fro of the Ping-Pong ball meant to echo an erstwhile intimacy between Theo and Julian? Is it meant to work as a point of contrast to the emotion of fright when they're set upon by lager-drinking louts?

Cuarón is all about leaving an auteur fingerprint all over *Children of Men,* and this seems to work to his extreme disadvantage when keying up its messianic under- and overtones. The little details of character names, clothing, shoes, dialogue, action, and technique (especially lighting and extradiegetic sound) all point toward a single-minded message: read the film as the scripture of the arrival of a new millennial messiah. The midwife, Miriam (who shares her name with an Old Testament prophetess and leader of Israelites), wears baggy clothing that evokes tai chi and yoga classes and fits perfectly with her New Age spiritualism. Waving her hands over Julian's dead body after an ambush, she offers the following syncretic prayer.

> O, save us, save us in our hour of need
> Blessed Mary, save us
> May all the ascended beings
> The bodhisattvas and saints
> And all those who have walked
> The surface of the earth
> In the light of eternal truth
> Come to the aid of our beloved sister, Julian.

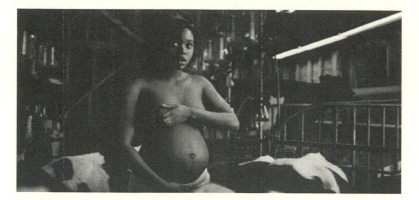

Fig. 26. Children of Men: Kee in a barn

Recall, too, that Cuarón's film is an adaptation of a novel by P. D. James, who is an outspoken Anglican. Significantly, although the adaptation bears only a faint resemblance to the original in most aspects of plot and characterization, Cuarón retains its Christological narrative line. It's fitting, then, that he also keeps the title, *Children of Men*—an oft-appearing phrase in the Bible as well as a psalm: "thou turnest man to destruction; and sayest, Return, ye children of men" (KJ Ps. 90:3). (Notably, too, in keeping with the messianic spirit of things, Cuarón released the film in the United States on December 25, 2006. *It's a Wonderful Life* or Cuarón's *Children of Men*—you choose.)

So far I have made several general observations. Now let me more carefully unpack how Cuarón serves up his heavenly bodies.

First, there is the choice of actors, and even the invention of characters. For instance, the character Kee, who does not exist in the novel, must stand in clearly as a symbol of our origins and humankind's new beginning: the great African Mother—or great black Mammy, if you want to see it from a slightly different angle. To make sure the audience reads her as just such a symbol, Cuarón has Theo first discover her pregnancy in a barn; a half-dozen or so cows part, and he sees her naked, rotund belly. Theo remarks, "Christ," and then "Jesus Christ."

If the Nativity mise-en-scène and Theo's divine expletives are not enough to ensure our Christological schematizing, Cuarón brings to the fore as extradiegetic music Christian composer John Tavener's choral work "Fragments of a Prayer." Music hits us hard at the subcortical level; neuroscientific research has demonstrated that music can "access directly the neural substrates that are associated with the primary reinforcers, such as food and sex,

Fig. 27. Children of Men: Kee on a swing

or with anticipation of danger."[17] It is not surprising, then, that Cuarón uses the choral extradiegetic music to trigger our feeling of epiphanic sublimity both quickly and deeply.

Indeed, as the sounds of the diegesis (Theo, the cows, and Kee) recede and the extradiegetic choral music fills out the filmic space, Cuarón aims to create a bridge for the audience to cross, moving from the banality of barnyard muck to the sublime vision of our Ghanaian Virgin Mary. He intends to use the music score (and hyperexposed and directed lighting enveloping Kee's tummy) as an aural-visual trigger of our automatic emotion reflexes. We are not told that this is miraculous (which would engage the cortex); rather, we feel it to be so (a process mediated by the amygdala). As the film unfolds, these visual and aural elements (superexposed lighting and choral score, respectively) increasingly mark Kee's presence. In one of Cuarón's deep-shot scenes at an abandoned schoolyard, he has Kee swinging in the background; she is bathed in overexposed light, which gives her and her surroundings a heavenly aura and glow.

Cuarón uses many other synch points or convergences between image and sound to lead viewers to feel the significance of Kee as the bearer of humanity's savior. When the baby is born, the overexposed lighting, the diegetic sound of the baby's cry, and the choral score make for what Jeff Smith calls "affective congruence,"[18] with all these devices intended to trigger a peak emotional response; the sequence comes just after one filled with sounds of guns firing and people screaming and shouting, so this quieting lull in the film's aural-visual pace is meant to bring us down again, allowing an even harder and more powerful appeal to our limbic systems.

Cuarón does offer us a blueprint to follow, though more by faith than by knowledge. The story's conceit, characters, and events appear as if out of nowhere, unexplained and unexplainable. We do not know why the infertility pandemic occurred or why Kee is suddenly fecund. We do not know whether the Human Project will, with Kee and her newborn at its side, save the world. Moreover, the plot does not tell us anything about the Human Project's goals, purpose, or resources. We do not know how the people—all aged and apathetic—have food to eat, power for their televisions, and fuel for their cars, motorcycles, and motorized rickshaws.

In a world without a sense of the future, most of us would stop creating, exploring, and discovering. Without that chain of solidarity between generations essential for humanity to identify itself as humanity—with both a past (memory) and a future (imagination and creativity)—we would not have the scientists who presumably work for the Human Project (which appears to be a major undertaking) to solve the mystery of the infertility pandemic. In this world we would not have a character such as Nigel collecting art like Michelangelo's *David* and Picasso's *Guernica*, because in a world without a future—one with no vitality, where we all are about to die anyway—there would be no value in painting, music, sculpture, and the like.

In all this the audience simply has to believe. The plot's twists and turns happen as if by the hand of God. For some reason, Cuarón uses these moments as opportunities to create a mise-en-scène where we see, for instance, the Battersea power station in the background, along with a pig balloon floating in the sky (an image from Pink Floyd's *Animals*; see fig. 24), torture scenes in Bexhill (evocative of Abu Ghraib), and Jasper wearing wire-rimmed glasses and shoulder-length hair (thus suggesting John Lennon) while listening to the Rolling Stones' "Ruby Tuesday" (written by Brian Jones and Keith Richards). There is also the overlay of the Ghanaian fugee with the Madonna; here she gives birth to the new millennial messiah, who turns out to be a girl, and whom she names after Theo's lost son, Dylan—another allusion to the 1960s counterculture.

Again, the film includes scenes of a desolated countryside, as when Theo and Jasper pass what appear to be charred horse or cow carcasses seemingly blown up by land mines. The holes in the blueprint again become apparent. No economic activity is visible; nobody toils on the land. So how does the country sustain itself? If the world has ceased providing what England needs, where do people get the material and tools, including airplanes, to produce these goods? Why travel to the Bexhill detention camp (see fig. 28), which is filled with danger? Why have Kee endure all this danger where she could be

Fig. 28. Children of Men: Bexhill prison camp

killed, raped, and so on, even though the area has miles of coastline providing any number of rendezvous points? Moreover, why would fugees want
to try to enter the United Kingdom in the first place, given that the whole
world is dying? People migrate for economic reasons with expectation that
they will make a better future, but there is no future in this world. Why, in
this last instance, detain and cage fugees when this is not, in such a world
of exploitation and oppression, the logical thing to do? They would best be
exploited as human labor to feed the Nigels of this world. The Fishes claim to
be defenders of fugees, yet they appear to be more violent, thuggish, intoler-
ant, and repressive than the army. Luke has Julian murdered, and he himself
murders Jasper in cold blood; he even shoots at Kee, who holds the promise
of humanity's future. How can a newborn child become the inspiration for a
movement centered on more humane treatment of refugees? How would the
birth of one person have the power to change a whole society? In all this the
film asks us simply to feel and have faith that it all works—and for a bigger
reason than it can explain or that its creator wants to explain.

Cuarón's recipe, in so many words, imagines an audience that is, well,
Cuarón. That is, his ideal audience is very limited, so his blueprint is limiting
in the way it seeks to cue and trigger the audience's cognitive and emotion
systems. All the elements that are willed into place by Cuarón as director, editor, and master screenwriter, and that are executed visually by Lubezki, rely
simply on a faith that the audience will believe in Cuarón, that viewers will
stop thinking and only reflexively emote.

As Patrick Colm Hogan states generally of our visual experience of film,
viewing *Children of Men* is "highly complex, but also structured in specifiable

ways."[19] These specifiable ways allow us to see more clearly how Cuarón's in-coherent, deus ex machina approach to building a filmic blueprint ultimately leads audiences to make little cognitive or emotional investment in the film.

Film viewing is a multilevel process, with the different elements of, say, Cuarón's film aimed to stimulate different subsystems in the brain as if each subsystem were engaged with reality. Further, human brains require a certain amount of coherence (logic, say) in the story's features if the different cortical and limbic systems and subsystems are to be activated. The more coherence, the more subsystems are activated and the more our cognitive and emotional responses take place.

Before the film slips into its mire of confused and unexplained details and unmotivated plot turns, it opens with Theo about to sip a coffee while standing by a trash can on one of London's sidewalks (a red double-decker bus and St. Paul's in the background identify the location) when a bomb explodes. He jumps. The sound and sight hit our limbic system, perhaps causing viewers to jerk forward in their seats. We hear screams and see a woman carrying her dismembered arm. Perhaps we feel shocked and horrified, but we also know that it is not real. Even if we do feel shock and horror, the neocortex will have done its job—the events are not real—and so we do not jump up and attempt run to the woman in pain. Here Cuarón has done his job. Using continuity editing, mise-en-scène, and diegetic sound, as well as actor body movement, he represents salient features of our world, to which we would react cognitively and emotively, knowing all along that our executive cortex will tell us it is only fiction. Then the title appears and credits roll, and the film is all downhill from there.

Besides the emotions generated by representations of the real world, there are others, including those that have been identified as "artifact emotions,"[20] which are triggered based on our response to technical aspects of the film, in the way Cuarón constructs his blueprint. These emotions are based on an appraisal of the technique, story, and so on, all the elements that Cuarón ultimately fails to deliver.

Cuarón wants his film to trigger both real world and artifact emotions. In interviews and the director's commentary on the film, he has frequently declared that his technique and mise-en-scène are aimed at conveying an extreme realism to match the experience of watching a "raw documentary." Thus, we get the blood-splattered lens during the long take of Theo looking for Kee in Bexhill and the long visceral take (199 seconds) of the birth of the child. Further, we get a London that looks much as it does now; Cuarón chose to shoot in London instead of using special effects or built sets. Notably, Cuarón mentions dressing up parts of East London to make it look "more run down" and "more Mexican."

Cuarón wants information to appear as it would in reality. For instance, we learn by happenstance—and in a series of television news flashes concerning the destruction of Paris, Moscow, Washington, Kuala Lumpur, Tokyo, New York, Jakarta, Stockholm, Rome, and Boston—that the world has collapsed and "only Britain soldiers on." Similarly, the background of one scene—Theo's abduction by the Fishes—includes a newspaper plastered on the wall that declares, "Africa devastated by nuclear fallout." All this information is presented too quickly and without enough detail, impeding any gap-filling activity that might build a stronger sense of the represented world. But, given all the holes in the film, instead we ask continually, why this and why that? As a result viewers likely will not invest world or artifact emotions in the film.

This lack of emotional engagement in *Children of Men* has certain other consequences that arguably diminish Cuarón's intent: to move his audience to feel compassion and, therefore, to open eyes to the social and political. The blueprint attempts to tell us something about today's predicament and thus offer a meritorious lesson in ethics and politics. Without emotional engagement, however, there is no empathy, and without empathy there is no sense of ethics or politics. Patrick Hogan sums up empathy thus: "It leads us to think of this other person in moral terms, as someone to whom we have obligations, someone who has rights—in short, as someone like ourselves."[21] We do not feel for Cuarón's characters because they're all stand-ins for something else: a Virgin Mary, a John Lennon, a you name it. We don't invest emotionally, empathetically, or ethically because the film does not ask this of us.

In a world without a future, the only forms of aggression are the incarceral, militarized state apparatus; the violence of the Fishes; and the impulsive/instinctive aggression of those within the Bexhill concentration camp. In a world without a future, however, why would we care about different forms of aggression and violence? The film fails to project a sense of ethics because it projects no sense of people as free agents held responsible for their actions. In a world where nobody cares, there is no balance between thought and emotion that might lead to, say, forms of premeditated aggression toward targets of oppression, that is, to violence in self-defense. There would be no sense of incarceration as bad, mistreatment as bad, and so on. No future necessarily means no moral compass. What the film does ask is that we simply have faith in the birth of a cure-all messianic "Tomorrow." And so, rather than opening eyes and moving audiences to compassion and action, the film disarms and takes away any means of understanding the present situation.

As I already mentioned, Cuarón insisted that everything in *Children of Men*, which is set in 2027, should look similar to the present-day reality of 2006: buses, clothing, army uniforms and weapons, coffee shops, and cars. This not only is an expression of his "extreme realism," but it also leads viewers to apprehend two things simultaneously: the film follows events and people that take place in the future (2027), but it also asks that they not disregard their contemporary world. Not only is this a clumsy demand on the viewer, one that offers no aesthetic reward, but it suggests something deeper about the worldview presented, namely, that capitalism is here today and will be here tomorrow, for all eternity. This message, coupled with the messianic narrative plot, feeds the myth that capitalism is simply a self-feeding mechanism, that there is no class struggle, so that the only way to make a better world out of the barbarism of capitalism is to await the birth of the new millennial messiah.

The capitalist crisis is reduced to a biological pandemic that leads to chaos and the disappearance of civilization everywhere except in a Britain that "keeps soldiering on." The pandemic is presented as the root of all the world's problems and all its solutions. The so-called solution arrives in the name of the ship, the *Tomorrow,* which will take Kee to the Azores, where humanity can get a new biological start. The problem is, therefore, biological, not social. It is a natural catastrophe, not one of our own making that arose because class warfare spun out of social relations based on the exploitive production of surplus value. To reestablish humanity we need not rebuild society from the ground up, on more solid foundations, but only await the birth of a child, the promise and fulfillment of the second coming.

In *Children of Men* Cuarón utterly fails in his attempt to critique the establishment, for he offers only a hodgepodge of New Age, eco-friendly spiritualism along with a story that is out of time and place and filled with weak ideas and characters. Civilization will be restored with the arrival of the messiah; perhaps, too, Cuarón's film will also be saved herewith.

Bubblegums That Pop;
Refritos That Go "Ah"

Perhaps surprisingly, the filmic sincerity and relevance informing *some* made-for-teens bubblegum films and adult-oriented refritos stand in sharp contrast to the *buena onda* alternative films of Cuarón and González Iñárritu. There are bubblegum and *refrito* films that renovate our perceptions, emotions, and cognitions related to the world. In several of such films, we see a strong presence of the will to style of directors who produce both form and content that can open our eyes, ears, thoughts, and feelings to something new. They exhibit refreshing novelty and provide clear cases of aesthetic success in Mexican filmmaking.

Bubblegums ... Being and the World

Amar te duele

The story of *Amar te duele/Loving You Hurts* (2002), takes place in our present day, in an area located on the outskirts of Mexico City that was built essentially in the last twenty years as a sort of gated community for the upper crust of the Mexican bourgeoisie, surrounded by lower-middle-class neighborhoods and, farther away, shantytowns. The wealthy people who inhabit this area, called Santa Fe, live behind high walls and are protected twenty-four hours a day, seven days a week, by armed bodyguards. This, of course, is part of our contemporary form of barbarism, a rebirth of the fortresses of the Middle Ages and seclusion of the very rich in the new ghettos. Fernando Sariñana's film shows certain aspects of this phenomenon.

Sariñana gives us a tragedy, though not a Shakespearean one of star-crossed lovers; instead, he offers us a present-day tragedy of young people

Fig. 29. Amar te duele: Renata's house in Santa Fe

who are not allowed to be young, that is, inquisitive, questioning, rebellious, exhilarated, hungry to know everything about themselves and the world they inhabit, and, most fundamentally, optimistic. All the protagonists are teenagers. One is Ulises (Luis Fernando Peña), an aspiring artist whose work in progress is a representation of his dream of a better world, which he paints on a street wall and in the pages of a comic book he is drawing.

The other protagonist is Renata (Martha Higareda), the wide-eyed, curious, adventurous elder daughter of a wealthy couple, capable of empathy toward people she is only beginning to know and having an affectionate attitude toward her sister, Mariana, her parents, and her schoolmates. Mariana (Ximena Sariñana) is younger but belongs to that growing category of people who are not just cynical but mentally and emotionally rotten at the core long before they have left their youth. She is also an alcoholic, and her behavior is rigidly dictated by all the prejudices and nearsightedness of the most retrograde members of her class.

Devoid of empathy and imagination, Mariana does not care to know anything about herself, others, or the world at large. But the society in which she lives has little room for people like Renata, and so it is the young Mariana (old before her time) who will live and the promising older Renata (young at heart) who will die.

La hija del caníbal

Antonio Serrano's use of voice-over narration as a central ingredient in *La hija del caníbal/Lucía Lucía / The Daughter of Canibal* (2003) allows the film to perform some extraordinary metaphysical acrobatics. Throughout the whole picture, the story is told completely in the realist mode. The style presented makes viewers feel that they are perceiving what is really happening within the storyworld.

Simultaneously and subtly, however, Serrano introduces clues that lead viewers to start doubting the truthfulness or reliability of the story and, therefore, of what they perceive on the screen. By the end of the film, audiences are entirely justified in reading the narrative as totally unreliable. Viewers come to doubt that the narrator-protagonist really is what they have encountered her to be.

In much of the film, Lucía (Celia Roth) seems to be much as her voice-over narration and the diegetic events suggest her to be: a writer in her late thirties/early forties who is experiencing a crisis in her life. This much is reliable, but it differs markedly from the image of Lucía in a photograph presented at the film's close, although this image also depicts, in a way that matches the rest of the film, her two neighbors and lovers: the young, virile Adrián (Kuno Beeker) and the old Spanish Civil War veteran, Félix (Carlos Álvarez-Nóvoa). Further, the background of the photograph corresponds to a location they visited on a road trip together. While Adrián and Félix appear to have a real existence within the fictional world of the film, the image of Lucía in the photograph does not match the Lucía we see in the fictional world of the film.

Lucía is a writer of fiction, so the audience may well wonder whether the guys in the photograph are real. Is she talking about people in the fictional world of the film? Is the lust for life and need for adventure that we see expressed in her character real in the fictional world of the film? Or is this all imagined by Lucía as she has reached an age when she is more settled and her life outlook in a way is tinted by her past? That is, when thinking about her past, she is thinking of herself as a compendium of a certain past. She sees this past as something positive, and she is simply extending the positivity of her past into the future in a settled and tranquil mode that tends toward closure.

Therefore, is it not possible that Lucía has only imagined a story in which she is married to a jerk, Ramón (José Elías Moreno), an incompetent thief and hustler who has to arrange his own kidnapping to get Lucía's money?

Fig. 30. La hija del caníbal: photograph of Adrián, Lucía, and Félix

Fig. 31. La hija del caníbal: Lucía's apartment

Fig. 32. La hija del caníbal: Lucía's apartment transformed

Fig. 33. La hija del caníbal: Lucía's apartment at the end of the film

When the movie begins, she is about to go on a trip to Brazil with Ramón. Is she perhaps simply imagining a story in which she is a mediocre, domesticated wife, and then Ramón is kidnapped, after which she launches herself out of this mediocre and dead-end life by trying to rescue him? Is she inventing this story? Maybe she is not married at all? Does she simply imagine this story so that she can bootstrap herself out of her humdrum life?

This unreliability is further emphasized when Serrano uses his camera to capture seamless changes in the décor of Lucía's apartment, as well as in her hair and clothes. On several occasions the furniture, fixtures, and wall color in her apartment change from one sequence to another, without apparent reason or explanation.

Perhaps the change of décor is an exteriorization of what Lucía wishes to have as her apartment. That is, the camera shows us the exteriorization (or material correlate) of wish fulfillment. Since constant changes in décor, clothes, and hairstyle are popularly considered to be features of women's behavior, perhaps the continual alterations of these features is Serrano's way of indicating that viewers are watching an unreliable narrative. These constant modifications would simply be the external or material correlate of Lucía's wishful thinking.

So Serrano makes a satisfying Mex-ciné puzzle film that asks the audience to contemplate whether there might be two narrators of the story. One is the camera (yielding the image as presented and manufactured by anyone we include under the umbrella of the implied author-director), and this is always present. The other, the voice-over of the character, is to an extent optional.

Finally, however, Serrano resists the audience's move to solve the puzzle. Both narrators are unreliable. The audience suspects Lucía to be unreliable for the reasons already stated. But the unreliability is sui generis and double, for the camera lens and Lucía are unreliable with respect to each other. Here the unreliability is generated by the contrast between what the camera shows and what the narrator tells and does. *La hija del caníbal* shows Serrano's will to style at work in the making of a playful puzzle film that incorporates a scrupulously realistic mode, all while subtly undermining its realism by presenting unreliability in the setting of the story.

Niñas and Mujeres . . . in Time and Place

Several contemporary Mex-ciné directors carefully detail vitally vivid times and places in their films. I will focus on two standouts: Marisa Sistach's *Per-*

fume de violetas/Violet Perfume (2001) and *La niña en la piedra* (2006; The girl on the stone) and María Novaro's *Sin dejar huella/Without a Trace* (2000).

It is important to consider how female Mexican directors make films that allow women in the audience to, in the words of Elissa Rashkin, "finally begin to recognize themselves in the Mexican cinema."[1] I am interested here in analyzing how Sistach (and the screenwriter José Buil) craft films that tell stories of women and girls firmly situated in specific times and places. Sistach does this so well that she engages and moves all sorts of filmgoers: male and female; old and young; American, European, and Mexican; and so on.

Perfume de violetas *and* La niña en la piedra

Marisa Sistach uses the bildungsroman form to portray the growing friendship between Yessica (Ximena Ayala) and Miriam (Nancy Gutiérrez) at a time when they are both exploring themselves and their world in new and changing bodies, from preteen to teen. While there are moments of joy and youthful discovery and adventure (one such moment portrays them innocently laughing and playing with bubbles while taking a bath), the contemporary Tlalpan (a suburb absorbed into Mexico City) they inhabit mostly invades and destroys this world. The tragedy: in this world of greed and violence, neither Yessica nor Miriam is allowed the full exploration of her body or imagination.

As the opening credits roll, Sistach superimposes actual newspaper articles of rapes and murders of young girls in Mexico City to remind audiences that the fictional lives of Yessica and Miriam are representative of the lives of young girls (often in working-class homes headed by single parents) in Mexico City today. Newspaper clippings establish a pact of truthfulness with the audience, one that is solidified in the choice of the Tlalpan setting, which is brought to gritty life by DP Servando Gajá's use of a handheld camera and Super 16 mm film that he then converted to 35 mm. These techniques give the film the poignancy of the directness associated with documentaries and allows Sistach to sidestep sentimentality.

Sistach's camera richly details the space of the action, giving the audience a road map of sorts to the movements, activities, and circumstances of the girls. It shows where they go to school and the kinds of kids who go there; the streets they walk between home, school, and the shops, as well as the vacant lots that connect these different spaces in the area known as San Angel; and the interiors of their respective homes, which show how economic circumstances affect the way each lives.

Fig. 34. Perfume de violetas: Yessica and Miriam take a bath

Indeed, the places where they live and in which they circulate reflect their social-class standing. Both girls have working-class single mothers, but Yessica's unnamed mother (María Rojo) works as a maid and thus lacks a steady income, whereas Miriam's mother, Alicia (Arcelia Ramírez), works as a salaried shoe store employee and thus does have a steady income, albeit a low one.

Sistach's careful eye for location reflects this nuanced difference in socioeconomic situation: Yessica lives in a one-room apartment shared with her mother and half brother, Jorge (Luis Fernando Peña). Miriam, however, lives alone with her mother in a two-bedroom apartment that even has a tub in the bathroom. The film's subtle though powerful representations of the different living environments cohere well with the class and characterizations of Yessica and Miriam.

By meticulously choosing actions, gestures, and emotional range, as well as camera techniques and shooting locations, Sistach firmly situates her story in place and time. The careful casting of actors solidifies this trait: the professional actors who play the mothers, Miriam and Yessica, and Yessica's stepbrother, along with the amateurs and nonprofessionals who play schoolchildren, are all average-looking Mexicans in terms of attractiveness and body type. Sistach keeps her end of the deal established with the film's opening credits: not to abstract this Mexican tragedy from time and space, not to sentimentalize or Europeanize the story.

The story unfolds in a solidly believable way. Yessica and Miriam are very much of their age: curious about the world, a bit rebellious, and with one foot

Fig. 35. Perfume de violetas: Yessica's apartment

still in the childlike world of make-believe. When Yessica first visits Miriam's house, Sistach shows that twinkle of delight in the discovery of new objects and the sheer joy of jumping on the bed together. Yet we see also in Yessica's body movement and facial expression the emergence of the seriousness of a young woman, that desperate sense of what awaits her when she is no longer a child.

While the film begins to show the progression from child to adult in subtle and nuanced ways, it brutally awakens the audience to the way particulars of time and place violently impact this healthy psychological development. Jorge accepts money (which he later uses to buy sneakers) to arrange the rape of Yessica in one of those vacant lots in San Angel. Yessica's body movements and facial expressions at the beginning of the film tell of a healthy adolescent's psychological interiority; those after the rape tell of a traumatized young girl.

La niña en la piedra is another film by Sistach (and José Buil) where all the parts, from technique and mise-en-scène to plot, action, and characterization, add up to a coherent whole that can powerfully move filmgoers in directed ways and with a great payoff. Sistach sets this film in the recognizable (to a Mexican filmgoer) tropical state of Morelos (south of Cuernavaca). Its characters are farmers or children of farmers, with one older brother who is a police officer and thus controls the area's narcotics traffic. As she does in *Perfume,* Sistach provides a day-in-the-life portrayal of violence experienced by two teenage Mexican girls, in this case Mati (Sofía Espinosa) and Perla (Ximena Ayala). Sistach (and Buil) connects the violence more directly to greed and codes of machismo by identifying the trigger of the brutalities in Mati's rejection of her schoolmate Gabino's (Gabino Rodríguez) sexual advances. He is rejected, and the code of machismo (here, of getting even) springs readily into place. Creating one of the most brutal scenes in Mex-ciné, Sistach shows Gabino, along with his friends, in a quasi-biblical and nearly lethal stoning of Mati. Gabino's choice of punishment is a visceral reminder of the violent and primitive codes of machismo still in play in Mexico and elsewhere in the world.

Sistach couples this macho-driven violence toward girls with the element of greed. (In *Perfume* Jorge has his sister raped twice, once for money to buy sneakers and again simply because he wants the money.) The machismo attached to Gabino is further exaggerated in his older brother, a police officer who struts his machismo all over the town while driving a car and dressing in clothes paid for by violent, greedy narcotics traffickers. And, of course, the older brother's access to drugs leads Gabino to get high and then stone and violate Mati.

Yet again, Sistach proves her filmmaking mettle, creating a film whose parts—the environment, class, characters, and action—all add up to a compelling and coherent whole. As a result Sistach creates a representation of violence against the community's weakest members—young girls like Yessica and Mati—that can affect audiences powerfully.

Sin dejar huella

Maria Novaro's *Sin dejar huella* similarly focuses on macho codes of violence, but in this case the violence is directed toward adult women. As was mentioned earlier, the story follows the Norteña (Northern Mexican) Aurelia and the expatriate Spaniard Ana, who deals in Mayan art forgeries, as they travel from El Paso to Cancún. As the film begins, we see the two women in very different situations, but Novaro portrays both as intelligent, bright, and courageous. Aurelia uses her wits to untangle herself from a web of domestic violence. She carefully plans all the details of her escape and the safety of her child, knowing that her violent, drug-dealing boyfriend and his thuggish sidekick will follow her. She knows that with Ana she can get to Cancún faster than if she had to take a bus, and Ana (with the car) knows that sharing the drive will allow her to get there faster as well; they can switch back and forth from driving to resting through the day and night. Ana uses her smarts to prevent becoming another rape victim of a slovenly border patrol agent, Mendizábel. As the story unfolds, we see how Ana and Aurelia use their intelligence to outfox and outdrive a line of tailgating macho types. In sum we see these two strong and smart women formulate a well-conceived plan to realize their goals: total emancipation, including Aurelia's reunion with her son.

In a scene showing one smart maneuver, the women use the natural landscape to rid themselves of the boyfriend. They lead him and his sidekick into the Yucatan jungle, to an area made up of organic, reeflike matter rife with pits, and the two men fall into one of these holes. Novaro uses the road trip to subtly and progressively show the audience different facets of Ana's and Aurelia's personalities, all while deemphasizing male characters, who typically enjoy the Mex-ciné limelight.

Novaro's story coincides perfectly with reality. There are no holes in the story. All the parts add up. And this includes, of course, her careful attention to conveying the sense of time it takes to travel from the border through northern Mexico to the Yucatan. In contrast to Cuarón's *Y tu mamá también*, where the director tries to force reality to conform to his fictional world, Novaro's road-trip story of Ana and Aurelia is given a strong sense of the journey's time and place. As a result Novaro needs no intellectual or technical tricks to smooth over gaping holes in her filmic blueprint. She can simply focus on creating complex and compelling women protagonists who viewers get to know better and with whom they can empathize more deeply as the film unfolds.

Marisa Sistach and María Novaro make films in time and place: from characterization to landscape to historical period. Their greater sense of reality allows filmgoers to breathe and experience along with the characters. These directors go deeply into their subjects; they richly and exhaustively show the particular in circumstances, characters, and so on with such seriousness and ability that their films matter to Mexican and non-Mexican filmgoers alike.

Niños and Hombres . . . Today's Return to the Middle Ages

This tradition of tangibly situating stories, events, and characters in the here and now encompasses films that focus on boys and men, too. Examples include Rodrigo Plá's *La zona* (2007; The zone) and Francisco Vargas's *El violín* (2005).

La Zona

Rodrigo Plá chooses to take us into the interior of quasi-medieval fortifications in *La zona*. Plá's story and camera spend most of their time behind the

Fig. 36. La zona: fortified walls protect manicured gardens and McVillas

Fig. 37. La zona: walls and surveillance cameras divide the haves from the have-nots

walls of the "haves," portraying how the rich in today's capitalist socioeconomic system are thoughtlessly creating threats to themselves by destroying any chance that those in the younger generation might develop healthy capacities for reason or emotion. Within this world of barbed-wire-topped concrete walls and surveillance cameras, Plá's direction, Laura Santullo's story, and Emiliano Villanueva's camera (handheld and occasionally lensed to replicate a surveillance camera) slowly uncover a world filled with violence, paranoia, and estrangement.

In this well-portrayed world, the women are as ruthless as the men. The camera shows how, as they seal their community from the outside world more and more, they condemn themselves to be prisoners both physically, in their fortified community, and emotionally, living according to a very stunted set of baseline reflex emotions, including fear and anger.

Nonetheless, although the wealthy elite of the film have reduced their sense of possibilities and aspirations to basic emotions and actions that lead to the killing of an innocent have-not, Miguel (Alan Chávez, who also plays a small role in *De la calle*), Plá shows a few who question and resist, providing the audience with the film's moral compass. When considering this as an environment in which to raise his little boy, Diego (Andrés Montiel) ponders, "I've often thought of why we're raising our son behind a wall." With Diego, Plá asks the filmgoing audience to consider how those living and growing up in *la zona* end up afraid of life—everything "out there"—and how they have given up all hope of changing things. With the exception of Alejandro (Daniel Tovar), who is deeply shaken by the hunting and killing of Miguel, the teenagers we see in *la zona* are much like Renata's little sister, Mariana, in *Amar te duele:* a form of rigor mortis has already frozen their emotions. Driven only by simple reflex emotions of fear and anger, the golf-club-wielding teenagers readily join their parents in hunting down Miguel.

Directors such as Gerardo Tort, Sariñana, and Plá make films that depict the fortification of a contemporary Mexico City. They choose to create aesthetic blueprints that can powerfully move audiences to consider the consequences of capitalism; that forcefully represent the historical involution of a decrepit and senile capitalism that sells itself as the road to success and happiness but, in fact, divides and lays waste to the haves and have-nots alike; and that accurately portray those environments as destructive to the emotion and reason systems of all people, whether rich, middle class, or poor.

These films are powerful not because they tell ageless tales of heroism, all-conquering love, or sacrifices made for the restoration of social harmony. No. *De la calle, La zona,* and *Amar te duele* acquire their power by fleshing out tragedies that critically reflect on a world where the healthy growth of imagination, curiosity, emotions, and ethics in adolescence no longer has a place.

El violín

In making *El violín*, director and screenwriter Francisco Vargas had the assistance of his longtime producer, Bertha Navarro; screenwriter, director, and promoter Victor Ugalde; and Mexican author Carlos Montemayor. With such help Vargas had no need to hold anything back. He opens the film with soldiers shown torturing and raping people in a barn. This resonates strongly with contemporary reality. In 2006 the Mexican media broke the story of soldiers not only violently harassing farmers of Nahua origin but also raping and

Fig. 38. El violín: Don Plutarco Hidalgo keeping an eye out for soldiers while retrieving bullets hidden in a cornfield

killing a seventy-year-old woman. Then President Felipe Calderón absolved the soldiers of the crime, declaring them "defenders of the people."

As the film unfolds, Vargas's script and camera follow the struggles of the violinist Don Plutarco Hidalgo (played by the eighty-four-year-old nonprofessional Ángel Tavira), his son Genaro (Gerardo Taracena), and his grandson Lucio (Mario Garibaldi), as well as the community of farmers generally as they try to fight this violently oppressive and murderous arm of the government.

While Vargas avoids identifying the location where the story transpires (for obvious political reasons), he does not set it outside time and place. First, the accents of the soldiers and farmers identify this as Mexico. Second, the mountain setting and the kinds of ponchos the farmers wear generally identify the region as Morelos, which lies between the states of Veracruz and Puebla; while not explicitly identified, this is probably in and around the mountain town Zongolica. So, while viewers will not know the exact place where these farmers are struggling against the army, they will see authentic representations of the extreme conditions in which these people have been forced to live, ones that lead to their decision to ignore the odds and fight the organized, trained, and well-armed military. The film conveys the facts forcefully: these people have only two options, to die one way or die another.

Vargas depicts this without any hint of sentimentality. He simply shows these poor people living high up in the inhospitable mountains, trying to survive on tiny crops. His camera, mise-en-scène, and choice of actors, actions, and events reflect what is really happening in Mexico.

Fig. 39. El violín: a sympathetic soldier speaks to Plutarco

Part of the film's power arises from Vargas's nuanced depiction of the soldiers. In conversations with Plutarco, the murderous Capitán (Dagoberto Gama) mentions that as a child he had almost nothing to eat and barely survived; he joined the army while still young because it offered a way to make a living. In general the soldiers' body movements, posture, and way of wearing their uniforms (hanging off their bodies) reveal a common peasant/ farmer origin. Scenes between lower-ranked soldiers and Plutarco include facial expressions, body movements, and actions that show the soldiers struggling with wrong and right; the audience gets the strong impression that they do what they do simply to survive and to send money home to families just like Plutarco's. In sympathy with Plutarco and the villagers' cause, one such soldier even surreptitiously slips the old man a gun.

Vargas's camera shows this in a neutral, nonsentimental manner by not using the film's visual and auditory elements to aestheticize the characters. The camera does shoot the landscape in slow, sweeping panoramas, but always to situate the characters in the story. Vargas's shots are completely integrated into the story. Unlike yesteryear's Gabriel Figueroa, then, Vargas employs shots of the landscape that authentically depict the area in which his characters live. The cinematography is always in synch with the narrative.

The film's grainy establishing sequence captures the soldiers as they torture and rape, but subsequent scenes indicate violence only indirectly; the blueprint directs us to fill gaps in ways that allow for a more forceful and visceral experience of the violence. Having caught Plutarco trying to smuggle bullets out of the village, which the military now controls, the Capitán asks

Fig. 40. El violín: Plutarco: "No more music"

Fig. 41. El violín: Lucio and a little girl walking down the road

him to play his violin. Plutarco knows his fate and refuses to play: "No more music." Vargas cuts to black and silence, leaving the viewer to fill in the blank: the captain pulls the trigger and murders Plutarco.

Vargas chooses not to end the film there, however. He includes an epilogue-like sequence that depicts the young Lucio singing a ballad about his village's struggle against the military; it ends with Lucio and a little girl walking down a road, and we catch a glimpse of Don Plutarco's gun.

El violín ends with children walking from the foreground to the background, along what would be the z-axis if this were a true three-dimensional space (in two-dimensional representations, movement from foreground to the background and vice versa helps establish a sense of three dimensions). The children also move up and away (along the z-axis), a vector that conveys a sense of heaviness and difficulty in the motion; they are effectively traveling against gravity if the direction across the two-dimensional screen is taken literally. The choice (whether the director's or the cinematographer's) to have them move up this axis is significant. It conveys a sense of the difficulty the children will face, uncomfortable lives spent working against gravity. This helps drive home the film's point: two generations of farmers have been wiped off the face of the earth, but Lucio and the little girl remain to tell the story and continue the hard struggle against oppression.

It's a Wrap

卐

Making, experiencing, interpreting, and judging twenty-first-century Mexican films requires us to use our perceptual, emotive, and cognitive faculties. As we have seen, these capacities lead to different artistic products. In this way Mexican films can be seen as a dialect of a planetary cinema. We can come to these conclusions because of an approach that carefully considers the composition of the Mexican film blueprint, as well as how it is made and consumed in time (history) and place (region), all this interfaced with questions of silver-screen backdrops, genres, trends, productions, distributions, and exhibitions.

At this point, I would like to reiterate several salient points.

First, Mexican filmmakers create blueprints or recipes for filmgoers to follow. There are many ingredients in the recipes; some of the more important include screenplay, cameras and lenses, type of shot, editing, music, mise-en-scène, casting, costumes, and score, among others that I touch on in detail at the beginning of this book.

Second, the filmmaking ingredients work together to trigger emotions in the audience. When the ingredients do not cohere, viewers often stop investing in the story either emotionally or cognitively. Such a disconnection may occur when, say, a twenty-four-year-old actress plays the part of a teen in González Iñárritu's *Babel* or a misguided body movement is used to indicate the hard-laboring class in Cuarón's *Rudo y Cursi*. If these elements are mixed well and with a strong sense of the way the parts add up to a whole, then a Mex-ciné film can become something spectacular. In making *Sin nombre,* for example, Fukunaga did his homework to be sure that all the parts cohere. First, he spent two years traveling the trains that migrants ride across Mexico; he then spent time writing and rewriting the screenplay with members of the Mara Salvatrucha, or MS-13, an extremely violent and dangerous transnational gang whose organized criminal networks involving drugs and prostitution extend from the United States into Central America.

Filmmakers such as Fukunaga make their films by testing their knowledge of reality against reality itself to create stories that work logically, sidestep sentimentality, and can move an audience powerfully. Fukunaga, for example, built his sturdy blueprint out of the harsh reality of migration across Central America and through Mexico, where people like Sayra and her family are mugged, raped, and killed by MS-13 and *la Migra*. And he adds to this experience his imagination, style, and skill as a director, orchestrating DPs, composers, sound designers, editors (in this case Luis Carballar and Craig McKay), casting directors, and costume designers, among many others, in his transformation of this all too common tragic story into a compelling Mexciné film.

All this effort and craft allowed Fukunaga to create one of the first films to depict the harsh reality of forced migration from Central and South American countries into and across southern Mexico's borders, littered with predatory gangs and corrupt *immigration officers;* he created a film that powerfully portrays the impossible struggle young people face in developing "healthy" emotional responses. Fukunaga understands his trade well and knows how to use all the elements of filmmaking to transform this story into a beautifully shaped artistic creation.

Conversely, when a Mex-ciné film fails to work (as *Babel* does), the failure quite likely arises because the director ignored connections between neurological emotion and reason systems. Noticeable incoherence interferes with the neurophysiological systems subtending emotional responses, yielding a less than captivating viewing experience. We finish watching a film like *Babel* and wonder why we wasted over two hours of our lives.

Third, as was already explained in the previous discussions of *Amar te duele, De la calle, and La zona,* without emotions there is no empathy, and without empathy there is no compass for acting positively or destructively toward others. Furthermore, only directors who possess a well-developed capacity to elicit emotional, empathetic, and ethical assessments in viewers can make films that, as does Francisco Vargas's *El violín,* trigger a series of contradictory responses in the audience: the captain is despicable, but we understand how his limited choices in life as a peasant led to his later choices and the destruction of his empathic system. Vargas's creation of a recipe filled with complex emotions and tensions makes the difference that *is* the difference between *El violín* and Jorge Colón's *Cansada de besar sapos:* the latter film presents a limited range of emotions, ethical dilemmas, and tensions, while the former is cognitively rich and complex and interestingly engaged with the world and its predicaments.

Fourth, directors with one eye on the Academy Awards and Cannes or other European festivals and the other eye on the box office tend not to make compelling filmic blueprints. Films such as *Todo el poder, Children of Men,* and *Babel,* for example, fail to achieve a sense of balance between industry and art.

Fifth, Mexican filmmakers can create, reframe, and transfigure real objects, real subjects, real experiences, and actual events that make up Mexican reality in ways that either *intensify* or *diminish* our apprehension of ourselves and the world in which we exist. Put simply, just as some Mexican films are well made, others are poorly made.

Sixth, we would be hard pressed to find a thread that unifies all twenty-first-century Mex-ciné films. I mentioned at the beginning of this book that I would focus on Mexican films made in the first decade of this century. I did this not because they share a common vision or follow the prescripts of a manifesto but only because, well, for the most part I like to watch, study, and teach them.

My point is that a Mex-ciné filmmaker can make a film about anything and set it anywhere. Moreover, filmmakers who were born or raised in Mexico can make films that fail to cohere or that slip into prepackaged sentimentality, just as directors born or raised elsewhere can make excellent films. Some of the best Mexican films are made by directors who are not Mexican by place of birth or heritage. Marisa Sistach was born to French and Spanish parents; Rodrigo Plá is from Montevideo, Uruguay; Luis Buñuel was a Spaniard; and Cary Joji Fukunaga was born in the United States to parents of Japanese and Swedish origins.

Racial, ethnic, or gender identity categories are not reason enough to exclude or include a director in the Mex-ciné film camp. What makes the difference here is a given director's sense of responsibility, will to style, and understanding of the world in imagining and then realizing the best damned film possible. Finally, I hope this book has shown that the films (good and bad) that make up a small sample of a twenty-first-century Mex-ciné landscape help constitute vital and necessary filmic idiolects that contribute deeply to the larger grammar of world cinema.

Afterword

✠

MICHAEL DONNELLY

I come to the pleasure of writing this afterword to *Mex-Ciné* from a history that crosses all dimensions of the filmmaking and filmgoing experience: from cinematic exhibitor and archivist to producer, DP (director of photography), and much more.

This odyssey began at an early age. As a kid I played with still cameras and Super 8 and made home movies and photographs as a form of personal expression. From the Chicago suburbs, where I went to practically every matinee I could get a ride to, I moved to Mexico City. Still a teenager, I was constantly exposed to the cinema and culture of that nation both as a spectator and a participant. Faced with watching awful dubbed versions of my previously favorite TV programs—a distinctly different experience in Spanish—I abandoned the habit, became a television invalid, and headed off to the city's many movie theaters. There in the dark I would indulge a continuous flow of international and Hollywood movies, subtitled, not dubbed, and for very little money.

After migrating back to the United States and living in Los Angeles, I joined a film collective that had leased the neighborhood Fox Theater in Venice, California. The resulting repertory movie theater became an instant local and even national success. For nearly a decade I virtually lived in the theater, working in all capacities, which included, for instance, creating film programs and music acts by day and watching said movies and music acts by night. Watching movies dancing in the dark with a different audience every night was spectacular.

Audience participation became my market research for the next month's bookings. Different screenings elicited different crowd reactions and energy. Why was this? Of course, certain onscreen events like the meditation of *La*

Jette (1962), the car chase in *Bullet* (1968), the violence of *A Clockwork Orange* (1971), or the raised hand in *Carrie* (1976) always got the same reaction, but the response to comedies and dramas often varied. And there was an external dimension to all this, too. Embedded in the audience and just to see what would happen, I found I could make people laugh by simply doing so in the dark along with the film. Maybe I was shilling; maybe my action gave them permission to express themselves. Either way, the insertion of my laughter—and coughs, on other occasions—was infectious.

I moved on to film distribution and built a classics film division for Azteca Films, selecting the best of Mexico's cinema history to service U.S. art theaters and museum venues. Later, for the UCLA Film and Television Archive and in conjunction with IMCINE (Instituto Mexicano de Cinematografía), I curated a four-year public touring package and catalog of nearly one hundred Mexican films covering the silent era up to the mid-1980s. That package became the foundation for the archival collection now held at UCLA's Powell Library.

I migrated to the technical side of film production, acting as producer of a number of feature films, serving as an executive with legacy Hollywood tech facilities CFI (Consolidated Film Industries) and Technicolor and frequently working as a director of and contributor to film festivals. In all this I have never forgotten the experiences I gained in the movie theater where the show all comes together.

Despite years and dollars spent on film production and critical studies classes, I still cannot profess to have a formal film education. What I learned came largely from a different place: studying enormous quantities of international films and learning from the filmmakers themselves. If something in a film interested me and I had it in my possession, I would study the reel, frame by frame. With access few others had, new worlds opened up for me that I never imagined possible. I developed great respect for the hidden technical mysteries of the creation of cinema art and entertainment.

Working hands-on and as an executive in the industry, I experienced the way films are a painstaking construct, an expensive and complicated human effort, planned and implemented with some semblance of control. Films are not just public experiences to be consumed and dismissed, although certainly that is not an entirely inappropriate fate for many.

We see reflected well in Frederick Luis Aldama's *Mex-Ciné* how producers, directors, and writers control their craft in order to present a more or less consistent and predictable experience other than just for themselves. Of course some producers, directors, and writers do this well—and some not so well; some films are created for a broad audience, others are made because they must be made, and a few seem to be made just for the filmmaker's friends. But every film that ends up before an audience (whatever the size) has a natural cycle of art and commerce. On some level, consciously or not, filmmakers are compelled to communicate a story (personal or otherwise) to elicit a reaction from others. Certainly, unexpected circumstances arise, but filmmakers simply do their best to follow a game plan, select a specific team for a project, and roll with the punches. If technical and financial resources hold out, a credible result is achieved. By whom, we might ask? A producer's or director's brute control of human and technical resources aside, intuition, experience, and wisdom all help to hedge bets along the way. Each step builds on another and reinforces what came before.

Outside one's own viewing experience, today the media tend to act as the arbiters of consumer behavior. Modern film journalism, sometimes (but mostly not) practiced by respected and thoughtful champions of cinema, has increasingly become more an extension of a commercial marketing imperative than a true commentary on the state and process of the creation of film. Film journalism is populated with reviewers and hardworking, enterprising film lovers. However, these "critics" are mostly verbal wizards caught up in the marketing spin to perpetuate media consumerism. Reviewers are populists, not analytical critics. I mean no disrespect to the trade of entertainment journalism—smart and supportive reviewers help sell movie tickets, for which I am thankful. There are indeed many excellent film critics. I think of the insightful wit of Pauline Kael, the intelligence of Andrew Sarris, the adventuresome experimental musings of J. Hoberman, and especially the few writings of Manny Farber. In these cases, however, each critic investigated a new way (or another way) to analyze film.

Yet we see even critics such as Kael, Sarris, and Hoberman, and Bresson come up short. For instance, with Sarris we might observe of his importation of the *auteur* theory that while it defines a signature property of individual vision, not everyone is an *auteur*, especially in Hollywood. As Aldama has shown so clearly, and is corroborated by my own experiences, this fails to consider all the parts that go into making a film. These predilections to film analysis are taught and validated in university critical studies programs, as well as in the mainstream media, where "keep it simple" is axiomatic.

This is where Aldama's work comes into significant play. In *Mex-Ciné* he directs his analysis to Mexican cinema at a point where I left off with my work on it in the late 1990s. He also investigates a new analytical structure that unifies and encompasses more elements of the filmmaking process. His concept and formulation of the "blueprint" matter. With them he explores a different structural relationship of the entirety of a film, from planning and creation to its public experience, that is relevant not just to Mexican filmmakers. He does not stand back from deeply informed critical—and here I mean *critical*—analyses of contemporary Mexican films. As such the book benefits serious filmmakers—and rejects outright any form of criticism that might further a marketing, consumerist agenda.

Let me return briefly to Aldama's concept of the blueprint. This is not a filmmaker's term—nor for that matter are filmmakers fluent in the recent advances in the neurosciences. That said, what Aldama does is to make more formally understood what we do to create our films so as to engage our viewers. It gives clarity to the way we make our "blueprints" *not* unmindful of circumstance. The more circumstance allows a director to be charged with keeping a unified vision of the many parts that make up a film the better his or her blueprint will function as a good measure during the journey of making a film. I leave the film selection and analyses of contemporary Mexican cinema to Aldama. For the rest I offer some further meditations.

Two good questions Aldama asks are have the filmmakers succeeded on their own terms and have they communicated the intention of their vision?

While we might hope that our film blueprints direct our audiences to experience a film in the ways we intend, audiences often find their own levels of engagement external to the carefully orchestrated elements presented in the film. Mocking sarcasm to outright rapture can be unintended viewer responses—responses that do not exist in the projected frames. Brain-numbing neurological responses to overmodulation of audio and IPS ("images per second," yes, it is a term) can more forcefully direct an audience's emotional response, but ultimately the audience responds as it pleases. And, I might add, while the media love to hype, box-office figures matter only as commerce, not as a filmmaker's benchmark indicator of winners or losers.

The blueprint concept captures well the *real* many creative minds that are involved in the making of films. In his book *Notes on Cinematography,* Robert Bresson captures this sense of the collective effort involved, too. Aldama and Bresson are thinking in the right direction. Construction of the magnificent churches of medieval Europe, which involved decades of labor by scores of craftspeople and artisans who never met, were motivated by glory, honor, and religion. Cinema is not much different.

It just makes sense to go beyond clichéd and misappropriated *auteurist* benchmarks or Grecian theater concepts. Many Shakespeare plays have five, not three, acts. Howard Hawks commented that with one great scene per reel, you have a movie. The world today is very cinema savvy. Once, the editorial cutting patterns in *Memento* (2000) or *Inception* (2010) would have been virtually inscrutable to popular audiences—no longer. Cinema logic as in *Apollo 13* (1995) or *Titanic* (1997) can create dramatic tension when the outcome is already known. Unlike a novel, where the reader can lower the book and pause to consider a passage, cinema is a slave to the clock. Film is relentless. A viewer must surrender to the real-time progressive sequence of experience—reflection is not an option. To travel around in "mind time," filmmakers rely on tricks of the trade, distractions, and the suspension of disbelief to sell their dramas. Yes folks, the space capsule is coming back with everyone on it and the *Titanic* is going down. But who is impacted? Audiences take sides, and the filmmakers set them up. History many not even matter. The words "Houston, we have a problem" were never uttered at Mission Control. Modern cinema analysis needs more tools for this exploration.

Genre cinema is known to require certain elements to satisfy audience expectations and viewing habits. A Hollywood "happy ending" is almost always a requirement. To protect their visions, or at least salvage some part of them, many filmmakers with allowable budgets will film several endings. The director's cut of *Blade Runner* (1982) shows Ridley Scott's vision to have been quite different from the studio's concept. Not only does the voice-over disappear and realign the point of view, but the fantasy ending teases with the idea that the bounty hunter may also be a closet android himself. Inevitably, the studio or distributors will press for a happy ending, or at least a positive upshot, especially if there is no alternative. Even *Thelma and Louise* (1991), while not ending "happy," at least closes somewhat "heroic"—same thing to Hollywood.

Story sleights of hand are required to divert audience attention away from foregone endings, such as those in *Titanic* and *Apollo 13*, or the tragedy of *Thelma and Louise*. But to pay for all that, a powerful voice with a commercial upside, such as Ridley Scott's, is required for the reissue of essentially another movie. Other directors, such as Clint Eastwood and Robert Altman, traded off their commercial dues to alternate with more personal films.

Different movies—romance, drama, action, art, horror, comedy, and so on—all have different formulas to satisfy audience expectations. Manipulated by skilled filmmakers, some formulas are far more sophisticated than others. Innovation and nuance notwithstanding, all formulas rely on proven stylistic continuities, popular references, and a common syntax. The image of the baby carriage bouncing down the steps in *The Untouchables* (1987) directly correlates to the scene in *Battleship Potemkin* (1925). While some in the audience may miss the reference and others get it, what the audience as a whole does experience is the sense of threat and intensification of tension that results from shared use of the formal technique.

Not all formulas are fanciful, transparent, or overly expository. With dramatic films, the design of the film must contain subtle but clear elements to move the audience forward in an engaging and convincing fashion. Audiences want to associate strongly with the characters; they want to feel where their emotional investment is going. Subplots, strong identifiable characters, engaging situations, and often technical accuracy help keep audiences' attention in the moment and not guessing too much about the ending.

Mysteries and thrillers are somewhat different. Not only did Alfred Hitchcock define the "McGuffin" (the unimportant, recurring distraction meant to throw the audience off the scent), but he brilliantly differentiated between "shock" and "suspense"—two fundamentally different formulas. When the audience knows something that the character does not, suspense is created as long as the audience is on the character's side. For instance, if the audience is acutely aware that some danger or horror lies behind a closed door and the character is not, when he approaches the door the reaction will be "Don't touch that door!" Suppose the character's hand reaches out but retracts by some sixth sense. As their creative intent, the director, actor, and editor can play with this condition for a long time, increasingly raising the stakes and the level of suspense. Further suppose that as the character retracts his hand, the filmmakers show a stranger lurking around the getaway car outside the house. Additionally, the audience has already been introduced to a phobic condition specific to the character. As long as the story advances interestingly while maintaining the suspense, you have a thriller, or possibly a mystery movie. If, however, the character opens the door and is devoured, or harmed, the suspense is lost and the audience goes into "shock." In that case we don't need a lurker outside or a neurotic condition because the character has become lunch, suspense is lost, and the actor, director, and editor have to start all over again.

A nonstop series of continuous "shocks" can become a solid horror or action film but with an entire other formula construct to keep an audience engaged. This works everywhere. *Jaws* (1975) is a good example—we never really see the shark. In *Vertigo* (1958), James Stewart is plagued by heights and must overcome this phobia to be a hero. The companion films *Alien* (1979) and *Aliens* (1986) differ in that the first is a psychological drama and suspense film, whereas the second is a hardware action movie with repeatedly shocking moments. Both are great films, each in a different way. And films may combine techniques as in Brian De Palma's *Carrie* (1976)—just when you thought it was all over, boom, up comes the hand from the grave. There is no resolution.

Film is more than a story, a director, and some performers. Directed actors personify and deliver the story and may dominate the premise of a film, but none alone is cinema. One expects a Jane Austen adaptation to be a good story and for the actors to behave according to a set of social and dramatic conceits—nothing wrong with that. However, original cinema asks for a wider field of vision, more disciplines, more circumstances, more money, and a different set of expectations. Today superheroes have rules and societal conceits as well.

What are those rules? Powerful technological tools help to place those conventions in the field of performance. The motion control in *Star Wars* (1977), the array of still cameras in *The Matrix* (1999), and *The Lord of the Rings'* (2001) computerized imaging technologies all provide a plastic context that may surprise us at first but is soon understood as a rule by which or the environment in which the character functions. Was Golem an actor or a visual effect? Such vivid depictions do more than just support the metaphysical underpinnings of the story in much the same way that the ancient Greeks did with choruses of gods and muses. The transformational functions of green screen and CGI (computer-generated imagery) can put a character in a time or place where the actor never set foot; 3D can put that character in your lap. These wizard tools are the heirs to the kind of movie magic that predated narrative, sound, and even performance. They are the foundation of the pure cinema of the moving image. These elements are always at work. While too often used as banal cheap tricks, over time these tools can become part of our cinematic language and syntax. After all, at one time cinema itself was considered nothing more than a parlor trick.

The producer entity functions as the prime mover. There is a movie industry axiom that the producer is the audience. The producer must first deal with taking on a project and going through the steps required to get it "set up" or approved by some financial group that has some idea of how to recoup its investment. There are many great "visions" that no one will touch as any kind of endgame is simply not on the horizon. With deadlines and obligations to investors, as well as a passion and vision for a project, the producer must be considered the prime mover and original owner of the blueprint. The producer usually finds a script, or property, hires a writer, determines a budget limitation, and may even package a cast before hiring a director.

While a director may be a writer and producer, thus a business partner with a producer, those additional skills may be more hats than one person can wear. A director may also take a project to a trusted producer for hire to deal with the organization, sales, and financing of the vision. Either way, as the most active force in physical production, a director's prime obligation, and artistic right, is to maintain a consistent creative overview through the many phases of production given the tools a producer allows. As a hired hand, a director is charged with creatively interpreting a script according to a game plan, in which he or she may or may not have had substantial input, in the making of the blueprint.

Despite everyone's best efforts to the contrary, film production is a fickle and circumstantial process. Another film industry axiom is that a film is never really finished, just abandoned when time, money, or creative drive runs out. Given this inevitability, a savvy producer will compensate for this degeneration of resources. Acting as a sounding board for the director and planning well for postproduction, editorial, postaudio, music, visual effects, and other tools pays off in keeping the long-term vision alive as the filmmaking fervor winds down. Just knowing that someone has this covered allows a director to do what must be done on set and nowhere else. There probably has never really been a movie for which a filmmaker would not want to redo this, that, or something else given the value of hindsight or additional money or technology.

There are war stories of übercontrolling directors (Aldama mentions Alejandro González Iñárritu) going to great lengths to shoot only what supports their vision, thereby limiting editorial changes and options and thwarting the interference of art savages, those by know-nothing, bottom-line obsessed producers. These reactions are not inventions. But equally true is that after production a director may move on to another film or elect to have limited involvement after delivering a director's first cut. A producer or studio then has the right to do as they want with that version and the producer must then finish the film. This is not always a bad thing as long as the producer/director vision is clear—that their blueprint remains functional. Good producers can be prime visionaries, too and there are many who have taken the film to a polished state that a director could not.

There are as many iterations of this practice as there are films. John Huston (famous for doing everything in the camera) once stated that he had never met many of the editors of his films. Other directors shoot only enough footage to cut one way and no other. Other directors are quite open to the collaborative process. A strong producer-director relationship is a fabulous asset.

Blueprint or not, a film must never become an orphan to luck. Luck often dictates what appears to have been a crucial decision. Pascal said, "Luck favors the prepared mind." Filmmakers know this well. For instance, Frank Sinatra was notorious for having one great take in him for any scene. Additional attempts to improve on his one take were usually fruitless and frustrating for the performer. Director John Frankenheimer likes to tell how such an incident played out in his film *The Manchurian Candidate* (1962). In the film Sinatra's character had discovered that his Korean War buddy, actor Laurence Harvey, would be transformed into an assassin when triggered by the sight of the queen of hearts. In a key scene Sinatra confronts Harvey with an entire deck of queens of hearts, sending the brainwashed ex–war hero into a delirious and dysfunctional hypnotic state and allowing Sinatra to unravel a dangerous plot to assassinate a presidential candidate intended to place a communist president in the White House. Sinatra's one take was superb, but an undiscovered camera mistake later revealed that his nose was quite out of focus! There was no way to improve a brilliant performance and no recourse for a reshoot. Devastated, Frankenheimer went with the only shot he had.

When the film was released, critics noticed and waxed ecstatic! What a brilliant use of point-of-view soft focus to depict Harvey's view of his tormentor as his disturbed mind disintegrated faced with an overload of the trigger queens of hearts card! Not what you expect from Hollywood. Luck made lemonade from lemons as the critic/audience invented an unexpected central story nuance from a huge technical faux pas.

These interpretations happen all the time as a film gains additional significance and meaning as it lives on past creative control. Possibly the greatest American film of all time, *Citizen Kane* (1941), was an unappreciated commercial disaster until the 1950s and 1960s! Why? Because the supposed subject of the film, William Randolph Hearst, hated the film and swore to destroy it because of a lurid reference to his mistress. Hearst enlisted every press person he could to pan the film and even bought the RKO studio with the specific purpose of destroying both director Orson Welles and that and subsequent films made by him. Thus, the suppressed masterpiece lay dormant away from mainstream viewers for more than two decades. These stories are legion.

I want to make passing reference to editing and audio tricks of the trade. The great fallback to production is postproduction. Some say this is where a film is really made. When Frank Sinatra's nose gets in the way, fix it in post? Not really. While postproduction may double as a great repair shop, its primary function should be to make a film sizzle. Put the icing on the cake and create another whole dimension to the process.

Postproduction reinforces production blueprints with organization, order, and enhancements. Innovative editing and shot arrangements polish and bring nuance to improve an actor's performance, or a writer's story idea. Audio and visual effects, often part of the original conception, add another dimension. The public at large is unaware of how all this works. Does an Academy Award for Best Editing or Best Sound Design mean anything to most people? No, unless you understand the craft. These craft artists thrive on their invisible impact. If you are watching the editing, or attuned to the sound design, you are probably out of the story to begin with.

Hitchcock and Luis Buñuel were famous for preconceiving movies in their heads. Hitchcock claimed he rarely went to the set—not true, but it could have been. To Buñuel editing was removing the slates from the production footage. To these directors, and John Huston, if what was in the script was shot, there was little need to do anything but stick the parts together. Things have changed. Today, especially with digital cinema capture, almost no one circles takes or projects dailies. Filmmakers shoot and assemble massive amounts of footage and make critical decisions in the editing room as much for creative reasons as business ones.

For some tech-savvy directors, like David Fincher, postproduction is now being brought onto the set with increasingly mobile equipment. Digital convergence of production and post is right around the corner, but that is another story. Here is a classic example of editing fundamentals. You have three pictures of a tough-looking, grizzled cowboy—not someone to fool with. In one picture he is smiling, in another he is frowning, and in another he is pointing an ugly gun at your head. Every picture is independent, the same person in the same costume in the same relative composition and color, but the order in which the shots are assembled and how long you look at them result in vastly different stories. You are either dead or forgiven. As an audience member, you do not know about the number of editorial choices that were possible; you only see the result. This description is the process in its simplest form—there might be a half dozen of these cowboys at different stages doing different things, as well as a sheriff and a damsel in distress.

Even more than action, comedy requires very specific timing. Editing does not create funny faces, but it creates order and timing among moving images; even a few frames can throw off a joke. Sight gags can only be on-screen for a short time, and they must build in sequence order to bring more impact. And rarely do gags and timing carry a comedy on their own without some common reference or context. I always like to remind people that the medium is called moving pictures, not filmed narrative—just a minor point to consider when evaluating a film.

While working in a film lab, I grew accustomed to seeing movies without any audio track; it is surprising how much you can tell about a film's successful storytelling when you just follow the picture editorial. This silent phase after picture cutting is a common step in color correction and visual effects. After editorial there is no need for sound as the final mix and music are added somewhere else. This is a great time to look at a movie and evaluate editorial pace and the power of the image. If all the editorial selections are reinforcing each other and the story, just imagine how much better the film will be with dialogue, music, and effects added. On your TV try turning off the volume on a DVD and see what you understand. A good director knows how to make use of this, just like good music producers know what a song sounds like played on a car stereo.

Genres vary in their editorial requirements, and specific formulas of shot length and transition constructions are known in the trade. Comedy almost always requires the threat of tragedy to succeed. Mysteries require great misdirection and audience participation. Action requires speed, surprise, timing, montage, and relentless building blocks. Romance requires long, lyrical moments and acute actor chemistry onscreen and enhanced in editorial. Pursuit films require advanced editing techniques like parallel cutting, unviewed assailants, and a specific editorial geography that does not leave the viewer behind. The list goes on, and the filmmaker's bag of tricks grows. Without realizing it, modern audiences have come a long way in their inherent understanding of editing. The editing in a film like *Memento* is key to understanding and participating in the main character's worldview. The film was a solid commercial success, whereas not too long ago it would have been unintelligible.

Famously, *High Noon* (1952) was not working well. As written the story spent too much time waiting around for the bad guy to show up. The solution, a strictly editorial creation, consisted of adding repeated cutbacks to a clock on the wall. As the clock advanced, tension built and pushed flat drama to the level of a Western classic. Similarly, *Jaws* was rumored to have begun conceived as an in-your-face action movie until the mechanical shark wouldn't work on command. No shark, no shock, so they went Hitchcockian for suspense and a potentially routine action film became a brilliant chase movie in which the pursuer (the shark) is rarely seen until deep into the film. Great editing makes these saves possible. *Memento* or *Inception* contains remarkably few computerized visual effects; brilliant editing helped not only to reinforce the story but to add a dimensional dynamic and revelation to the storytelling. Christopher Nolan works this way, planning everything in advance and keeping in the effects in-camera as much as possible.

Audio is like the haiku of cinema. Audio and cinematography each bring strength to fill the spaces among the narrative, staging, and performance. Axiomatic in cinema is that audio supports the rest of the film. If one is paying too much attention to the music, then likely the film structure has slipped away from the director. Audio can bring it back. But a pushy mix can make a film play like a disk jockey's song list—one after another the lyrics reiterate exactly what you see onscreen to work up nostalgia with the target audience. This experience tells you to go buy the soundtrack and signals an excess that rarely integrates into an overall textured experience of a film. Likely this is a patchwork not the blueprint.

A filmmaker has a vast arsenal with which to realign his or her film after production. Common uses of music and audio in a film are score, songs, sound effects, and stings. The creative choice may be to enhance existing footage or finalize production concepts. Layer on layer of recorded audio effects build to create a single screen moment. The sound of the discharge of a pistol may have a dozen or more components. These may be the wind, a creaky door, or an auto driving off. Audiences are usually rapt in the action and may not notice, but they know when the effects are not there!

Greater emotional depth can be brought to bear with a score that really supports the story. A score is music written for a particular film. The composer seeks to follow the emotion and tone designed for the film. Individual songs are more familiar licensed music written by others and deemed appropriate for a particular moment or character. Sound effects are just that, painstakingly manufactured nonmusical audio of the world around us, or audio designed to create the world of the story. Stings are abrupt instrumental or sonic accents that create a reaction to reinforce some onscreen moment as in a genre film.

Then there are films that have little or no musical score at all, and in them silence becomes its own voice. *Alien* is a good example—there is no sound in space. Musicals are usually lip-synched after the fact by vocalists who cover the actors who sing (or not) onstage to audio playback. Other than in intimate close-ups and important dialogue, actors' performances are not necessarily recorded with great fidelity as their live performances often are used only as guide tracks for later postsynch rerecording. That said, directors and actors almost always prefer to try and use set performance, but that is not always possible.

In the rerecording studios, nearly all nondialogue audio is designed, en-hanced, and built painstakingly, layer on layer, after the film has been shot, edited, and cut to length and everyone else has gone home. The resulting power of the soundtrack is huge and may even define a film. Stanley Ku-brick's works are especially powerful in this regard: the near silence of the apes discovering the bone to the Strauss waltz to the final electronic sonic ef-fects all bring an especially powerful and memorable texture to *2001: A Space Odyssey* (1968).

Postproduction is where much of the drama and wonder are created in movies. In its earliest days, editorial storytelling was enabled by masters like D. W. Griffith, Edwin S. Porter, Sergei Eisenstein, and Vsevolod Pudovkin. The edit room was their home turf. Here the pieces of the puzzle are com-pleted. It is where one shot following another tells a whole other story. The developed frames remain the same, but their relationship to one another is a whole other thing. And of course there is montage and the volumes written about that. Visual effects take us places and open up a director's palette like never before. All these and other tools give the director and the editor ways to improve and create the timing and tension in a story, to linger a moment on a face or place, or to give the audience a rest and a transition in montage. Shoot-ing a film is like writing a score, but editorial is the performance, and a good director is the virtuoso who knows this, plans for it, and shoots accordingly.

Aldama's decision to apply his blueprint to Mexican cinema brings up spe-cific considerations that do not apply everywhere or necessarily at all to overly commercial cinema. Most films are well served by suggesting common audi-ence experiences that are shorthand paths to deeper communication. Audi-ences may not have gone to the moon, had a romance with Sophia Loren or María Félix, been mortally wounded in action, or been brainwashed, but they must share a common sense of what such an experience would be like. This condition is central to film as a universal language and one quite apart from spoken narrative.

It often happens that the subtleties of language become lost in translation or cultural differentiation, but if viewers can find context for those universal sensibilities somewhere between the lines they may adopt their own versions. Michael York's book (with Adrian Brine) *A Shakespearean Actor Prepares* is illuminating. The occasional film actor, a formidable performer of the Bard's works the world over, was astonished to find so many variations of Shake-speare that had been adopted, even coopted, by national cultures that laid claim to the works and considered their versions to be the right ones. Film is different. Remakes are occasional but are usually different beasts. Stories are more commonly adapted from other art forms and retold from a different viewpoint, as Akira Kurosawa is famous for doing, utterly transforming many of these stories in the process.

Subtitles distract the viewer's eye, and dubbing eliminates an actor's performance. Comedies traditionally do not travel well among cultures. Humor is many layered, often culturally specific, and quite dependent on timing. One of the most enduring American comedic entertainers, Johnny Carson, was a flop when his show was broadcast in England. The British did not get Carson's humor.

Historically Mexico's social cinema relies on comedy; Tin Tan, Cantinflas, and many contemporary comics' best work lashes out at class and economic distinctions in a folkloric, associative manner. Mexican language and culture are famous for their folkloric manners, rhythms of speech, and puns. Fernando Eimbcke's *Duck Season* (2004) captured youthful noncommunication, and Alfonso Cuarón's *Y tu mamá también* (2001) succeeded in Mexico as a language, personal buddy story, and striking social commentary. The latter film's exceptional U.S. and international success came mostly on its merits, which were not language specific; its great idiomatic nuance was notable and generally understood but operated on fewer levels. *Duck Season* barely caught on. *Mex-Ciné* analyzes both films in depth.

The Mexican Government and its film industry have a complicated marriage, an arranged marriage perhaps. Almost since the beginnings of the medium (which more or less coincided with the Mexican Revolution), a private and a public sector have coexisted, a condition common to other business sectors in Mexico. Simplistically, in the marketplace the government is less involved in manufacturing and more so in areas of financing, marketing, and price control.

Loosely, all things radio, television, and cinema fall to Radio, Televisión, Cinematografía (RTC), which is part of the Department of State. Some have pushed to move control to the Mexican Department of Education (SEP), but constitutionally that seems to be too much. To one extent or another, then, cinema is considered a cultural patrimonial to the world at large. Perhaps the closest U.S. model would be the Corporation for Public Broadcasting or its television network PBS.

Beginning as far back as the 1930s, with support for Paul Strand's *Redes* (1936) by the SEP; the largely government financed Estudios Clasa, which produced and provided military equipment and services for Fernando de Fuentes's *Vámanos Con Pancho Villa/Let's Go with Pancho Villa* (1936); the Independent Film Festival of 1960; government appropriation of the film industry infrastructure and the creation of the National Film Bank in the 1970s; and finally the realignment that established IMCINE in 1983, Mexican government administrations have repeatedly attempted to assure financing and infrastructure to achieve a cinema patrimony that reflects Mexican art and cultural values. In that regard, the programs have succeeded.

Such lofty and ambitious goals have been always complicated by the government's struggle to monetize its industry acquisitions with a saleable product that supports a labor-intensive industry. The government's flirtation with the operation and ownership of studios, as well as distribution and exhibition systems, peaked in the 1970s, to the extent of buying out large private businesses, but since the 1990s this trend has been reversed. In its heyday this industry produced some 150 to 200 films per year.

Today the private sector is pretty much free to do as it pleases and make the films it wants. Over the years private-sector producers have had much success in creating a financing and distribution infrastructure for their commercial genre productions but less success in most areas of innovation and creativity. Mostly, the private producers know how to dominate the marketplace, especially the U.S. marketplace where a captive audience pays for its tickets in dollars, not pesos.

More serious or less commercially oriented filmmakers usually require government support for financing and marketing. The approval process is complex, and a filmmaker's concept may be compromised by institutional realities, but that is the general idea. Many of the Mexican films seen at major international film festivals have taken this path. For many serious filmmakers, institutional support is hugely important, as are government-negotiated international coproduction arrangements.

Today, with the infrastructure gone and government roles diminished, a double blow has reduced Mexico's film output to mere dozens per year, most without any reliable access to screens. Mexican films today rely on the same distribution networks as any other film from any other country—a sad state of affairs for filmmakers and producers looking to recoup their investments. For this reason there has been an exodus of sorts, with younger filmmakers leaving Mexico, where they learned their craft, and heading for Hollywood or Europe to earn a living from their talents.

The point of this "business-side" excursion is to indicate that Aldama's blueprint for Mexico has many masters. For now a single visionary director may not always be in control of the myriad of elements required to make a film. *Mex-Ciné's* focus on contemporary Mexican films necessarily must include those with some level of government support. These films are of a more singular vision, with manageable budgets; not by-the-numbers, market-dictated constructs; or the harbormaster technological feats of many of to-day's Hollywood offerings. Thus the blueprint is easier to trace through the process. Aldama wisely includes expatriate Mexican filmmakers who left to work in Hollywood and have found substantial international success.

Mexico's geographic and cultural proximity to Hollywood is always a lure. The national filmmaking culture is historically linked to its northern neighbor. Additionally, the United States has a vital Mexican art and entertainment culture thriving inside its borders. Since the 1980s, Mexico's film industry has atrophied at the same time that Mexican film schools have turned out innovative, freethinking, and highly trained students. But there is no way for them to make a living outside of television or advertising.

There is a gap between the filmmakers of the 1970s and the emerging filmmakers of the 2000s. In this gap Mexico lost an entire generation of creative talent to Britain and France but mostly to Los Angeles. The 1970s directors continued to make great cinema, and their crews learned a lot, but few could follow in their footsteps.

Disciple actors, directors, and cinematographers left to find creative outlets and professional remuneration unavailable to them at home. Several have left an important mark. Astutely, Aldama interprets the hybrid nature of their work. These talented expatriates in Hollywood display flair and skill in their output of essentially Hollywood movies with no specific intent to cater directly to a specific national audience. To make a real Mexican movie, Alfonso Cuarón went back to Mexico.

Numerous Mexican directors of photography have succeeded in Hollywood as well as at home. Camera artists have found a way to excel at their craft in Hollywood, where the industry always seems to have a place for international talents.

The mechanics of 35 mm film, cameras, and lighting equipment are based on common, universal technologies proven basically since the 1930s. The visual communication of cinematography neutralizes other film components such as language, commercial best practices, local customs, and so on. With the new digital cinematographic technologies, it is only a matter of time until these, too, are common and universal. Falling costs and increased access to new digital equipment will give more impoverished national cinemas more professional options. The common commercial film cameras continue to be manufactured in the United States, Germany, and France, while most digital ones come from Japan. Adequate production equipment is available everywhere. The visual language of cinema is universal and easily understood, and adequate tools exist for almost any individual interpretation by a director, cinematographer, or art director.

Kodak, Fuji, and Agfa film stocks dominate. The increased quality and exposure range of modern film is almost impossible to mess up. Still, the first-class labs on every continent require careful handling and shipping. And the higher cost of 35 mm film processing has digital cinema on the rise. Still, digital postproduction technology is expensive and equipment is not immediately available. And there is expertise involved.

Good lenses are expensive and rare. Few are interchangeable between film and video cameras. Most movies can get by with a handful of lenses, a zoom and a selection of four to six primes. The few options for film formatting—Widescreen Scope, American 1.85 to 1., European 1.66 to 1, and the high-definition digital 1.77 to 1—are pretty much dictated by theatrical and broadcast standards.

Lens selection, framing, focus, and proximity of the camera are pretty much the syntax of the visual language. A wide-shot or a pan sets up the geography of a scene so the audience knows where it is and who else is there, something like a descriptive passage in fiction. A two-shot is like a sentence with a noun and a verb; two characters, one active and the other reactive, trade primary emphasis within the frame. Their images may be supported, referenced, or counterreferenced by means of dialogue. These shots advance the story. A close-up is like an adjective or adverb that further enhances a character's reaction or inner emotion. Books have been written about the close-up. Usually this is where real movie acting comes in to let the audience know where the character stands emotionally, unless the close-up is a point of view, whereby the characters tell each other where they stand while letting the audience in on it. An extreme close-up is like an exclamation point, question mark, or specific a point of view of something a character sees that the director wants the audience to see (though maybe not the other character). Focus pulling, zooms, and depth-of-field alterations allow emphasis changes within a scene without editing no matter what the framing. And on and on it can go. Everyone has a language he or she sets up and hopefully sticks to throughout the film.

Although no actual pictures or renderings of the Old Globe Theatre exist, Michael York described Shakespeare's design as extremely wide for its day so as to amplify the staging of works and the audience experience. The greater breadth of the stage allowed more mobility for the actors and space for the director or playwright to isolate onstage actions, develop subplots and discrete dialogue, and play with the geography of blocking a scene to keep audience interest active and moving left to right, especially in the ground-lings pit. The dynamics of the x- and y-axes were more important than stage depth (the z-axis). True or not, to my movie mind such a layout functionally mirrors the cinema effects of stereo sound or the wide screen or even the split-screen image.

Stanley Kubrick thought the opposite. He disliked wide-screen and ste-reo formats. Reissues have violated his wishes, although 70 mm prints of *2001: A Space Odyssey* (1968) used that format and *Spartacus* (1960) was a proj-ect he took over, but the director himself always wanted the audience pointed directly at the screen, with no distractions left or right. This concept is just as evident in his balanced photographic compositions in-camera. Straight-on right off the screen is how he wanted it from the beginning. His indelible and powerful images are the result.

My intention here has been illustrate some applied workings that support a broader interpretation of film such as Aldama puts forth with his blueprint. I do not dislike film journalists and don't mean to wax ecstatic over dated, ob-scure movies; to present classics as superior films to those of today; or even to suggest that there are not better examples to put forth. In fact I purposefully stuck to examples with which many readers are likely familiar. I only hope to attach a historical and universal context to the work of *Mex-Ciné*. I trust the casual reader will learn more about the world of Mexican film, develop an insight into the challenges that filmmakers face, and perhaps discover how it all comes together.

It may seem like many of the world's masters had to paint with their hands tied, or that the stories they had to tell were dull and irrelevant, but the fundamental desire to create cinema and the cerebral process of doing so have varied little since the inception of the form in the 1890s. It is a basic human creative drive to express life and imagination in motion and to some-how harness all the powers available to realize a vision; that has not changed, but the tools have become more varied and available, though more complex intellectually. We see the intricacies of film creation and its consumption in Aldama's *Mex-Ciné*.

Michael Donnelly is a cinematographer, exhibitor, editor, photographer, and archivist.

Mex-Ciné Filmography

☁

This is not conclusive. Generally, films that do not mention actors are documentaries. English titles are given if distributed as such.

2000

Amores Perros
Director: Alejandro González Iñárritu
Cinematography: Rodrigo Prieto
Script: Guillermo Arriaga
Editor: Luis Carballar, Alejandro González Iñárritu, Fernando Pérez Unda
Music: Gustavo Santaolalla
Stars: Emilio Echevarría, Gael García Bernal, Goya Toledo

De ida y vuelta/Back and Forth
Director: Salvador Aguirre
Cinematography: Geronimo Denti
Script: Salvador Aguirre, Alejandro Lubezki
Editor: Moises Ortiz-Urquidi.
Music: Jorge Fratta
Stars: Gerardo Taracena, Ricardo Esquerra, Tiaré Scanda, Mario Zaragoza

Las olas del Tiempo
Director: Carlos Salcés
Cinematography: Chuy Chávez
Script: Carlos Salcés, Blanca Montoya
Editor: Carlos Salcés, Jaime Ramos
Music: Eduardo Gamboa
Stars:Ana Karen Fernández, Jaime Ramos

Sin dejar huella/Without a Trace
Director: María Novaro
Cinematography: Sergei Saldívar Tanaka

Script: María Novaro
Editor: Angel Hernandez Zoido
Music: Juan Borrel
Stars: Aitana Sánchez-Gijón, Tiaré Scanda, Jesús Ochoa

Todo el poder/Gimme the Power
Director: Fernando Sariñana
Cinematography: Eduardo Martínez Solares
Script: Enrique Renteria, Carolina Rivera
Editor: Alex Rodríguez
Music: Enrique Quezadas
Stars: Demián Bichir, Cecilia Suárez, Luis Felipe Tovar

2001

Y tu mamá también/And Your Mom Too
Director: Alfonso Cuarón
Cinematography: Emmanuel Lubezki
Script: Carlos Cuarón, Alfonso Cuarón
Editor: Alex Rodríguez, Alfonso Cuarón
Music: Various Artists
Stars: Maribel Verdú, Gael García Bernal, Diego Luna

Inspiración
Director: Ángel Mario Huerta
Cinematography: Jose Casillas
Script: Angel Mario Huerta
Editor: Hernán Contreras, Gael Geneau, Angel Mario Huerta
Music: Guillermo Méndez Guiú
Stars: Arath de la Torre, Bárbara Mori, Rodrigo Oviedo

Alex Lora, esclavo del rocanrol
Director: Luis Kelly
Cinematography: Pedro Castillo
Script: Federico Chao, Luis Kelly
Editor: Unavailable
Music: Alex Lora (Saúl Almaráz, post production sound)
Stars: Alex Lora, Chela Lora

Ciudades oscuros
Director: Fernando Sariñana
Cinematography: Salvador "Chava" Cartas
Script: Enrique Rentería, Fernando Sariñana
Editor: Robert Bolado
Music: Eduardo Gamboa
Stars: Alejandro Tomassi, Alonso Echánove, Demián Bichir, Diego Luna, Dolores
  Heredia

Devil's Backbone
Director: Guillermo del Toro
Cinematography: Guillermo Navarro
Script: Guillermo del Toro, Antonio Trashorras, David Muñoz
Editor: Luis del la Madrid
Music: Javier Navarrete
Stars: Fernando Tielve, Eduardo Noriega, Marisa Paredes, Federico Luppi

Francisca . . . ¿De qué lado estas?
Director: Eva López-Sánchez
Cinematography: Javier Morón
Script:Jorge Goldenberg, Eva López Sánchez, Pierre Salvadori, Mayra Santiago
Editor: Sigfrido Barjau, Santiago Torre
Music: Leonardo Heiblum, Jacobo Lieberman
Stars: Fabiola Campomanes, Ulrich Noethen, Arcelia Ramirez, Juan Ríos

El misterio del Trinidad
Director: José Luis García Agraz
Cinematography: Pedro Juan López
Script: Carlos Cuarón
Editor: Carlos Espinosa (assistant to editor)
Music: Nacho Mastretta
Stars: Eduardo Palomo, Rebecca Jones, Alejandro Parodi

La virgen de la lujuria
Director: Arturo Ripstein
Cinematography: Esteban de Llaca
Script: Paz Alicia Garciadiego
Editor: Fernando Pardo
Music: Leoncio Lara
Stars: Ariadna Gil, Luis Felipe Tovar, Juan Diego

Corazones rotos/Broken Hearts
Director: Rafael Montero
Cinematography: Rafael Ortega
Script: Rafael Montero
Editor: Oscar Figueroa
Music: Pedro Gilabert and André Moraes
Stars: Verónica Merchant, Rafael Sánchez, Carmen, Montejo

Nicotina
Director: Hugo Rodríguez
Cinematography: Marcelo Iaccarino
Script: Martín Salinas
Editor: Alberto de Toro
Music: Fernando Corona
Stars: Diego Luna, Marta Belaustegui, Rosa María Bianchi

La passion de María Elena
Director: Mercedes Moncada Rodriguez
Cinematography: Javier Morón,
Script: Mercedes Moncada Rodriguez
Editor: Viviana Garcia-Besné, Mercedes Moncada Rodríguez
Music: Martín Chávez, Samuel Larson, Café Tacuba
Stars:

El segundo aire/A Second Chance
Director: Fernando Sariñana
Cinematography: Patrick Murguia
Script: Carolina Rivera
Editor: Roberto Bolado
Music: Enrique Quezadas
Stars: Jesús Ochoa, Lisa Owen, Jorge Poza

Sin ton ni Sonia
Director: Carlos Sama
Cinematography: Federico Barbabosa
Script: Carlos Sama
Editor: Alex Rodriguez
Music/Sound: Antonio Diego, Emmanuel Romero, Rodolfo Romero
Stars: Juan Manuel Bernal, Cecilia Suárez, Mariana Gajá

2002

Dame tu cuerpo
Director: Rafael Montero
Cinematography: Lohengrin
Script: Enrique Renteria
Editor: Óscar Figueroa
Music: Ricardo Mancilla, Luis Medina
Stars: Rafael Sánchez Navarro, Luz María Zetina, Pedro Alvarez Tostado

Vivir mata/Life Kills
Director: Nicolás Echevaría
Cinematography: Pablo Reyes
Script: Juan Villoro,
Editor: Tlacateotl Mata, Mario Sandoval
Music/Sound: Ruy Garcia, Mario Lavista
Stars: Daniel Giménez Cacho, Susana Zebaleta, Luis Felipe Tavar

La habitacion azul/The Blue Room
Director: Walter Doehner
Cinematography: Serguei Saldívar Tanaka
Script: Walter Doehner, Vicente Leñero, George Simenon (novel)

Editor: Walter Doehner, Juan Fernandez
Music/Sound: Doug Browne, Ruy García
Stars: Juan Manuel Bernal, Patricia Llaca, Elena Anaya

A Thousand Clouds of Peace
Director: Julián Hernández
Cinematography: Diego Arizmendi
Script: Julián Hernández
Editor: Emiliano Arenales Osorio, Jacopo
Music/Sound: Basilio Garcia, Aurora Ojeda, Enrique L. Rendón Jaramillo
Stars: Juan Carlos Ortuño, Juan Carlos Torres, Salvador Alvarez

El Tigre de Santa Julia/The Tiger of Santa Julia
Director: Alejandro Gamboa
Cinematography: Alfredo Kassem
Script: Alejandro Gamboa, Francisco Sánchez
Editor: Óscar Figueroa
Music/Sound: Santiago Ojeda
Stars: Miguel Rodarte, Irán Castillo, Isaura Espinosa

Amar te duele/Loving You Hurts
Director: Fernando Sariñana
Cinematography: Chava Cartas
Script: Carolina Rivera
Editor: Roberto Bolado
Music/Sound: Enrique Quezadas
Stars: Luis Fernando Peña, Martha Higareda, Ximena Sariñana

Japón
Director: Carlos Reygadas
Cinematography: Diego Martínez Vignatti, Thierry Tronchet
Script: Carlos Reygadas
Editor: Daniel Melguizo, Carlos Serrano Azcona, David Torres
Music/Sound: Gilles Laurent, Ramón Moreira,
Stars: Alejandro Ferretis, Magdalena Flores, Yolanda Villa

De la Calle/Streeters
Director: Gerardo Tort
Cinematography: Héctor Ortega
Script: Jesús González Dávila, Marina Stavenhagen
Editor: Carlos Hagerman, Juan Carlos Solórzano, Gerardo Tort
Music/Sound: Diego Herrera
Stars: Luis Fernando Peña, Maya Zapata, Armando Hernández

El Crimen del padre Amaro/The Crime of Padre Amaro
Director: Carlos Carrera
Cinematography: Guillermo Granillo

Script: Vicente Leñero
Editor: Óscar Figueroa
Music/Sound: Rosino Serrano
Stars: Gael García Bernal, Ana Claudia Talancón

Ladies' Night
Director: Garbriela Tagliavini
Cinematography: Javier Zarco
Script: Issa López
Music/Sound: Ruy García, Rodrigo Garibay
Stars: Anna de la Reguera, Ana Claudia Taloncón, Luis Roberto Guzmán, Fabián
    Corres

La tregua
Director: Alfonso Rosas Priego
Cinematography: Arturo de la Rosa Eduardo Flores Torres
Script: Mario Benedetti
Editor: Carlos Puente
Music/Sound: Amparo Rubín
Stars: Gonzalo Vega, Adriana Fonseca, Guillermo Murray

Sin Destino/Without Destiny
Cinematography: Jorge Rubio Cazarín
Script: Leopoldo Laborde
Editor: Leopoldo Laborde
Music/Sound: Clímax, Encefálisis, Ogo, Richard Wagner
Stars: Francisco Rey, David Valdez, Roberto Cobo

2003

Zapata: El sueño del héroe/Zapata: The Dream of a Hero
Director: Alfonso Arau
Cinematography: Vittorio Storaro
Script: Alfonso Arau
Editor: Carlos Puente
Music/Sound: Ruy Folguera
Stars: Alejandro Fernández, Lucero, Patricia Velásquez

21 Grams
Director: Alejandro González Iñárritu
Cinematography: Rodrigo Prieto
Script: Guillermo Arriaga
Editor: Stephen Mirrione
Music/Sound: Gustavo Santaolalla
Stars: Sean Penn, Naomi Watts, Benicio del Toro

La Hija del Caníbal/Lucía Lucía
Director: Antonio Serrano
Cinematography: Xavier Pérez Grobet
Script: Antonio Serrano (screenplay), Rosa Montero (novel)
Editor: Jorge Garcia
Music/Sound: Nacho Mastretta
Stars: Cecilia Roth, Carlos Alvarez-Nóvoa, Kuno Becker

Adán y Eva (todavía)
Director: Iván Ávila Dueñas
Cinematography: Ciro Cabello, Alejandro Cantú
Script: Iván Avila Dueñas
Editor: Ivonne Fuentes, Iván Avila Dueñas
Music/Sound: Herminio Gutiérrez, Rosino Serrano, Valeria Palomino
Stars: Junior Paulino, Diana Lein, Raúl Adalid

Club eutanasia
Director: Agustín Tapia
Cinematography: Javier Morón
Script: Agustín Tapia
Editor: Roberto Bolado, Agustín Tapia
Music/Sound: Leoncio Lara, Jaime Pavon
Stars: Rosita Quintana, Héctor Gómez, Lorenzo de Rodas

Como tú me has deseado
Director: Juan Andrés Bueno
Cinematography: Xavier Cruz Ruvalcaba
Script: Juan Andrés Bueno
Editor: Carlos Puente
Music/Sound: Karen Roel
Stars: Delia Casanova, Carlos Cobos, Isaura Espinoza

Conejo en la luna
Director: Jorge Ramírez Suárez
Cinematography: Luis Sansans Arnanz
Script: Jorge Ramírez-Suárez
Editor: Alex Rodríguez
Music/Sound: Eduardo Gamboa
Stars: Bruno Bichis, Lorraine Pilkington, Jesús Ochoa, Adam Kotz

Corazón de melon
Director: Luis Velez
Cinematography: Oscar Palacios
Script: José Ignacio Valenzuela Chascas
Editor: Sigfrido García
Music/Sound: Eduardo Gamboa, Botellita de Jeréz

Stars: Christina Pastor, Daniel Martínez, Ludwika Paleta, Aldonza Velez, Juan
  Carlos Colombo

Desnudos
Director: Enrique Gómez Vadillo
Cinematography: Alberto Lee
Script: Maurioco Pichardo, Juan Criatian Ortega, Enrique Gómez Vadillo,
Editor: Francisco Guerrero
Music/Sound: José Ramos
Stars: Karime Lozano, Rafael Amaya, Carmen Rodríguez, Juan Vidal

Un día sin mexicanos
Director: Alfonso Arau
Cinematography: Alan Caudillo
Script: Yareli Arizmendi, Sergio Arau, Sergio Guerrero
Editor: Daniel A. Fort
Music/Sound: Juan José Colomer
Stars: Tony Abatemarco, Caroline Aaron, Fernando Arau, Brian Brophy

Digna . . . hasta el ultimo aliento
Director: Felipe Cazals
Cinematography: Hugo Díaz, Miguel Garzón.
Script: Felipe Cazals
Editor: Moisés Carrillo
Music/Sound: Pedro Villalobos
Stars: Vanessa Bauche

Espinas
Director: Julio César Estrada
Cinematography: Arturo de la Rosa
Script: Guillermo González Montes
Editor: Óscar Figueroa
Music/Sound: Federico Terán
Stars: Guillermo Gil, Esteban Soberones, Marianela Cataño

El mago
Director: Jaime Aparicio
Cinematography: Diego Arizmendi
Script: Jaime Aparicio, Enrique Rentería
Editor: Jaime Andrade, Humberto Delgado
Music/Sound: Rosino Serrano
Stars: Erando González, Julissa, Gustavo Muñoz, Maya Zapata

Magos y gigantes
Director: Andrés Couturier y Eduardo Sprowls
Cinematography: Robert Jaimes (lead animator)
Script: Francisco Hirata, Martinez Vara Adolfo
Editor: Jorge Hernandez S.

Music/Sound: Xavier Asali
Stars: Rossy Aguirre (voice), Francisco Colmenero (voice), Miguel Couterier (voice)

Manos libres (Nadie te habla)
Director: José Buil
Cinematography: Servando Gajá
Script: José Buli
Editor: José Buil, Mayte Ponzanelli
Music/Sound: Eduardo Gamboa
Stars: Alejandro Clava, Luis Gerardo Méndez, José Carlos Femat

Puños rosas / Pink Punch
Director: Beto Gómez
Cinematography: Héctor Osuna
Script: Beto Gómez, Alfonso Súarez Romero
Editor: Óscar Figueroa
Music/Sound: Daniele Luppi
Stars: José Yenque, Rodrigo Oviedo, Cecilia Suárez, Isela Vega

Siete días/Seven Days
Director: Fernando Kalife
Cinematography: Gonzalo Amat
Script: Fernando Kalife
Editor: Juan Carlos Garza
Music/Sound: Jeff Cardoni
Stars: Jaime Camil, Eduardo Arroyuelo, Martha Higareda, Julio Bracho

Tú te lo pierdes
Director: Salim Nayar
Cinematography: Jaime Reynoso, Miguel López
Script: Salim Nayer
Editor: Carlos Puente
Music/Sound: Juan Peña, Walter Meyenberg
Stars: Fernando Luján, Patricia Pereyra, Lolita Cortés, Alec Von Bargen

Zurdo
Director: Carlos Salcés
Cinematography: Chuy Chávez
Script: Blanca Montoya and Carlos Salcés
Editor: Carlos Salcés
Music/Sound: Saúl Almaráz, Jaime Baksht, Gabriel Coll Barberis
Stars: Álex Perea, Alejandro Camacho, Arcelia Ramírez, Giovanni Florido

2004

Temporada de Patos/Duck Season
Director: Fernando Eimbcke

Cinematography: Alex Zabé
Script: Fernando Eimbcke
Editor: Mariana Rodriguez
Music/Sound: Alejandro Rosso
Stars: Daniel Miranda, Diego Cataño, Enrique Arreola, Danny Perea

Hellboy: Sword of Storms
Director: Guillermo del Toro.
Cinematography: Guillermo Navarro
Script: Guillermo del Toro
Editor: Peter Amundson
Music/Sound: Marco Beltrami
Stars: Ron Perlman, Doug Jones, Selma Blair

Matando Cabos/Killing Cabos
Director: Alejandro Lozano
Cinematography: Juan José Saravia
Script: Tony Dalton, Kristoff Raczynski, Alejandro Lozano
Editor: Alberto de Toro
Music/Sound: Santiago Ojeda
Stars: Tony Dalton, Ana Claudia Talancón, Pedro Armendáriz Jr

El misterio de los almendros/The Almond Tree Mystery
Director: Jaime Humberto Hermosillo
Cinematography: Jorge Z. López
Script: Arturo Villaseñor
Editor: Jaime Humberto Hermosillo, David Villalazo
Music/Sound: Omar Guzmán
Stars: Maria Rojo, Alejandro Tomassi, Juan José Meraz, Manuel Medina

Al otro lado/The Other Side
Director: Gustavo Loza
Cinematography: Gerónimo Denti, Serguei Tanaka, Patrick Murguía
Script: Gustavo Loza
Editor: Roberto Bolado, Juan Fernández
Music/Sound: Héctor Ruiz
Stars: Carmen Maura, Héctor Suárez, Sanaa Alaoui, Susana González

7 mujeres, 1 homosexual y Carlos
Director: Rene Bueno Camacho
Cinematography: Alberto Less
Script: Rene Bueno Camacho
Editor: Rene Bueno Camacho, Rodrigo Zapién
Music/Sound: Luis Salazar, Giovanni Arreola, Carlos Tachiquín
Stars: Mauricio Ochmann, Adriana Fonseca, Ninel Conde, Luis Felipe Tovar

Acme & Co
Director: Gregorio Rocha Valverde

Cinematography: Eugenio Polgowsky, Ramón Orozco
Script: Gregorio Rocha
Editor: Gregorio Rocha
Music/Sound: Isabel Muñoz, Mario Garnier (sound)/Music-Various Artists
Stars: Felix Padilla and Edmundo Padilla

American visa
Director: Juan Carlos Valdivia
Cinematography: Ernesto Fernández Telleria
Script: Juan Carlos Valdivia, based on the novel by Juan de Recacoechea
Editor: Horacio Quiroz
Music/Sound: José Stephens
Stars: Demián Bichir, Kate del Castillo, Alberto Etcheverry, Jorge Ortiz

Atrás de las sombras
Director: Óscar Ramírez González
Cinematography: Hugo Villa Smythe, Luis David Sansans Arnaiz, Carlos Salom
    Freixas
Script: Ozcar Ramírez González, Olga Cáceres
Editor: Gabo Baudet, Ozcar Ramírez González
Music/Sound: Enrique Greiner, José Wolfer
Stars: Adolfo Ramírez, Alfredo Cruz Ruvalcaba, Armando Castillán, Andres
    Tavira

Fuera del cielo
Director: Javier Patrón
Cinematography: Patrick Murguía
Script: Guillermo Ríos, Vicente Leñero
Editor: Jorge García, Javier Patrón
Music/Sound: Emmanuel del Real, Ramiro del Real, Renato del Real
Stars: Demián Bichir, Armando Hernández, Dolores Heredia, Elizabeth Cer-
    vantes

Bienvenido Welcome 2
Director: Gabriel Retes, Lourdes Elizarrarás
Cinematography: Eduardo Flores Torres
Script: Gabriel Retes, María del Pozo
Editor: Sebastián Garza
Music/Sound: Osvaldo Montes
Stars: Ramón Almodóvar, Lourdes Elizarrarás, Daisy Granados

En el hoyo
Director: Juan Carlos Rulfo
Cinematography: Juan Carlos Rulfo
Script: Juan Carlos Rulfo
Editor: Valentina Leduc
Music/Sound: Leonardo Heiblum
Stars: Unavailable

Guchachi
Director: Abraham Oceransky
Cinematography: Abraham Oceransky
Script: Abraham Oceransky
Editor: Moisés de la Peña, Abraham Oceransky
Music/Sound: Joaquín López Chas
Stars: Ernesto Gómez Cruz, Abel Woolrich, Juana María Garza, Gerardo Trejo
    Luna, Marco Pérez

La guerilla y la esperanza: Lucio Cabañas
Director: Gerardo Tort
Cinematography: Héctor Ortega
Script: Marina Stavenhagen
Editor: Sebastian Hofmann, Juan Carlos Solórzano, Gerardo Tort
Music/Sound: Diego Herrera

Hijas de su madre: Las Buenrostro
Director: Busi Cortés
Cinematography: Alberto Lee
Script: Consuelo Garrido
Editor: Óscar Figueroa
Music/Sound: Benjamin Shwartz
Stars: Ramon Barragan, Patricio Castillo, Lumi Cavazos

Imaginum
Director: Alberto Mar and Issac Sandoval
Cinematography: Unavailable
Script: José Carlos García de Letona, Francisco Hirata Kitahara, Adolfo Martínez
    Vara
Editor: Alberto Rodríguez
Music/Sound: Xavier Asali
Stars: Eugenio Derbez (voice), Ilse (voice), Giovanni Florido (voice)

Las lloronas
Director: Lorena Villareal
Cinematography: Alejandro Cantu
Script: Enrique Renteria, Lorena Villareal
Editor: Abraham Marcos, Christopher Gernon
Music/Sound: Leoncio Lara-Bon
Stars: Raúl Adalid, Elizabeth Avila, Rosa Maria Bianchi, Francisco Gattorno,
    Rodrigo Mejia

Mezcal
Director: Ignacio Ortiz
Cinematography: Serguei Saldívar Tanaka
Script: Ignacio Ortiz
Editor: Ignacio Ortiz, Sigfrido Barjau, David Torres

Music/Sound: Lucía Álvarez
Stars: Dagoberto Gama, Ana Graham, Angelina Peláez, Ricardo Blume

Batalla en el cielo/Battle in Heaven
Director: Carlos Reygadas
Cinematography: Diego Martínez Vignatti
Script: Carlos Reygadas
Editor: Benjamin Mirguet, Adoración G. Elipe, Nicolás Schmerkin
Music/Sound: John Travener
Stars: Marcos Hernández, Anapola Mushkadis, Bertha Ruíz, David Bornstein

Muxes: Auténticas, intrépidas buscadoras del peligro
Director: Alejandra Islas
Cinematography: Alejandro Quesnel
Script: Alejandro Islas
Editor: Alejandro Islas y Alejandro Quesnel
Music/Sound: Alejandro Herrera
Stars: Clara Chagorua, Victor Chirinos, Alicia de Sales

La niña en la piedra (Nadie te ve)
Director: Marisa Sistach
Cinematography: Servando Gajá, Ciro Cabello
Script: José Buil
Editor: José Buil
Music/Sound: Eduardo Gamboa
Stars: Arcelia Ramírez, Gabino Rodríguez, Sofía Espinosa, Ricardo Polanco

Noticias lejanas
Director: Ricardo Benet
Cinematography: Martín Boege
Script: Ricardo Benet
Editor: Lucrecia Gutiérrez
Music/Sound: Guillermo González Phillips
Stars: David Aarón Estrada, Mayahuel del Monte, Martín Palomares

Parejas
Director: Enrique Arroyo Schroeder
Cinematography: Serguei Saldívar Tanaka
Script: Enrique Arroyo Schroeder
Editor: Luis Patlán Vizcaíno, Enrique Arroyo Schroeder
Music/Sound: Alejandro Giacoman de Neymet
Stars: Victor Huggo Martín, Mónica Dionne, Erika de la Llave, Rodrigo Murría

*Preguntas sin respuesta: Los asesinatos y desparaciciones de mujeres en
ciudad Juárez y Chihuahua*
Director: Rafael Montero
Cinematography: Miguel Angel Nava, Guillermo Juárez, Armando Herrera,
    Marco, Gomez, Lohengrin Zapiain, Sergio Franco, Mario Mendoza

Script: Rafael Montero
Editor: Jorge Vargas
Music/Sound: Ramón Arcos
Stars: Unavailable

Rosario Tijeras
Director: Emilio Maillé
Cinematography: Pascal Martí
Script: Marcelo Figueras, based on the novel by Jorge Franco
Editor: Irene Blecua
Music/Sound: Roque Baños
Stars: Flora Martínez, Unax Ugalde, Manolo Cardona, Rodrigo Oviedo

Santos peregrinos
Director: Juan Carlos Carrasco Aguayo
Cinematography: Ignacio Prieto Palacios
Script: Juan Carlos Carrasco Aguayo, José Antonio Carreón Rivera
Editor: Juan Pablo Córtés Alvarez
Music/Sound: Agustín Barbabosa
Stars: Carmen Salinas, Isaura Espinoza, Arturo Beristain, Julieta Egurrola Adal
    Ramones

Sólo Dios sabe/Only God Knows
Director: Carlos Bolado
Cinematography: Federico Barbabosa
Script: Carlos Bolado, Diane Weipert
Editor: Carlos Bolado, Manuela Dias
Music/Sound: Otto, Julieta Venegas
Stars: Diego Luna, Alice Braga, Cecilia Suárez, José María Yazpik, Renata Zha-
    neta

Ver, oír y callar
Director: Alberto Bravo García
Cinematography: Lars Hermann
Script: Alberto Bravo García, Arturo A. Bravo
Editor: Alberto Bravo
Music/Sound: Arturo A. Bravo, Alejandro Marín,
Stars: Mauricio Ochmann, Luis Felipe Tovar, Paola Núñez

Las vueltas del citrillo
Director: Felipe Cazals
Cinematography: Angel Goded
Script: Felipe Cazals
Editor: Óscar Figueroa
Music/Sound: Omar Guzmán
Stars: Damián Zaragoza, José María Yazpik, Vanessa Bauche, Jorge Zárate, Mario
    Zaragoza

Cero y van 4
Director: Alejandro Gamboa, Antonio Serrano, Carlos Carrera, Fernando Sari-
ñana
Cinematography: Chava Cartas, Andrés León Becker
Script: Antionio Armonía
Editor: Roberto Bolado, Óscar Figueroa
Music/Sound:Santiago Ojeda, Alvaro Ruiz, Rodrigo Barberá, Juan Cristóbal
Pérez Grobet
Stars: Alexis Ayala, Raquel Morell, René Campero, Ana Ciochetti, Juan Claudio
Retes

Así
Director: Jesús Mario Lozano
Cinematography: Emiliano Villanueva
Script: Jesús Mario Lozano
Editor: Óscar Montemayor
Music/Sound: Rubén Linder
Stars: Roberto García Suárez, Oliver CantúRoel, David González Zorrilla-
Santiago

Cicatrices/Scars
Director: Paco del Toro
Cinematography: Alberto Lee
Script: Verónica Maldonado, Paco del Toro
Editor: Alejandro Navarrete
Music/Sound: Victor Peña
Stars: Rodrigo Abed, Nora Salinas, Susana González, Bryan Rangel, Leonor
Bonilla, Marta Aura

La mujer de mi hermano/The Wife of my Brother
Director: Ricardo de Montreui
Cinematography: Andrés Sánchez
Script: Jaime Bayly, Sanjay Jaiswal
Editor: Jaime Bayly
Music/Sound: Aravind-Shankar, Angelo Milli
Stars: Bárbara Mori, Christian Meier, Manolo Cardona

La tragedia de Macario/The Tragedy of Macario
Director: Pablo Véliz
Cinematography: Brian Gonzalez
Script: Pablo Véliz
Editor: Pablo Véliz
Music/Sound: Carlos Sanchez, Pablo Véliz
Stars: Rogelio T. Ramos, Victor Agustin, Juanita Castro

Bajo Juárez (Ni una más)
Director: Alejandra Sánchez, José Antonio Cordero

Cinematography: Érika Licea
Script: Alejandra Sánchez, Érika Licea
Editor: José Antonio Cordero, Alejandra Sánchez
Music/Sound: Tareke Ortiz
Stars: Unavailable

Bienvenido paisano
Director: Rafael Villaseñor Kuri
Cinematography: Ignacio Prieto
Script: Luis Bekris Gutiérrez, Rafael Villaseñor Kuri, Antonio Orellana
Editor: Max Sánchez
Music/Sound: Salvador Toache
Stars: Rafael Inclán, María Sorté, Juan Angel Esparza, Giovani Florido

Cañitas, presencia
Director: Julio César Estrada Lopez
Cinematography: Arturo de la Rosa
Script: Gabriel González Meléndez, Xavier Robles, based on the novel by Carlos
    Trejo
Editor: Óscar Figueroa
Music/Sound: Eduardo Gamboa
Stars: Armando Hernández, Mariana Ávila, Francesca Guillén, Angélica Aragón

Carambola
Director: Kurt Hollander
Cinematography: Rafael Ortega
Script: Kurt Hollander
Editor: Jorge García
Music/Sound: Alex Ruiz, Juan Pablo Medina, Alejandro Contreras
Stars: Daniel Martínez, Diego Luna, Jesús Ochoa, Laura Hidalgo, Roberto Cobo

El carnaval de Sodoma
Director: Arturo Ripstein
Cinematography: Unavailable
Script: Paz Alicia Garciadiego, Pedro Antonio Valdez
Editor: Alejandro Ripstein
Music/Sound: Mikael Carlsson (executive soundtrack producer)
Stars: Marta Aura, María Barranco Alejandro Camacho

El cielo dividido
Director: Julián Hernández
Cinematography: Alejandro Cantú
Script: Julián Hernádez
Editor: Emiliano Arenales Osorio, Julián Hernández
Music/Sound: Arturo Villela Vega
Stars: Miguel Ángel Hoppe, Fernando Arroyo, Alejandro Rojo, Clarisa Rendón,
    Pilar Ruíz

El cobrador (In God We Trust)
Director: Paul Leduc
Cinematography: Josep M. Civit, Ángel Goded, Diego Rodriguez
Script: Rubem Fonseca, Paul Leduc
Editor: Natalia Bruschtein, Valentina Leduc Navarro, Juan Carlos Macías
Music/Sound: Tom Zé
Stars: Peter Fonda, Lázaro Ramos, Antonella Costa

Cuatro labios
Director: Carlos Marchovich
Cinematography: Carlos Marchovich
Script: Carlos Marchovich
Editor: Carlos Marchovich
Music/Sound: Juan Carlos Prieto
Stars: Ari Borovoy, Óscar Schwebel, Mariana Ochoa, Mbalia Marichal, Lidia
   Ávila

Desierto adentro
Director: Rodrigo Plá
Cinematography: Serguei Saldívar Tanaka
Script: Laura Santullo, Rodrigo Plá
Editor: Ana García, Rodrigo Plá
Music/Sound: Jacobo Lieberman, Leonardo Heiblum
Stars: Mario Zaragoza, Diego Cataño, Memo Dorantes, Eileen Uáñez, Luis
   Fernando Peña

Dos abrazos
Director: Enrique Begné
Cinematography: Federico Barbabosa
Script: Paula Markovitch
Editor: Samuel Larson
Music/Sound: Antonio Fernández Ross
Stars: Maya Zapata, Giovanni Florido, Ximena Sariñana, Jorge Zárate

Efectos secundarios
Director: Issa López
Cinematography: Carlos Aguilera
Script: Issa López
Editor: Jorge García
Music/Sound: Jermaine Stegall
Stars: Mariana de Tavira, Arturo Barba, Alejandra Gollás, Pedro Izquierdo

Equinoccio y la pirámide mágica
Director: Soccoro Méndez
Cinematography: Ignacio Prieto
Script: Socorro Méndez Díaz
Editor: Óscar Figueroa

Music/Sound: Omar Guzmán
Stars: Jesús Ochoa, Gabriela Canudas, Gabriel Porras, Enrique Arreola

Eréndira Ikikunari
Director: Juan Mora Catlett
Cinematography: Toni Kuhn
Script: Juan Mora Catlett
Editor: Juan more Catlett, Carlos Rodrigo Montes de Oca
Music/Sound: Andrés Sánchez
Stars: Xochiquétzal Rodríguez, Justo Alberto Rodríguez, Roberto Isidro Rangel

El garabato (Un fin de semana involvidable)
Director: Adolfo Martínez & Adolfo Martínez Orzynski
Cinematography: Keith Holland Alberto Lee
Script: Vicente Leñero, Adolfo Martínez Solares, based on the novel by Vicente
    Leñero
Editor: Adolfo Martínez Solares, Adolfo Martínez Orzynski
Music/Sound: Emiliano Marentes, Nahum Velásquez M.
Stars: Juan Pablo Medina, Mariana Ávila, Margarita Sanz, José Alonso

El guapo
Director: Marcel Sisniega
Cinematography: Diego Arizmendi
Script: Marcel Sisniega, Daniel Sada, based on the novel by Daniel Sada
Editor: Carlos Puente
Music/Sound: Leoncio Lara Bon
Stars: Carlos Corona, María del Carmen Félix, Ernesto Gómez Cruz, Martín
    Altomaro

Los heroes y el tiempo
Director: Arturo Ripstein
Cinematography: Esteban de Llaca
Script: Alejandro Ripstein
Editor: Alejandro Ripstein
Music/Sound: Leoncio Lara
Stars: René Arredondo, Saul López de la Torre, Alberto Ulloa, Romeo Valentin

Historias del desencanto
Director: Alejandro Valle, Felipe Gómez
Cinematography: Carlos Arango
Script: Alejandro Valle
Editor: Alejandro Valle, Felipe Gómez, Roberto Bolado
Music/Sound: Jacobo Liberman
Stars: Fabiana Perzabal, Mario Oliver, Jimena Ayala, Jorge Zárate

Los laberintos de la memoria
Director: Guita Schyfter
Cinematography: Sebastián Hiriart

Script: Guita Schyfter
Editor: Miguel Schverdfinger
Music/Sound: Diego Monk

Malos hábitos
Director: Simón Bross Soriano
Cinematography: Eduardo Martínez Solares
Script: Ernesto Anaya, Simón Bross
Editor: Adolfo Ibarrola, Raúl Martínez Reséndez
Music/Sound: Daneile Luppi
Stars: Jimena Ayala, Elena de Haro, Marco Treviño, Elisa Vicedo, Aurora Cano

Más que a nada en el mundo
Director: Javier Solar & Andrés León Becker
Cinematography: Unavailable
Script: Andrés León Becker, Javier Solis
Editor: Luciana Jauffred Gorostiza
Music/Sound: Herminio Gutiérrez
Stars: Elizabeth Cervantes, Juan Carlos Colombo, Julia Urbini

Mejor es que Gabriela no se muera
Director: Sergio Umansky
Cinematography: Celiana Cárdenas
Script: Ricardo Hernández Anzola
Editor: Max Chamberlain
Music/Sound: Renaud Barbier
Stars: Alejandro Barros, Dagoberto Gama, Mauricio Isaac, Martín Lasalle

Mi vida dentro
Director: Lucía Gajá
Cinematography: Érika Licea, AMC
Script: Lucía Gajá
Editor: Lucía Gajá
Music/Sound: Leonardo Heiblum, Jacobo Lieberman
Stars: Unavailable

Morirse en domingo
Director: Daniel Gruener
Cinematography: Guillermo Granillo
Script: Antonio Armonía
Editor: Gabriel Rodríguez
Music/Sound: Gabriel González Meléndez
Stars: Silverio Palacios, Humberto Busto, Maya Zapata, Fernando Becerril

Morirse está en hebreo
Director: Alejandro Springall
Cinematography: Celiana Cárdenas
Script: Jorge Goldenberg, Alejandro Springall, Ilán Stavans

Editor: Madeleine Gavin
Music/Sound: Jacobo Lieberman
Stars: Blanca Guerra, Martha Roth, Sergio Klainer, Guillermo Murray

Mosquita muerta
Director: Joaquín Bissner
Cinematography: Santiago Barreiro
Script: Joaquín Bissner
Editor: Joaquín Bissner, Aldo Rohlfs
Music/Sound: Chacho Gaytán
Stars: Bruno Bichir, Odiseo Bichir, Denisse Gutiérrez, Rocío Verdejo

Un mundo maravilloso
Director: Luis Estrada
Cinematography: Guillermo Granillo
Script: Vicente Leñero, Víctor Bartoli Herrera
Editor: Roberto Bolado
Music/Sound: Miguel Hernández (supervising sound editor)
Stars: Sergio Basañez, Tony Dalton, Dolores Heredia

Los pajarracos
Director: Héctor Hernández & Horacio Rivera
Cinematography: Chuy Chávez
Script: Horacio Rivera
Editor: Mayte Ponzanelli
Music/Sound: Eugenio Toussaint
Stars: Miguel Rodarte, Itati Cantoral, Regina Orozco Luis de Alba

Pamela por amor
Director: Rodolfo Galindo Ubiema
Cinematography: Unknown
Script: Unknown
Editor: Mayte Ponzanelli
Music/Sound: Carlos Cano (sound editor)
Stars: Sergio Bustemante, Carlos Cardán, Fabián Corres

Polvo de angel
Director: Óscar Blancorte
Cinematography: Arturo de la Rosa
Script: Óscar Blancarte
Editor: Mónica Romero
Music/Sound: Jose Miguel Enriquez Rivaud
Stars: Julio Brancho, Khristian Clausen, Miguel Couturier

Sangre
Director: Amat Escalante
Cinematography: Alejandro Fenton
Script: Amat Escalante

Editor: Amat Escalante
Music/Sound: Martín Hernández (supervising sound editor)
Stars: Cirilo Recio Dávila, Claudia Orozco, Martha Preciado

Súper amigos
Director: Arturo Pérez Torres
Cinematography: Mario Gallegos
Script: Arturo Pérez Torres
Editor: Cameron Esler
Music/Sound: Rob Hutchins
Stars: Unavailable

Toro negro
Director: Carlos Armella & Pedro González Rubio
Cinematography: Pedro González-Rubio
Script: Unknown
Editor: Carlos Armella
Music/Sound: Morgan Szymanski
Stars: Fernando Pacheco, Romelia Sosa Mario Tello

Trazando Aleida
Director: Christiane Burkhard
Cinematography: Christiane Burkhard
Script: Christiane Burkhard
Editor: Lucrecia Gutierrez
Music/Sound: Matias Barberis

La última mirada
Director: Patricia Arriaga-Jordán
Cinematography: Héctor Ortega
Script: Patricia Arriaga-Jordán
Editor: Miguel Lavandeira
Music/Sound: Rodrigo Sigal
Stars: Sergi Mateu, Marisol Centeno, Alexa Damián

La vida immune
Director: Ramón Cervantes
Cinematography: Tonatiúh Martínez
Script: Ramón Cervantes
Editor: Ramón Cervantes
Music/Sound: Unavailable
Stars: Carmen Beato, Rocío Verdejo, Sandra Rodríguez

El violín
Director: Francisco Vargas
Cinematography: Martín Boege, Oscar Hijuelos
Script: Francisco Vargas Quevado
Editor: Ricardo Garfias, Francisco Vargas

Music/Sound: Armando Rosas, Cuauhtémoc Tavira
Stars: Ángel Tavira, Gerardo Taracena, Dagoberto Gama

2006

Amor Xtremo/Xtreme Love
Director: Chava Cartas
Cinematography: Beto Casillas
Script: Carolina Rivera, Carlos Sariñana
Editor: Unavailable
Music/Sound: Unavailable
Stars: Aarón Díaz, Irán Castillo, Plutarco Haza

Así del precipio/So the Precipice
Director: María Teresa Suárez Maceiras
Cinematography: Jaime Reynoso
Script: María Teresa Suárez Maceiras
Editor: Roberto Bolado
Music/Sound: Rodrigo Barbera
Stars: Ana del Reguera, Ingrid Martz, Gabriela Platas

Babel
Director: Alejandro González Iñárritu
Cinematography: Rodrigo Prieto
Script: Guillermo Arriaga, Alejandro González Iñárritu
Editor: Douglas Crise, Stephen Mirrione
Music/Sound: Gustavo Santaolalla
Stars: Brad Pitt, Cate Blanchett, Gael García Bernal

El brassier de Emma
Director: Maryse Sistach
Cinematography: Arturo de la Rosa
Script: José Buil, Maryse Sistach
Editor: José Buil
Music/Sound: Salvador Toache, Gerardo Rosado
Stars: Sofía Espinosa, Arcelia Ramírez, Marco Treviño, Miguel Nájera

Buscando a Leti/Looking for Leti
Director: Dalia Tapia
Cinematography: Jose Luis Rios, Meena Singh
Script: Tadeo Garcia, Dalia Tapia
Editor: Johanna Chacón, Lucy Cordon
Music/Sound: Wanda DeCwikeil-Avila
Stars: Yovanny Cabarcas, Carmen Cenko, Juan Manuel De la Torre

Cansada de besar sapos/Tired of Kissing Frogs
Director: Jorge Colón

Cinematography: Jaime Reynoso
Script: Joaquín Bissner, Isabel Guerrero, Manuel Huici, Christopher Hool
Editor: Alexis Gudiño
Music/Sound: Santiago Ojeda
Stars: Anna Serradilla, Ana Layevska, José María de Tavira, Miguel Rodarte, Itatí Cantoral

Cementerio de papel
Director: Mario Hernández
Cinematography: Jorge Rubio Cazarín
Script: Xavier Robles, based on the book by Fritz Glockner
Editor: Óscar Figueroa
Music/Sound: Pamela Hersch, Graciela Rivas
Stars: Rosario Ibarra de Piedra, Alberto Estrella, José Juan Meraz

Children of Men
Director: Alfonso Cuarón
Cinematography: Emmanuel Lubezki
Script: Alfonso Cuarón, Timothy J. Sexton, David Arata, Mark Fergus, Hawk Ostby
Editor: Alfonso Cuarón, Alex Rodríguez
Music/Sound: John Tavener
Stars: Julianne Moore, Clive Owen, Chiwetel Ejiofor

Cochochi
Director: Israel Cárdenas & Laura Amelia Guzmán
Cinematography: Israel Cárdenas, Laura Amelia Guzmán
Script: Israel Cárdenas, Laura Amelia Guzmán
Editor: Laura Guzmán, Israel Cárdenas, Yibran Asuad
Music/Sound: Leonardo Heiblum, Juan Nevares, José, Ángel Rodríguez
Stars: Luis Antonio Lerma Torres, Evaristo Corpus Lerma Torres, José Ángel Torres

Conozco la cabeza de Juan Pérez
Director: Emilio Portes
Cinematography: Ramon Orozco
Script: Emilio Portes
Editor: Yibran Assaud, Emilio Portes, Rodrigo Ríos
Music/Sound: Alfredo Loaeza
Stars: Silverio Palacios, Dolores Heredia, José Sefami

Cuando las cosas suceden
Director: Antonio Peláez
Cinematography: Luis Sansans
Script: Antonio Peláez
Editor: Antonio Peláez
Music/Sound: Arturo Rodríguez

Stars: Alejandro Tommasi, Marcela Guirado, Juan Ferrara, Mar Carrera

Cumbia callera
Director: René U. Villarreal
Cinematography: Antonio Beltrán Hernández
Script: Ana Rebuelta, René U. Villarreal
Editor: René Villareal
Music/Sound: Luis Manuel López Carrera, José Manuel Mendoza, Javier de Lira
Stars: Fernando García Castañeda, Oliver Cantú, Andul Zambrano

Drama/Mex
Director: Gerardo Naranjo
Cinematography: Tobías Datum
Script: Gerardo Naranjo
Editor: Yibran Asaud
Music/Sound: Lynn Fainchtein
Stars: Diana García, Fernando Becerril, Miriana Moro, Emilio Valdez

Los demonios del Edén
Director: Alejandra Islas
Cinematography: Alejandro Quesnel
Script: Alejandra Islas
Editor: Alejandra Islas
Music/Sound: Charlie Cuevas

El evangelista
Director: Juan Daniel Zavaleta
Cinematography: Juan Daniel Zavaleta
Script: Juan Daniel Zavaleta
Editor: Juan Daniel Zavaleta
Music/Sound: Unavailable
Stars: J. Salome Martinez, Nicolás Guzmán, Esmirna García

Entre caníbales
Director: Rodrigo González Mendoza
Cinematography: Robert Humphreys
Script: Lourdes LópezCastro
Editor: Mario Sandoval
Music/Sound: Bonanza
Stars: Plutarco Haza, Roberto Sosa, Regina Orozco, Ludivina Velarde

Eros una vez María
Director: Jesús Magaña
Cinematography: Carlos Aquilera
Script: Jesús Magaña Vázquez
Editor: Edna H. Lee
Music/Sound: Héctor Ruiz, Giovanni Escalera
Stars: Julio Bracho, Ana Serradilla, Mahalat Sánchez, Mónica Dionne

Espérame en otro mundo
Director: Juan Pablo Villaseñor
Cinematography: Martín Boege
Script: Juan Pablo Villaseñor
Editor: Miguel Lavanderia
Music/Sound: Jimena Giménez Cacho
Stars: Natalia Esperón, Margarita Sanz, Fernando Becerril, Hernán Mendoza

Famila tortuga
Director: Rubén Imaz
Cinematography: Gerardo Barroso Alcalá
Script: Rubén Ímaz Castro, written with the collaboration of Gabriela Vidal
Editor: León Felipe González Sanchez
Music/Sound: Galo Durán
Stars: José Ángel Bichir, Luisa Pardo, Manuel Plata López, Dagoberto Gama

La frontera infinita
Director: Juan Manuel Sepúlveda
Cinematography: Víctor Dávila
Script: Juan Manuel Sepúlveda
Editor: Roberto Bolado
Music/Sound: Arturo Villela Vega
Stars: Unavailable

Hasta el viento tiene miedo
Director: Gustavo Moheno
Cinematography: Arturo de la Rosa
Script: Alfonso Suárez Romero, Ángel Pulido, Mario P. Székely, Gustavo Moheno
Editor: Óscar Figueroa Jara
Music/Sound: Eduardo Gamboa
Stars: Martha Higareda, Verónica Langer, Danny Perea, Mónica Dionne

Los ladrones viejos: Las leyendas del artegio
Director: Everardo González
Cinematography: Martín Boege, Everardo González, Gerardo Montiel Klint
Script: Everardo González
Editor: Juan Manuel Figueroa
Music/Sound: Rodrigo Garibay, Matías Barberis
Stars: Jorge Calva Márquez, Efraín Alcaraz Montes, Raymundo Moreno Reyes

La leyenda de la Nahuala
Director: Ricardo Arnaiz
Cinematography: Unavailable
Script: Omar Mustre de León, Antonio Garci
Editor: Ricardo Arnaiz, Gabriel Villar
Music/Sound: Gabriel Villar
Stars: Ofelia Medina (voice), Germán Robles (voice), Jesús Ochoa (voice)

Luz silenciosa/Silent Light
Director: Carlos Reygadas
Cinematography: Alexis Zabé
Script: Carlos Reygadas
Editor: Natalia López
Music/Sound: Raúl Locatelli
Stars: Cornelio Wall, Miriam Toews, María Pankratz

Llamando a un angel
Director: Rodolofo Guzmán, Héctor Rodríguez, and Francisco Rodríguez
Cinematography: Héctor Osuna, Raúl Ramón, Carlos Davis Colin
Script: Rodolfo Guzmán, Héctor Rodríguez, Francisco Rodríguez
Editor: Rodolfo Guzmán, Héctor Rodríguez, Francisco Rodríguez
Music/Sound: Mario Osuna, Josué M. Martin
Stars: Luis Felipe Tovar, Patricia Llaca, Mónica Dionne, Julio Bracho

Más vale maña que fuerza
Director: María del Carmen de Lara
Cinematography: Jorge Suárez, Fernando Acuña, Antonio Uruñuela
Script: María del Carmen de Lara
Editor: Unavailable
Music/Sound: Eduardo Aparicio, Latino Cumbia Boys
Stars: Unavailable

Ópera
Director: Juan Patricio Riveroll
Cinematography: Jorge Senyal, AMC, Beto Macías
Script: Juan Patricio Riveroll
Editor: Roberto Garza Angulo, Alejandro Molina
Music/Sound: Carusso, Mozart
Stars: Mariana Margo Soto, Arturo Ríos, Magdalena Flores, Martín La Salle

Pan's Labyrinth
Director: Guillermo del Toro
Cinematography: Guillermo Navarrete
Script: Guillermo del Toro
Editor: Bernat Vilaplana
Music/Sound: Javier Navarrete
Stars: Ivana Baquero, Doug Jones, Sergi López, Maribel Verdú

Párpados azules
Director: Ernesto Contreras
Cinematography: Tonatiuh Martínez
Script: Carlos Contreras
Editor: Ernesto Contreras, José Manuel Cravioto
Music/Sound: Iñaki
Stars: Cecilia Suárez, Enrique Arreola, Ana Ofelia Murguía, Tiaré Scanda

Partes usadas
Director: Aarón Fernández
Cinematography: Javier Morón
Script: Aaron Fernández
Editor: Ana Laura Calderón
Music/Sound: Nacao Zumbi
Stars: Eduardo Granados, Alan Chávez, Carlos Ceja, Damayanti Quintanar

Una película de huevos
Director: Gabriel Riva Palacio Alatriste & Rodolfo Riva Palacio Alatriste
Cinematography: Unknown
Script: Rodolfo Riva Palacio Alatriste, Gabriel Riva Palacio Alatriste
Editor: Valeria Foster, Leandro Spatz
Music/Sound: Carlos Zepeda
Stars: Bruno Bichir (voice), Carlos Espejel (voice), Angelica Vale (voice)

Propiedad ajena
Director: Luis Vélez
Cinematography: Chava Cartas
Script: Luis Vélez, José Antonio Olvera
Editor: Sigfrido García
Music/Sound: Gabriel Chávez H., Miguel Ángel Cañizo, Paola Rosado, Gerardo
    Australia
Stars: Ludwika Paleta, Rib Hillis, Plutarco Haza, Gizeht Galatea

Quemar las naves
Director: Francisco Franco
Cinematography: Erika Licea, AMC
Script: María Reneé Prudencio, Francisco Franco
Editor: Sebastián Garza
Music/Sound: Alejandro Giacomán
Stars: Irene Azuela, Angel Onésimo Nevares, Claudette Maillé, Bernardo
    Benítez

Un retrato de Diego
Director: Diego López & Gabriel Figueroa
Cinematography: Manuel Alvarez Bravo, Gabriel Figueroa Flores
Script: Margarita Mancilla, Diego López
Editor: Unavailable
Music/Sound: Arturo Márquez, Silvestre Revueltas, Julian Carrillo
Stars: Unavailable

La sangre iluminada
Director: Iván Ávila Dueñas
Cinematography: Ciro Cabello, Alejandro Cantú
Script: Iván Avila Dueñas, José Ignacio Valenzuela
Editor: Elena Pardo, Pedro Jiménez

Music/Sound: Fernando Corona
Stars: Gustavo Sánchez Parra, Joustein Roustand, Enoc Leaño, Flor Payán

Sultanes del Sur
Director: Alejandro Lozano
Cinematography: Juan José Saravia
Script: Tony Dalton
Editor: Luis de la Madrid
Music/Sound: Javier Capellas
Stars: Tony Dalton, Jordi Mollá, Silverio Palacios, Ana de la Reguera

Todos los días son tuyos
Director: José Luis Gutiérrez Arias
Cinematography: Ignacio Prieto
Script: José Luis Gutierrez
Editor: Roque Azcuaga, Jose Luis Gutierrez
Music/Sound: Paco Aveleyra
Stars: Mario Oliver, Emma Suárez, Alejandro Camacho

El viaje de la Nonna
Director: Sebastián Silva
Cinematography: Guillermo Rosas
Script: Antonio Armonía, Sebastián Silva
Editor: Carlos F. Rossini
Music/Sound: Daniel Hidalgo
Stars: Ana Ofelia Murguía, Verónica Langer, Rodrigo Murray, Julio Bracho

2007

A propósito de Alexa
Director: René Bueno Camacho.
Cinematography: Unavailable
Script: Rene Bueno Camacho
Editor: Rene Bueno, Zeiddy Silva Ríos
Music/Sound: Paul Bidault
Stars: Angélica Aragón, Magi Avila, Jaime Camil

El aliento de Dios
Director: Isabel Cristina Fregoso
Cinematography: Miguel Angel García, Armando Padilla
Script: Isabel Cristina Fregoso
Editor: Patricia Garcia Barragán
Music/Sound: Mario Osuna

Amar
Director: Jorge Ramírez Suárez
Cinematography: Luis Sansans Arnanz, AMC
Script: Jorge Ramírez Suárez

Editor: Roberto Bolado, Jorge Ramírez Suárez
Music/Sound: Chetes, Eduardo Gamboa, Kerigma, et al.
Stars: Luis Ernesto Franco, Diana García, María Aura, Martín Altomaro

Amar a morir
Director: Fernando Lebrija
Cinematography: Masanobu Takayanagi
Script: Fernando Lebrija, Harrison Reiner
Editor: Radu Ion, Paulo Carballo
Music/Sound: Edward Rogers
Stars: José María de Tavira, Martina García, Alberto Estrella, Raúl Méndez

Amor, dolor y viceversa
Director: Alfonso Pineda Ulloa
Cinematography: Damián García
Script: Alex Marino
Editor: Jorge Macaya
Music/Sound: Roque Baños
Stars: Bárbara Mori, Leonardo Sbaraglia, Marina de Tavira, Joaquín Cosío

Ángel caído
Director: Arturo Anaya Treviño
Cinematography: Juan Castillero Botello
Script: Arturo Anaya Treviño
Editor: Raúl Vásquez Mojica
Music/Sound: Luis Leñero
Stars: Sebastián Zurita, Emiliano Zurita, Humberto Zurita, José Alonso, Carlos
    Cacho

Arráncame la vida
Director: Roberto Sneider
Cinematography: Javier Aguirresarobe
Script: Roberto Sneider
Editor: Aleshka Ferrero
Music/Sound: Arturo Márquez, Leonardo Heiblum, Jacobo Lieberman
Stars: Ana Claudia Talancón, Daniel Gimén Cacho, José María de Tavira, Isela
    Vega

Arresto domiciliario
Director: Gabriel Retes
Cinematography: Nacho Elizarrarás, Arturo Ortiz Soldado
Script: María del Pozo, Gabriel Retes
Editor: Laura López, Lourdes Elizarrarás
Music/Sound: Osvaldo Montes
Stars: Lucila Balzaretti, Gabriel Retes, Lourdes Elizarrarás, Idalmis del Risco

Ausencia
Director: Alfonso Suárez
Cinematography: Guilén Errecalde

Script: Alfonso Suárez
Editor: Mario Martínez Cobos
Music/Sound: The Seamus, Projector
Stars: Eduardo España, Lori Skoda, Bob Barnes, Peter Constantini

Bajo la sal
Director: Mario Muñoz
Cinematography: Serguei Saldívar Tanaka
Script: Angel Pulido Alonso, Mario Muñoz Espinoza
Editor: Jorge García
Music/Sound: Federico Bonasso
Stars: Humberto Zurita, Plutarco Haza, Irene Azuela, Emilio Guerrero

El Búfalo de la noche/The Night Buffalo
Director: Jorge Hernández Aldana
Cinematography: Héctor Ortega
Script: Guillermo Arriaga, Jorge Hernández Aldana, based on the novel by Guillermo Arriaga
Editor: Alex Márquez
Music/Sound: Omar Rodríguez López
Stars: Diego Luna, Liz Gallardo, Camila Sodi, Gabriel González, Irene Azuela

Las buenas yerbas
Director: María Novaro
Cinematography: Gerardo Barroso
Script: María Novaro
Editor: Sebastián Garza, María Novaro
Music/Sound: Alejandro de Icaza
Stars: Ursula Prunedda, Ofelia Medina, Ana Ofelia Murguía

Cinco días sin Nora
Dirctor Mariana Chenillo Alazraki
Cinematography: Alberto Anaya
Script: Mariana Chenillo Alazraki
Editor: Óscar Figueroa, Mariana Chenillo
Music/Sound: Darío González Valderrama
Stars: Fernando Luján, Cecilia Suárez, Ari Brickman, Enrique Arreola

Cómo no te voy a querer?
Direcor: Victor Avelar
Cinematography: Héctor Maeshiro
Script: Victor Jesús Avelar Martínez
Editor: Lourdes Rébora, Víctor Avelar
Music/Sound: Alejandro Marcovich, Panteón Rococó,
Stars: Alejandro Belmonte, Siouzana Melikián, Daniel Martínez

Cosas insignificantes
Director: Andrea Martínez Crowther

Cinematography: Josep María Civit
Script: Andrea Martínez Crowther
Editor: Angel Hernández Zoido
Music/Sound: Leo Heiblum, Jacobo Lieberman
Stars: Bárbara Mori, Fernando Luján, Carmelo Gómez, Lucía Jiménez

Chamaco
Director: Miguel Necoechea
Cinematography: Guillermo Granillo
Script: Klirk Harris, Miguel Necoechea, Carl Bessai
Editor: Mario Sandoval
Music/Sound: Evan Evans
Stars: Martin Sheen, Alex Pera, Kirk Harris, Danny Perez, Gustavo Sánchez
     Parra

Enemigos íntimos
Director: Fernando Sariñana
Cinematography: Chava Cartas
Script: Ana Carolina Rivera
Editor: Óscar Figueroa
Music/Sound: Miguel Sandoval
Stars: Demián Bichir, Ximena Sariñana, Verónica Merchant, Blanca Sánchez

Esperame en otro mundo/Wait for Me in Another World
Director: Juan Pablo Villaseñor
Cinematography: Martín Boege
Script: Juan Pablo Villaseñor
Editor: Miguel Lavandeira
Music/Sound: Jimena Giménez Cacho
Stars: Natalia Esperón, Margarita Sanz, Fernando Becerril, Hernán Mendoza

Flores para el soldado
Director: Javier Garza Yáñez, Iván García, Daniel Galo
Cinematography: Guillermo G. Garza
Script: Javier Garza Yáñez, Iván García
Editor: Samuel Larson
Music/Sound: Dan Radlauer
Stars: Joe Cappelletti (narrator)

HavanYork
Director: Luciano Larobina
Cinematography: Emiliano Villanueva Rabotnikof
Script: Luciano Larobina
Editor: Juan Manuel Figueroa, Haydee Montaño, Natalia López, Aldo Alvarez
Music/Sound: Pablo Valero, Descember Bueno, Kelvis Ochoa, Anónmio Consejo
Stars: DJ Tony Tone, Familias Cuba Represent, The Fantastic Aleems, Supanova
     Slom

Juegos inocentes (Un fin de semana involvidable)
Director: Adolfo Martínez Orzynski
Cinematography: Esteban de Llaca
Script: Luis Bekris, Gibrán Portela, Francisco Santos
Editor: Mayte Ponzanelli
Music/Sound: Salvador Toache, Gerardo Rosado
Stars: Ignacio Riva Palacio, Abril Reyes, Eréndira Ibarra, Alan Fernando

Kada kien su karma
Director: León Serment
Cinematography: Esteban de LLaca
Script: León Serment
Editor: Óscar Figueroa
Music/Sound: Luis Guzmán
Stars: Blanca Guerra, José Alonso, Rocío Verdejo, Alfredo Sevilla

KM 31: Kilometre 31
Director: Rigoberto Castañeda
Cinematography: Alejandro Martínez Reséndez
Script: Rigoberto Castañeda
Editor: Alberto del Toro
Music/Sound: Carles Cases
Stars: Iliana Fox, Adria Collado, Raúl Méndez, Carlos Aragón, Luisa Huertas

Ladrón que roba a ladrón/To Rob a Thief
Director: Joe Menendez
Cinematography: Adam Silver
Script: JoJo Henrickson
Editor: Joe Menendez
Music/Sound: Andrés Levin
Stars: Fernando Golunga, Miguel Varoni, Julie Gonzalo

El libro de piedra
Director: Julio César Estrada
Cinematography: Unavailable
Script: Gustavo Moheno, Mario P. Székely, Julio César Estrada, Enrique Renteria,
Editor: Óscar Figueroa
Music/Sound: Eduardo Gamboa
Stars: Ludwick Paleta, Plutarco Haza, Marta Aura

Me importas tú . . . y tú (El barco de la ilusión)
Director: Adolfo Martínez Solares & Adolofo Martínez Orzynski
Cinematography: Keith Holland, Alberto Lee
Script: Adolfo Martínez Solares
Editor: Unavailable
Music/Sound: Tin Tan
Stars: José Alonso, Rafael Amaya, Khristian Clausen

La Misma Luna/Under the Same Moon
Director: Patricia Riggan
Cinematography: Checco Varese
Script: Ligiah Villalobos
Editor: Aleshka Ferrero
Music/Sound: Carlos Siliotto
Stars: Eugenio Derbez, Kate del Castillo, Adrian Alonso

Morenita
Director: Alan Jonsson Gavica
Cinematography: Emiliano Villanueva
Script: Alan Jonsson Gavica, Annabel Oakes
Editor: Ana García
Music/Sound: Leoncio Lara
Stars: Mario Almada, Everardo Arzate, Michelle Marie

Naco es chido
Director: Sergio Arau
Cinematography: Gerardo Barroso
Script: Sergio Arau, Armando Vega Gil, Tihui Arau, Francisco Barrios
Editor: Sebastian Hofmann
Music/Sound: Saúl Almaráz
Stars: Sergio Arau, Yareli Arizmendi, Flavia Atencio

Naica
Director: Gonzalo Infante Castañeda
Cinematography: Manuel Gálvez, Lucca Masa
Script: Gonzalo Infante Castañeda, Angeles Necoechea
Editor: Etla Post
Music/Sound: Alejandro Giacoman
Stars: Tullio Bernabei, Giovanni Badinno, Paolo Forti, Saúl Villasante

Nesio
Director: Alan Cotton
Cinematography: Esteban de Llaca
Script: Alan Coton
Editor: Óscar Figueroa
Music/Sound: Sr. Bikini, Fuera de Servicio, Luis Leñero
Stars: Claudette Maillé, Tenoch Huerta, Jorge Adrián Espíndola, Charly Valentino

Niño Fidencio de Roma a Espinoza
Director: Juan Farré Rivera
Cinematography: Mar Farré Fernández, Humberto García López, Juan Farré Rivera
Script: Curry Fernández Bueno
Editor: Martín Bautista M.

Music/Sound: Philip Glass
Stars: Unavailable

Niñas Mal/Charm School
Director: Fernando Sariñana
Cinematography: Chava Cartas
Script: Issa López (story), Carolina Rivera (screenwriter)
Editor: Óscar Figueroa
Music/Sound: Miguel Angel Molina
Stars: Martha Higareda, Blanca Guerra, Camila Sodi

Otro tipo de música
Director: José Rosalío Gutiérrez
Cinematography: Chucho González
Script: José Gutiérrez Razura
Editor: Pablo Valadez, Alberto Ponce
Music/Sound: Sutra, Leo Marín, Jesús Hernández
Stars: Marisol Padilla, Rubén Radilla, Carlos Hoeflich, Mely Ortega, Mauricio
    Cedeño

7 Soles
Director: Pedro Ultreras
Cinematography: Vladimir Van Maule
Script: Pedro Ultreras
Editor: Rocío Zambrano, Ignacio Decerega
Music/Sound: Rosino Serrano
Stars: Gustavo Sánchez Parra, Evangelina Sosa

Soneros del Tesechoacán
Director: Rolando Inti Cordera
Cinematography: Amir Galván
Script: Alejandro Albert Fernández, Diego, Sheinbaum
Editor: Ricardo Vergaza
Music/Sound: Soneros del Tesechoacán
Stars: Unavailable

Spam
Director: Charlie Gore
Cinematography: Carlos Hidalgo
Script: Charlie Gore
Editor: Oscar Figueroa
Music/Sound: Haggai Cohen Millo
Stars: Sebastián Sariñana, Gloria Navarro, David Ostrosky, Verónica Merchant

Todos hemos pecado
Director: Alejandro Ramírez
Cinematography: Omar García
Script: Alejandro Ramírez

Editor: David Aragón, Juan Carlos Blanco
Music/Sound: Dan Levi
Stars: Aleyda Gallardo, Alberto Estrella, Mario Almada, Angélica Aragón, Julio
Bracho

El último silencio: The Last Silence
Director: Jeoshua Gil Delgado
Cinematography: Unavailable
Script: Gibran Viradi Ramirez, Joshua Gil
Editor: Idzin Xaca
Music/Sound: Darío Arcos
Stars: Luis Fernando Peña, Diana Golden, Guillermo Quintanilla

La última y nos vamos
Director: Eva López-Sánchez
Cinematography: Javier Morón
Script: Alfredo Mier y Terán, Eva López-Sánchez
Editor: Mario Sandoval
Music/Sound: Renato del Real, Ramiro del Real
Stars: Juan Pablo Campa, Gabino Rodríguez, Sebastián Hiriart, Manuel García-
Rulfo

La Zona/The Zone
Director: Rodrigo Plá
Cinematography: Emiliano Villanueva
Script: Laura Santullo, Rodrigo Plá
Editor: Bernat Vilaplana
Music/Sound: Fernando Velázquez
Stars: Daniel Giménez Cacho, Daniel Tovar, Alan Chávez, Carlos Bardem, Mario
Zaragoza

Hellboy II: Blood and Iron
Director: Guillermo del Toro
Cinematography: Guillermo Navarro
Script: Guillermo del Toro, Mike Mignola
Editor: Bernat Vilaplana
Music/Sound: Danny Elfman
Stars: Ron Perlman, Selma Blair, Doug Jones, Jeffery Tambor, Luke Goss

2008

Enemigos íntimos
Director: Fernando Sariñana
Cinematography: Chava Cartas
Script: Unavailable
Editor: Mauricio Sarinana

Music: José Villar
Stars: Blanca Sanchez, Giovanna Zacarias, Demián Bichir

Spam
Director: Carlos Sarinana
Cinematography: Carlos Hidalgo
Script: Charlie Gore
Editor: Óscar Figueroa
Music/Sound: Miguel Angel Molina
Stars: Luis Gatica, Veronica Merchant, Gloria Navarro

Kada kien su karma
Director: Leon Serment
Cinematography: Esteban de Llaca
Script: Leon Serment
Editor: Oscar Figueroa
Music: Luis Guzman
Stars: Blanca Guerra, Jose Alonso, Rocio Verdejo

Dusk
Director: Gary Alaraki
Cinematography: Serguei Saldívar Tanaka
Script: Guillermo Arriaga
Editor: Mario Sandoval
Music/Sound: Enrique Greiner
Stars: Jose Maria Yazpik, Iliana Fox

Lokas
Director: Gonzalo Justiniano
Cinematography: Andrés Garretón
Script: Gonzalo Justiniano, Rodrigo Bastidas, Julio Rojas
Editor: Carolina Quevedo
Music: Cuti Aste
Stars: Rodrigo Bastidas, Coco Legrand, Raimundo Bastidas

Morenita, el escandalo
Director: Alan Jonsson
Cinematography: Emiliano Villanueva
Script: Alan Jonsson, Annabel Oakes
Editor: Ana Garcia
Music: Leoncio Lara
Stars: Mario Almada, Everardo Arzate, Michelle Marie Benoit

Todos hemos pecado
Director: Alejandro Ramirez
Cinematography: Omar García
Script: Alejandro Ramirez
Editor: David Aragon

Music: David Ramos
Stars: Mario Almade, Rafael Amaro, Angélica Aragón

Llamando a un angel
Director: Rodolfo Guzman, Hector Rodriguez,
Cinematography: Carlos Colin, Hector Osuna, Raul Ramon
Script: Pancho Rodriguez, Rodolfo Guzman, Héctor Rodriguez
Editor: Rodolfo Guzman, Héctor Rodriguez, Pancho Rodriguez
Music: Giovanni Escalera, Josue M. Martin
Stars: Monica Dionne, Eduardo Espena, Andres Montiel

Fallen Gods
Director: Ernesto Daranas
Cinematography: Rigoberto Senarega
Script: Ernesto Daranas
Editor: Pedro Suarez
Music: Magda Rosa Galvan, Juan Antonio Leyva
Stars: Silvia Aguila, Carlos Ever Fonseca, Héctor Noras

Meet the Head of Juan Perez
Director: Emilio Portes
Cinematography: Ramón Orozco
Script: Emilio Portes
Editor: Yibran Assaud, Emilio Portes, Rodrigo Rios
Music/Sound: Alfredo Loaeza
Stars: Silverio Palacios, Dolores Heredia, José Sefami

Shakespeare and Victor Hugo's Intimacies
Director: Yulene Olaizola
Cinematography: Ruben Imaz, Yulene Olaizola
Script: Yulene Olaizola
Editor: Yulene Olaizola
Music: Emiliano Gonzalez de Leon, Emiliano Motta
Stars: Rosa Elena Carbajal, Florence Vega Moctezuma

Matilda
Director: María Fernanda Rivero
Cinematography: Victor Dávila
Script: María Fernanda Rivero
Editor: María Fernanda Rivero Gutiérrez
Music: Unavailable
Stars: Unavailable

Desbocados
Director: René Cardona III
Cinematography: Alberto Lee
Script: René Cardona III, Óscar González
Editor: Óscar González

Music: Unavailable
Stars: Gerardo Alabarrán, Armando Araiza, Gregorio Cazais

Viva High School Musical
Director: Eduardo Ripari
Cinematography: Rolo Pulpeiro
Script: Pablo Lago, Susana Cardozo
Editor: Rosario Suarez
Music: Alejandro Kauderer, Emilio Kauderer
Stars: Fernando Dente, Agustina Vera, Delfina Peña

Limbo
Director: Horacio Rivera
Cinematography: Gerardo Ruffinelli
Script: Horacio Rivera
Editor: Fernando Benitez, Ismar Figueroa, Horacio Rivera
Music/Sound: Luis Arguelles
Stars: Francisco Barcala, Ruben Cristiany, Fátima Díaz

Como no te voy a querer
Director: Victor Avelar
Cinematography: Hector Maeshiro
Script: Victor Avelar
Editor: Victor Avelar, Lourdes Rébora
Music/Sound: Óscar Acosta
Stars: Alejandro Belmonte, Natalia Esperón, Daniel Martínez

40 días
Director: Juan Carlos Martín
Cinematography: Miguel Lopez
Script: Pablo Soler Frost
Editor: Juan Carlos Martín, Mario Sandoval
Music: Ruy Garcia
Stars: Andrés Almeida, Hector Arredondo, Elena de Haro

Three Little Pigs
D-Enrique Vargas Celis
Cinematography: Martha Celis Mendoza
Script: Roald Dahl
Editor: Pablo Abitia
Music: Unavailable
Stars: Ruy Cirigo (narrator), Odeth Casanova, Cecilia Castaneda

X-mas, Inc.
Director: Fernando Rovzar
Cinematography: Alejandro Martinez
Script: Fernando Rovzar
Editor: Jessica Valencia

Music: David Lawrence
Stars: Alejandra Ambrosi, Pedro Armendáriz Jr., Mauricio Barrientos

Verano 79
Director: Rodrigo Oviedo
Cinematography: Daniel Jacobs
Script: Rodrigo Oviedo, Anwar Safa
Editor: Jeanette Russ
Music/Sound: Emilio Cortes
Stars: Alejandro Cervantes, Victor Kaim, Victor Rivera

Roma
Director: Elisa Miller
Cinematography: Christian Rivera, Maria Secco
Script: Elisa Miller
Editor: Ares Botanch
Music: Federico Schmucler
Stars: Marcela Cuevas, Jaime Estrada

La muerte de Vanessa
Director: Mauricio Calderon
Cinematography: Jorge Ramírez
Script: Mauricio Calderon
Editor: Jorge Ramírez and Mauricio Calderon
Music: Jose Juan Mendoza
Stars: Rosario Cruz, Luis Gerardo Mendez García

Fade to Black
Director: Alejandro Sugich
Cinematography: Alejandro Sugich
Script: Alejandro Sugich
Editor: Unavailable
Music: Unavailable
Stars: Fernando Biscalchin, Heidi Bradi

Dos mil metros (sobre el nivel del mar)
Director: Marcelo Tobar
Cinematography: Juan Bernardo Sanchez Mejia
Script: Marcelo Tobar
Editor: Marcelo Tobar, David Torres
Music/Sound: Adan Herrera
Stars: Ari Brickman, Mónica Huarte, Xavier Therrien

El ultimo guión. Buñuel en la memoria
Director: Gaizka Urresti, Javier Espada
Cinematography: Pablo Marquez
Script: Javier Espada
Editor: Unavailable

Music: Martin J. Guridi
Stars: Juan Luis Buñel, Jean-Claude Carrière, Angela Molina

Fuera de Control/Out of Control
Director: Sofia Carrillo
Cinematography: Paola Chaurand
Script: Sofia Carrillo
Editor: Uri Espinoza Cueto
Music/Sound: Raul Atondo
Stars: Unavailable

24 cuadros de terror
Director: Christian Gonzalez
Cinematography: Rafael Sanchez
Script: Christian Gonzalez
Editor: Carlos Espinosa
Music: Nahum Velasquez
Stars: Rafael Amaya, Jesus Arriaga, Raquel Bustos

Corazón de campeón
Director: Joel Vallie, Carlos Mesta
Cinematography: Jan Kuijt
Script: Juan Carlos
Editor: Carlos Mesta, Joel Vallie
Music: Eric Pizana
Stars: Mónica Almanza, Charly Balderas, Luís Antonio Barajas

Nesio
Director: Alan Coton
Cinematography: Esteban de Llaca
Script: Alan Coton
Editor: Óscar Figueroa
Music: Senor Bikini, El Grupo Zass, Luis Lenero
Stars: Jorge Adrián Espindola, Tenoch Huerta, César Jaime

Where Have All the Flowers Gone?
Director: Arturo Perez Jr.
Cinematography: Arturo Perez Jr.
Script: Arturo Perez Jr.
Editor: Arturo Perez Jr.
Music: Joel Sadler, Natalia Perez, Drew Nix, Kristin Mueller, Michael Franti
Stars: Joel Sadler, Billy Troy, Arturo Perez Jr.

Peleas de gallos
Director: Gabriel Pontones
Cinematography: Leon Chiprout
Script: Gabriel Pontones.
Editor: Aina Calleja, Nicolás Dyszel

Music: Jeronimo Gorraez
Stars: Dagoberto Gama, Eligio Meléndez and Héctor Norman

Raices torcidas
Director: Javier Ortiz
Cinematography: Skye Borgman
Script: Javier Ortiz, Cesar Rodriguez
Editor: Oscar Zapata
Music: Juan Manuel Leguizamon, Arturo Solar
Stars: Mauricio Quintana, Cesar Rodriguez, Adriana Leal

Pamela por amor
Director: Rodolfo Galindo Ubierna
Cinematography: Rodolfo Galindo Ubierna
Script: Rodolfo Galindo Ubierna
Editor: Mayte Ponzanelli
Music/Sound: Carlos Cano
Stars: Sergio Bustamante, Carlos Cardan, Fabian Corres

Piece of Heaven
Director: Félix Barbosa, Misael Barbosa
Cinematography: Michel Amado Carpio
Script: Samuel Reyes, Felix Barbosa
Editor: Unavailable
Music: Adrian Bravo
Stars: J. Felix Barbosa R., Graciela Vazquez, Luis Carlos

Más allá de mí
Director: Jesús Mario Lozano
Cinematography: Pierre Stoeber
Script: Jesús Mario Lozano
Editor: Oscar Montemayor
Music: Miguel Almaguer
Stars: Humberto Bustos, Fernando Noriega, Flor Payán

El refrigerador
Director: Carlos Escamilla
Cinematography: Edgar Luzanilla
Script: Carlos Escamilla
Editor: Carlos Escamilla
Music: Roberto Salomon
Stars: Gabriela Fraire, Miguel Romo, Oscar Lopez

El desconocido
Director: Rafael Piñero
Cinematography: Jorge Ramirez
Script: Rafael Piñero
Editor: Rafael Piñero

Music: Bonanza
Stars: Juan Acosta, Raúl Castellanos, Elias Chiprout

Chiles xalapeños
Director: Fabrizio Prada
Cinematography: Gerardo Ruffinelli
Script: Renato Prada Oropeza, Fabrizio Prada
Editor: Hector Ferreiro
Music/Sound: Rafael Arcos
Stars: Iran Castillo, Maria Rebeca, Al Castillo

Animecha kejtzitakua
Director: Julian Antunano
Cinematography: Diego Velasco
Script: Alan Gutierrez, Rafael Gonzalez,
Editor: Julian Antunano, Alan Gutierrez
Music/Sound: Alan Gutierrez
Stars: Alan Gutierrez, Miguel Urtiaga

Dulces perversions
Director: Edgar Castañeda
Cinematography: Edgar Castañeda
Script: Edgar Castañeda
Editor: Edgar Castañeda
Music: Carla Bezi, Jesús de Magallanes, Alberto Estrella
Stars: Carla Bezi, Jesus de Magallanes, Alberto Estrada

Peregrinación
Director: Enrique Arroyo
Cinematography: Serguei Saldivar Tanaka
Script: Enrique Arroyo
Editor: Enrique Arroyo, Berenice Ubeda
Music: Alejandro Giacoman
Stars: Mayahuel del Monte, José Carlos Ruiz, Mario Zaragoza

Un día da estos
Director: Miguel Ángel Sánchez
Cinematography: Maria Eugenia Fernandez
Script: Miguel Ángel Sánchez
Editor: Unavailable
Music/Sound: Daniel Sanchez Caballero
Stars: Loreto Blazquez, Maria del Carmen Felix, Antonio Lopez

El deseo
Director: Marie Benito
Cinematography: Vidblain Balvas
Script: Marie Benito
Editor: José De La Torre, Marie Benito

Music: Rodrigo Márquez
Stars: Keyla Wood, Paloma Woolrich

Floppy
Director: Francisco Payo Gonzalez
Cinematography: Héctor Osuna
Script: Celso R. Garcia, Francisco Payo Gonzalez
Editor: Ricardo Neri
Music: Mario Osuna
Stars: Lucca Biegai, Marius Beigai, Gerardo Rodriguez Gerko

Los niños devoran lobos
Director: Antonio Isordia
Cinematography: Fernando Acuna, Antonio Isordia
Script: Antonio Isordia
Editor: Juan Manuel Figueroa, Ana García
Music: Unavailable
Stars: Unavailable

El caso de la Rubia Platino. Justicia ambiental
Director: Adolfo Cardenas, Salvador Lopez
Cinematography: Adolfo Cardenas, Rodrigo Murray
Script: Jesús Ochoa (narrator), Omar Monroy
Editor: Adolfo Cardenas, Salvador Lopez, Alfredo Vargas
Music: Gus Reyes
Stars: Gustavo Carvajal, Gabriel Calvillo, Gustavo Alanís,

Inadaptado
Director: Raul Gallardo Flores
Cinematography: Russell Menkes
Script: Raul Gallardo Flores
Editor: Unavailable
Music: Carlos Ramos
Stars: Raul Gallardo Flores

Soy mi madre
Director: Phil Collins
Cinematography: Damián García
Script: P. David Ebersole, Todd Hughes,
Editor: Cristovao Dos Reis
Music: Nick Powell
Stars: Veronica Langer, Sonia Couoh, Miriam Calderon

Paloma
Director: Roberto Fiesco
Cinematography: Mario Guerrero
Script: Julian Hernandez
Editor: Emiliano Arenales Osorio

Music: Arturo Villela
Stars: Columba Domínguez, Manuel Martinez Ruiz, Humberto Mendoza López

El jardin
Director: Erick Delgado
Cinematography: Ricardo Villareal
Script: Erick Delgado
Editor: Erick Delgado & Salvador Medina
Music: Salvador Medina
Stars: Erick Delgado, Mariana Maria Fernanda Alvarez

Café paraiso
Director: Alonso Ruiz Palacios
Cinematography: Damián García
Script: Alonso Ruiz Palacios
Editor: Juan Manuel Figueroa
Music: Tomas Barreiro, Freddie Stevenson
Stars: Tenoch Huerta, José Safami, Sophie Alexander

Respeto
Director: Jose Leandro Cordova
Cinematography: Alejandro Tapia Fenton
Script: Unavailable
Editor: David Torres
Music: Andrés Almeida
Stars: Brenda Lozano

El vengador
Director: Jorge Orozco
Cinematography: Alberto Anaya
Script: Jorge Orozco
Editor: Fernando Perez Unda
Music: Unavailable
Stars: Alejandro Calva, Juan Rios, Mahalat Sanchez

Salvador
Director: Victor Salcido
Cinematography: Luis Adan Zayas
Script: Victor Salcido
Editor: Rogelio Ortega
Music: Pablo Mondragon
Stars: Hugo Albores

El cuatro oscuro
Director: Enrique Rodríguez
Cinematography: Edgar Flores
Script: Enrique Rodríguez
Editor: Gerardo Garza

Music: Unavailable
Stars: Susana Alanís, Emma Mirthala Cantú, Erick Hinojosa

Corazoncito
Director: Clementina Campos
Cinematography: Clementina Campos
Script: Dorian Neyra
Editor: Dorian Neyra
Music: Dorian Neyra
Stars: Miguel Alcaraz, Paulina Grajeda, Itary Neyra

Beyond the Mexique Bay
Director: Jean-Marc Rousseau Ruiz
Cinematography: Santiago Sanchez
Script: Lucie Fournie, Jean-Marc Rousseau Ruiz
Editor: Alexandre Donot
Music/Sound: Paul Bidault
Stars: Marc Duret, Sofia Espinosa

Primer movimiento para veinte hombres en un cuarto vacio
Director: Gabriel Herrera
Cinematography: Santiago Torres
Script: Gabriel Herrera
Editor: Moises Magos
Music: Unavailable
Stars: Joaquin Chable, Miguel Couturier

El ultimo evangelio
Director: Juan Carlos Valdivia
Cinematography: Esteban de Llaca
Script: Alejandro Orozco
Editor: Unavailable
Music: Gus Reyes
Stars: Fernando Ciangherotti, Joaquín Garrido, Germán Robles

Trazando Aleida
Director: Christiane Burkhard
Cinematography: Christiane Burkhard
Script: Cristiane Burkhard
Editor: Lucrecia Gutierrez Maupomé
Music: Matías Barberis
Stars: Unavailable

Volver a morir
Director: Miguel Angel González, Avilla Benigno Piñera, Gabriel Romo
Cinematography: Unavailable
Script: Miguel González, Benigno Pinera, Gabriel Romo
Editor: Benigno Piñera, Gabriel Romo, Miguel Angel González Avila

Music: Unavailable
Stars: Unavailable

Wadley
Director: Matias Meyer
Cinematography: Gerardo Barroso
Script: Matias Meyer
Editor: Matias Meyer
Music: Galo Duran
Stars: Leonardo Ortizgris

Omisión
Director: Joe Rendón
Cinematography: Krystian Olivares, Julio Carlos Zapata Ramos
Script: Joe Rendón
Editor: Joe Rendón
Music: Marcos Zavala
Stars: Sophie Alexander-Katz, Irene Alvarez

Resistencia
Director: Francisco Javier Padilla
Cinematography: Jose Antonio Salazar Gary
Script: Francisco Javier Padilla
Editor: Reginaldo Chapa
Music: Unavailable
Stars: Alex Lora

Entrevista con la tierra
Director: Nicolas Pereda
Cinematography: Sebastian Hiriart
Script: Nicolas Pereda
Editor: Nicolas Pereda
Music: Marcela Rodriguez
Stars: Unavailable

Francisca y la muerte
Director: Oscar Fernandez
Cinematography: Unavailable
Script: Oscar Fernandez
Editor: Oscar Fernandez
Music: Unavailable
Stars: Unavailable

Nariz loca
Director: Adrian Corona
Cinematography: Unavailable
Script: Adrian Corona
Editor: Unavailable

Music: Alejandro Vela
Stars: Adrian Corona, Venda D'Abato, John Lambert

No Way
Director: Oliver Meneses
Cinematography: Oliver Meneses
Script: Oliver Meneses
Editor: Oliver Meneses
Music: Oliver Meneses
Stars: Antonio Arroyo, Jose Luis Barraza

Manantial
Director: Gabriel Govela
Cinematography:
Script: Ernesto Anaya Adalid, Gabriel Govela
Editor: Ivan Espana, Gabriel Govela
Music: Unavailable
Stars: Unavailable

The Legend of the Bat
Director: Lucia Morgan
Cinematography: Unavailable
Script: Lucia Morgan
Editor: Unavailable
Music: Sacha Atkinson
Stars: Esteban Rogel

Novre
Director: Carlos Olmos Carrillo
Cinematography: Carlos Olmos Carrillo
Script: Carlos Olmos Carrillo
Editor: Carlos Olmos Carrillo
Music: Carlos Olmos Carrillo
Stars: Karen Elizabeth Horta Navarro, Gerardo Velazquez Melendez

Septiembre aún
Director: Bulmaro Osornio
Cinematography: Gerardo Barroso
Script: Bulmaro Osornio, Matias, Meyer
Editor: Leon Felipe Gonzalez
Music: Unavailable
Stars: Miriam Balderas, Dagoberto Gama, Sebastian L. Medrano

Suripanta
Director: David Rodriguez Estrada
Cinematography: Dimitris Bogiantzis
Script: David Rodriguez Estrada
Editor: Carmen Cabana

Music: Martin Gonzalez
Stars: Fernando Arroyo, Edward E. Cohen, Paola Ochoa

La noche es clara
Director: Rafael Elizalde
Cinematography: Manuel Martinez
Script: Rafael Elizalde
Editor: Rafael Elizalde
Music: Rafael Elizalde
Stars: Orlando Moguel, Raul Mendez

La curiosa conquista del ampere
Director: Ramón Orozco Stoltenberg
Cinematography: Beto Casillas
Script: Ramon Orozco, Sonia Couoh, Alfredo Herrera
Editor: Roque Azcuaga
Music: Paulina Marquez
Stars: Eduardo Cassab, Sonia Couoh, Alfredo Herrera

Niño Fidencio . . . de Roma a Espinazo
Director: Juan Farre
Cinematography: Juan Farre, Mar Farre, Humberto Garcia, Salvador Ramirez
Script: Curry Fernandez
Editor: Martin Bautista
Music: Unavailable
Stars: Unavailable

De como los niños pueden volar
Director: Leopoldo Aguilar
Cinematography: Unavailable
Script: Leopoldo Aguilar
Editor: Ceasr O.G. Valdez
Music: Mario Martinez
Stars: Unavailable

Vert d'automne
Director: Eduardo Hernandez-Garza
Cinematography: Noah Pankow
Script: Eduardo Hernandez-Garza
Editor: Khaled Salem
Music: Eduardo Arbide
Stars: Mikel Albisu, Txema Blasco, Mia Dancey

Pepperoni
Director: Fausto Estrada Guerrero
Cinematography: Bobby Webster
Script: Fausto Estrada Guerrero
Editor: Fausto Estrada Guerrero

Music: Jacques Davidovici
Stars: Linn Bjornland, Samantha Cullen, Ernie

La pesadilla
Director: Ary Hernandez
Cinematography: Ary Hernandez
Script: Ary Hernandez
Editor: Ary Hernandez
Music: Ary Hernandez
Stars: Ary Hernandez

Colors
Director: Andrés Ibáñez
Cinematography: Scott Miller
Script: Andrés Ibáñez
Editor: Unavailable
Music: Paulina Marquez
Stars: Unavailable

El grupero–La muerte de un cantante
Director: Francisco Joel Mendoza
Cinematography: Diego Arizmendi, Manuel Tejada
Script: Julio Escalero, Victor Garibay, Raul Kennedy
Editor: Unavailable
Music: Unavailable
Stars: Unavailable

La madrina
Director: Tavo Ruiz
Cinematography: Sergio Mariscal
Script: Tavo Ruiz
Editor: Irene Morezi
Music: Unavailable
Stars: Mara Cuevas, Ignacio Guadalupe, Adriana Olmos

La canción de los niños muertos
Director: David Pablos
Cinematography: Hatuey Viveros
Script: David Pablos
Editor: David Pablos
Music: Unavailable
Stars: Sebastian Aguirre, Rodrigo Azuela, Daniel Corkidi

2009

La última y nos vamos
Director: Eva López Sánchez

Cinematography: Javier Moron
Script: Eva López Sánchez, Alfredo Mier y Teran
Editor: Mario Sandoval
Music/Sound: Odin Acosta
Stars: María de los Ángeles Ayuso, Antonio Bassols, Rossa Camhi

Amar a morir
Director: Fernando Lebrija
Cinematography: Masanobu Takayanagi
Script: Fernando Lebrija, Harrison Reiner
Editor: Radu Ion
Music: Edward Rogers
Stars: Jose Maria de Tavira, Martina Garcia, Alberto Estrella

Boogie
Director: Gustavo Cova
Cinematography: Unavailable
Script: Robert Fontanarrosa, Mercelo Paez-Cubells
Editor: Andrés Fernandez
Music: Diego Monk
Stars: Pablo Echarri (voice), Nancy Duplaa (voice), Nicolas Frias (voice)

Paradas continuas
Director: Gustavo Loza
Cinematography: Jeronimo Denti
Script: Gustavo Lora, Juan Meyer
Editor: Camillo Abadia
Music: Federico Bonasso
Stars: Ramon Valdez, Luis Arrieta, Cassandra Ciangherotti

El cartel
Director: Brian J. Bagley
Cinematography: Peter Biagi
Script: Brian J. Bagley
Editor: Todd Busch
Music: Russ Howard III
Stars: Jose Luis Franco, Freddy Douglas, Mauricio Islas

El estudiante
Director: Roberto Girault
Cinematography: Gonzalo Amat
Script: Roberto Girault, Gaston Pavlovich
Editor: Roberto Girault, Ariana Villegas Brown
Music: Juan Manuel Langarica
Stars: Jorge Lavat, Norma Lazareno, José Carlos Ruiz

2033
Director: Francisco Laresgoiti

Cinematography: Luis David Sansans
Script: Jordi Mariscal
Editor: Carlos Puente, Pedro G. García
Music: Daniel Hidalgo
Stars: Miguel Couturier, Sandra Echeverría, Alonso Echánove

Recien cazado
Director: Rene Bueno
Cinematography: Unavailable
Script: Rene Bueno
Editor: Rene Bueno, Zeiddy Silva Rios
Music: Paul Bidault
Stars: Angélica Aragón, Magi Avila, Jaime Camil

Rage
Director: Sebastian Cordero
Cinematography: Enrique Chediack
Script: Sergio Bizzio (novel), Sebastian Cordero (screenplay)
Editor: David Gallart
Music: Lucio Godoy
Stars: Martina Garcia, Gustavo Sanchez Parra, Tania de la Cruz

Alamar
Director: Pedro González-Rubio
Cinematography: Pedro González-Rubio
Script: Pedro González-Rubio
Editor: Pedro González-Rubio
Music: Diego Benlliure
Stars: Natan Machado Palombini, Jorge Machado, Nestor Marin

The Kid: Chamaco
Director: Miguel Necoechea
Cinematography: Guillermo Granillo
Script: Carl Bessai, Kirk Harris,
Editor: Mario Sandoval
Music: Shaun Drew
Stars: Martin Sheen, Kirk Harris, Alex Perea

El traspatio / Backyard
Director: Carlos Carrera
Cinematography: Martin Boege, Everardo González
Script: Sabina Berman
Editor: Óscar Figueroa
Music: Fernando Corona
Stars: Ana de la Reguera, Asur Zagada, Marco Pérez

The Maid
Director: Sebastián Silva

Cinematography: Sergio Armstrong
Script: Sebastián Silva
Editor: Danielle Fillios
Music: Ruy Garcia
Stars: Catalina Saavedra, Claudia Celedón, Alejandro Goic

Daniel y Ana
Director: Michel Franco
Cinematography: Chuy Chávez
Script: Michel Franco
Editor: Óscar Figueroa
Music/Sound: Santiago Nuñez
Stars: Dario Yazbek Bernal, Marimar Vega, José Maria Torre

Otra película de huevos y un pollo
Director: Gabriel Riva Palacio Alatriste, Rodolfo Riva Palacio Alatriste
Cinematography: Unavailable
Script: Rodolfo Riva-Palacio Alatriste
Editor: Joaquim Martí
Music/Sound: Matías Barberis
Stars: Bruno Bichir (voice), Patricio Castillo (voice), Carlos Espejel (voice)

Rabioso sol, rabioso cielo
Director: Julián Hernández
Cinematography: Alejandro Cantú
Script: Julián Hernández
Editor: Emilliano Arenales Osorio
Music: Arturo Villela
Stars: Jorge Becerra, Javier Oliván, Guillermo Villegas

Amar
Director: Jorge Ramírez Suárez
Cinematography: Luis David Sansans
Script: Jorge Ramirez Suarez
Editor: Roberto Bolado, Jorge Ramírez Suárez
Music: Héctor Martínez, Jorge Ramírez Suárez
Stars: Luis Ernesto Franco, Diana García, Tony Dalton

Northless
Director: Rigoberto Perezcano
Cinematography: Alejandro Cantú
Script: Edgar San Juan, Rigoberto Perezcano
Editor: Miguel Schverdfinger
Music: Ruy García
Stars: Harold Torres, Alicia Laguna, Sonia Couoh

La Linea
Director: James Cotton

Cinematography: Miguel Bunster
Script: R. Ellis Frazier
Editor: Miklos Wright
Music: David Tom
Stars: Ray Liotta, Andy Garcia, Esai Morales

Tres Piezas de amor en un fin de semana
Director: Salvador Aguirre
Cinematography: Guillermo Granillo
Script: Salvador Aguirre, Jose Angel Montiel
Editor: Roberto Bolado
Music/Sound: Fernando Camara
Stars: Adriana Barraza, Juan Carlos Barreto, Lusi Ernesto Franco

The Last Death
Director: David Ruiz
Cinematography: Juan Jose Saravia
Script: David Ruiz
Editor: Jorge Macaya
Music: Lynn Fainchtein (supervisor)
Stars: Kuno Becker, Manolo Cardona, Luis Arrieta

Heights Dweller
Director: Fernando C. Finck, J. Xavier Velasco, Alejandro Vooruin
Cinematography: Joshua Gil
Script: J. Xavier Velasco, Alejandro Voorduin,
Editor: Fernando C. Finck, J. Xavier Velasco, Alejandro Voorduin
Music: Alejandro Bonilla
Stars: Arcelia Ramírez, Ana Layevska, Martín Zapata

Condones.com
Director: Abraham Mancilla
Cinematography: Arturo de la Rosa
Script: Abraham Mancilla, Rosa María Chávez
Editor: Unavailable
Music: Unavailable
Stars: Martha Acuña, Gerardo Albarrán, Irene Arcilla

Perpetuum Mobile
Director: Nicolás Pereda
Cinematography: Alejandro Coronado
Script: Nicolás Pereda
Editor: Nicolás Pereda
Music: John Camino
Stars: Gabino Rodríguez, Teresa Sanchez, Francisco Barreiro

El libro de piedra
Director: Julio Cesar Estrada

Cinematography: Jorge Rubio Cazarín
Script: Gustavo Moheno, Mario P. Székely, Julio Cesar Estrada, Enrique Renteria,
    Carlos E. Taboada
Editor: Óscar Figueroa
Music: Eduardo Gamboa
Stars: Ludwika Paleta, Miguel Coututier, Evangelina Sosa

Sin retorno
Director: Guillermo Ivan
Cinematography: Jorge Román
Script: Guillermo Ivan, Eric Hayser
Editor: David Constantino
Music: Daniel Medina
Stars: Guillermo Ivan, Eric Hayser, Rosa Najera

Black Sheep
Director: Humberto Hinojosa Ozcariz
Cinematography: Kenji Katori
Script: Humberto Hinojosa Ozcariz
Editor: Joaquim Martí
Music: Ernesto Paredano
Stars: Carlos Aragón, Iván Arana, Rodrigo Corea

La mitad del Mundo
Director: Jaime Ruiz Ibáñez
Cinematography: Alejandro Ramierez Corona
Script: Jaime Ruiz Ibanez
Editor: Victor Velázquez
Music: Armando Rosas
Stars: Luisa Huerta, Hansel Ramírez, Susana Salazar

La Yuma
Director: Florence Jaugey
Cinematography: Unavailable
Script: Edgar Soberón Torchia, Florence Jaugey
Editor: Mario Sandoval
Music: Rodrigo Barbera
Stars: Alma Blanco Rigoberto Mayorga, Gabriel Benavides

Viaje Redondo
Director: Gerardo Tort
Cinematography: Héctor Ortega
Script: Beatriz Novaro, Marina Stavenhagen
Editor: Sebastian Hofman
Music/Sound: Alejandro de Icaza
Stars: Teresa Ruiz, Cassandra Ciangherotti, Gina Morett

El agente 00-P2
Director: Andres Couturier

Cinematography/Art Direction: Jorge Carrera
Script: Andrés Couturier, Martinez Vara Adolfo, Alberto Rodriguez
Editor: Unavailable
Music: Alejandro de Icaza
Stars: Jorge Badillo (voice), Jaime Camil (voice) Mario Castañeda Partido (voice)

Vaho
Director: Alejandro Gerber Bicecci
Cinematography: Alberto Anaya
Script: Alejandro Gerber Bicecci
Editor: Juan Manuel Figueroa, Rodrigo Ríos
Music: Matías Barberis, Rodrigo Garibay
Stars: Marta Aura, Sonia Couoh, Aldo Estuardo

Me importas tú . . . y tú
Director: Adolfo Martínez Solares
Cinematography: Keith Holland
Script: Fritz Glöckner
Editor: Unavailable
Music/Sound: Carlos Cano
Stars: José Alonzo, Rafael Amaya, Khristian Clausen

Macho
Director: Rafael Palacio Illingworth
Cinematography: Autumn Durald
Script: Rafael Palacio Illingworth
Editor: Daniel Raj Koobir
Music: Joseph Bauer
Stars: Michael Teh, Jolene Anderson, Rafael Palacio Illingworth

Cabeza de buda
Director: Salvador Garcini
Cinematography: Alfredo Kassem
Script: Salvador Garcini, Antonio Abascal, Marimar Oliver Coindreau
Editor: Luciana Jauffred Gorostiza
Music: Xavier Asali
Stars: Kuno Becker, Alberto Agnesi, Irene Arcila

Chilango Chronicles
Director: Carlos Enderle
Cinematography: Arturo de la Rosa
Script: Carlos Enderle
Editor: Roberto Bolado, Carlos Enderle
Music: Pablo Mondragon
Stars: Pablo Abitia, Claudio Acuña, Cristian Aguado

Bala Merdida / Bitten Bullet
Director: Diego Muñoz

Cinematography: Carlos Hidalgo
Script: Diego Muñoz
Editor: Felipe Gomez
Music: Pablo Valero
Stars: Damián Alcázer, Octavio Castro, Alexander Dahm

The General
Director: Natalia Almada
Cinematography: Chuy Chavez
Script: Natalia Almada
Editor: Natalia Almada
Music: Shahzad Ismaily, Marc Ribot, John Zorn
Stars: Unavailable

Un mexicano más
Director: René Cardona III
Cinematography: Alberto Lee
Script: Rene Cardona III, Ramon Obon, Juan Sanchez Andraca (novel)
Editor: Rafael Mendoza
Music: Unavailable
Stars: Tonatiuth Avilez, René Campero, Khristian Clausen

Flores en el desierto
Director: José Álvarez
Cinematography: Pedro Gonzalez-Rubio, Fernanda Romandia
Script: Unavailable
Editor: José Luis Fernandez Tolhurst
Music: Martin Delgado
Stars: Unavailable

Corazón del tiempo / Heart of Time
Director: Alberto Cortés
Cinematography: Marc Bellver
Script: Alberto Cortés, Hernan Bellinghaussen
Editor: Alberto Cortés, Lucrecia Gutierrez
Music: Descember Bueno, Kelvis Ochoa
Stars: Rocío Barrios, Francisco Jiménez, Marisela Rodríguez

El Arbol
Director: Carlos Serrano Azcona
Cinematography: David Valldeperez
Script: Carlos Serrano Azcona,
Editor: Manuel Munoz, Carlos Reygadas, Carlos Serrano Azcona
Music: Ginferno
Stars: Antonio Martin Beato, David Bermejo, Ana Casado Boch

Nikté
Director: Ricardo Arnaiz

Cinematography: Ricardo de la Rosa
Script: Omar Mustre, Antonio Garci
Editor: Ricardo Arnaiz, Gabriel Villar
Music: Gabriel Villar
Stars: Sherlyn, Pierre Angelo, Pedro Armendáriz Jr.

Serpent and the Sun: Tales of an Aztec Apprentice
Director: Shaahin Cheyene
Cinematography: Mike Goedecke, Aaron Platt, Marc Shap
Script: Unavailable
Editor: Brian Dodge
Music: Austin Wintory
Stars: Gerardo Aldana, Santiago Ortelas Aumeinto, Elena Avila

Euforia
Director: Alfonso Corona
Cinematography: Arturo de la Rosa
Script: Alfonso Corona
Editor: Óscar Figueroa
Music: Anthony Guefen
Stars: Enrique Arreola, Elizabeth Avila, Francisco Cardoso

Watch'em Die
Director: Adrián García Bogliano, Ramiro García Bogliano
Cinematography: Fabricio Basilotta
Script: Adrián García Bogliano, Ramiro García Bogliano, Hernan Moyano
Editor: Adrián García Bogliano, Hernan Moyano
Music: Rodrigo Franco
Stars: Federico Aimetta, Diego Aroza, Diego Cremonesi

Welcome
Director: Fausto Estrada Guerrero
Cinematography: Fausto Estrada Guerrero
Script: Fausto Estrada Guerrero
Editor: Fausto Estrada Guerrero
Music: Mario Rodriguez Jaramillo
Stars: Laura Dooling, Nahui Estrada Guerrero, Eva Pribylova

Chinango
Director: Peter Van Lengen
Cinematography: Erika Licea Orozco
Script: Peter Van Lengen, Talina Tinoco
Editor: Nestor Braslavsky, Rafa Devillamagallon
Music: Cody Westheimer
Stars: Marko Zaror, Hugo Stiglitz, Susana González

Perdida
Director: Viviana García-Besné

Cinematography: Vivana García-Besné
Script: Viviana García-Besné, Edson Lechuga
Editor: Viviana García-Besné, Joaquim Marti
Music: Anahit Simonian
Stars: Guillermo Calderón, José Luis Calderón, Pedro A. Calderón

Juegos inocentes
Director: Adolfo Martinez Orzynski
Cinematography: Esteban de Llaca
Script: Luis Bekris, Luis Bekris Gibran Portela, Francisco Santos
Editor: Mayte Ponzanelli
Music/Sound: Carlos Cano
Stars: Miguel Couturier, Alan Fernando, Erendira Ibarra

9 meses, 9 días / 9 Months 9 Days
Director: Ozcar Ramírez González
Cinematography: Unavailable
Script: Unavailable
Editor: Unavailable
Music: Michael Nyman
Stars: Unavailable

In Pursuit of Panama
Director: Garrett Martin, J. Garrett Martin, Ryan Swan
Cinematography: Cody Smith
Script: Ryan Swan, J. Garrett Martin
Editor: Garrett Martin, J. Garrett Martin, Ryan Swan
Music: Ryan Swan
Stars: J. Garrett Martin, Muhammad Radwan, Karina Laetita Arriaga Samano

Un tigre en la cama
Director: Rafael Montero
Cinematography: Alberto Lee
Script: Unavailable
Editor: Tania Rojas
Music: Diego Westendarp
Stars: Brenda Angulo, Cristina Bernal, Juan Carlos Casasola

Ghostown
Director: Kenneth Castillo
Cinematography: Mike Testin
Script: Kenneth Castillo
Editor: Unavailable
Music: Andrea Bari, Enrico Cacace
Stars: Daniela Melgoza, Eddie Ruiz, Lauren Birriel

Juntos / Together
Director: Nicolás Pereda

Cinematography: Alejandro Coronado
Script: Nicolás Pereda
Editor: Nicolás Pereda
Music: Unavailable
Stars: Francisco Barreiro, Luisa Pardo, Polly

Oscuridad / Darkness
Director: Fernando Barreda Luna
Cinematography: Francisco MacSwiney Almazan
Script: Fernando Barreda Luna
Editor: Fernando Barreda Luna
Music: Fernando Barreda Luna, Luis Marza
Stars: Sergio Mar, Jorge Adam Nader, Reyna Perez

The Strange Case of DJ Cosmic
Director: John Celona
Cinematography: Unavailable
Script: John Celona
Editor: Unavailable
Music: John Celona
Stars: Duncan Regehr, Thea Gill, Miles Meadows

Borderline
Director: Diego Ibarrola
Cinematography: Mirko Zlatar
Script: Adriana Diaz Chapa, Diego Ibarrola
Editor: Miguel Salgado
Music: Matias Barberis, Lisette Martel
Stars: Adriana Diaz Chapa, Pedro Hossi, Litzy

Castrato
Director: Sohrab Akhavan
Cinematography: Unavailable
Script: Unavailable
Editor: Sohran Akhavan
Music: Unavailable
Stars: Miguel Angel Lopez, Edwin Calderon, Gaston Yanes

1956
Director: Joseph Hemsani
Cinematography: Rodrigo Sandoval
Script: Joseph Hemsani, Ivan Lowenberg
Editor: Unavailable
Music: Unavailable
Stars: Mariana Penalva, Jose Carlos Montes

Quiero saber la verdad
Director: Laura Sevilla

Cinematography: Alejandro Arrioja
Script: Laura Sevilla
Editor: Guillermo Camacho
Music/Sound: Novelli Jurado
Stars: Francisco Otero, Laura Sevilla, Jose Ramon Berganza

A Trivial Exclusion
Director: Grant Sui Wonders, Jeannie Sui Wonders, Clark Sui Wonders, Jackson Sui
Cinematography: Clark Sui Wonders, Grant Sui Wonders, Jackson Sui
Script: Jackson Sui, Clark Sui Wonders,
Editor: Clark Sui Wonders, Grant Sui Wonders, Jackson Sui
Music/Sound: Clark Sui Wonders
Stars: Chase Sui Wonders, Jackson Sui, Jeannie Sui Wonders

Reencuentros: 2501 migrantes
Director: Yolanda Cruz
Cinematography: John Simmons
Script: Yolanda Cruz
Editor: Mako Kamitsuna
Music: Unavailable
Stars: Unavailable

Plan B
Director: Sergio Arau
Cinematography: Gerardo Barrios
Script: Sergio Arau
Editor: Adrian Salinas
Music: Unavailable
Stars: Sergio Arau, Yareli Arizmendi, Francisco Barrios

The Forgotten Tree
Director: Luis Rincón
Cinematography: Arturo R. Jimenez
Script: Diana Medina, Luis Rincón
Editor: Luis Rincón
Music: Unavailable
Stars: Unavailable

Scarlett
Director: Jhasua A. Camarena
Cinematography: Unavailable
Script: Jhasua A. Camarena
Editor: Jhasua A. Camarena
Music: Unavailable
Stars: Unavailable

Marea de arena / Tides of Sand
Director: Gustavo Montiel Pagés

Cinematography: Carlos Rossini
Script: Unavailable
Editor: Fernando Pardo
Music: Martin Capella, Pablo Chemor
Stars: Damián Alcázar, Carmen Beato, Edurne Ferrer

Melted Hearts
Director: Jorge Ramirez Rivera
Cinematography: Rafael Sanchez
Script: Jorge Ramirez Rivea, Rafael Vázquez
Editor: Jorge Ramirez Rivera
Music: Shaun Barrowes, Adrian Gutierrez, Carlos Madrigal
Stars: Jesus Eduardo Alvarez, Mariana Avila Gomez, Grecia Bautista

Entre líneas
Director: Maru Buendia-Senties
Cinematography: Roy Rutngamlug
Script: Maru Buendia-Senties
Editor: Trey Barth, Maru Buendia-Senties
Music: Xavier Solorio
Stars: Sergio Bonilla, Fatima Paola, Eréndira Ibarra

Elvira
Director: Javier Solórzano
Cinematography: Enrico Bonanno, David R. de la Mora, David García
Script: Unavailable
Editor: Gabriel Rodriguez de la Mora
Music: Unavailable
Stars: Elvira Arellano

(N)
Director: Ana Méndez, Francisco Westendarp
Cinematography: Unavailable
Script: Francisco Westendarp, Ana Méndez
Editor: Ana Mendez, Francisco Westendarp
Music: Unavailable
Stars: Unavailable

Buroinfierno / Hellbureau
Director: Daniel Sametz
Cinematography: Renata Gutiérrez
Script: Daniel Sametz
Editor: Daniel Sametz
Music/Sound: Alejandro Lopez (editor)
Stars: Marco Antonio Treviño, Martha Claudia Moreno, Humberto Velez

Con los pies en el cielo
Director: Vidal Cantu
Cinematography: Angel Barroeta, Guillermo Garza

Script: Adolfo Franco, Vidal Cantu
Editor: Nicolenca Beltran
Music: Emilio Estefan
Stars: Romero Britto, Emilio Estefan Jr., Emilio Estefan

Life Sucker
Director: Gabriel Avina
Cinematography: Gabriel Avina
Script: Gabriel Avina
Editor: Gabriel Avina
Music: Joel Ides
Stars: Amanda Axelson, Israel Colon, Sean Ervin

The Beetle and the Fly
Director: Fausto Estrada Guerrero
Cinematography: Fausto Estrada Guerrero
Script: Unavailable
Editor: Fausto Estrada Guerrero
Music: Mario Rodriguez Jaramillo
Stars: Unavailable

Fuego de Medianoche
Director: Daniel Däliger
Cinematography: Daniel Däliger, Alejandro Neyra
Script: Giselle Maia, Giselle Dominguez
Editor: Daniel Daliger
Music: Inner Turbulence
Stars: Estefanía Cantarell, Julio Tamez, Martín Pretalia

Fray Justicia
Director: René Cardona III
Cinematography: Alberto Lee
Script: René Cardona III, Alfredo Solares, Ahleli Gomez
Editor: Ernest Flores, Tania Rojas
Music: Jorge Gebel, Emiliano Marentes
Stars: Eduardo Rivera, Eric del Castillo, Carlos Bonavides

El armadillo fronterizo
Director: Miguel Anaya Borja
Cinematography: Unavailable
Script: Miguel Anaya Borja
Editor: Miguel Anaya Borja
Sound: Martinez Jacobo
Stars: Unavailable

El día que conoci a Batman
Director: Memo García-Naranjo Urzaiz
Cinematography: Memo García-Naranjo Urzaiz

Script: Memo García-Naranjo Urzaiz
Editor: Memo García-Naranjo Urzaiz
Music/Sound: Memo García-Naranjo Urzaiz (editor)
Stars: Memo García-Naranjo Urzaiz (voice)

Sara
Director: Alejandro Montes
Cinematography: Alejandro Montes
Script: Alejandro Montes
Editor: Alejandro Montes
Music: Unavailable
Stars: Unavailable

Sin nombre / Without Name
Director: Cary Joji Fukunaga
Cinematography: Adriano Goldman
Script:Cary Joji Fukunaga
Editor: Luis Carballar, Craig McKay
Music: Marcelos Zarvos
Stars: Paulina Gaitan, Marco Antonio Aguirre, Leonardo Alonso

Sincronia
Dirctor: Jorge Ivan Morales
Cinematography: Yaasib Vasquez
Script: Jorge Ivan Morales, Adan Lerma
Editor: Adan Lerma, Jorge Ivan Morales
Music: Omar Juarez
Stars: Hugo Catalan, Marisol Centeno, Mario Heras

Free Jolito
Director: Marcus Bucay
Cinematography: Lorena Rosendo
Script: Marcos Bucay, Moises Aisemberg
Editor: Diego Cohen
Music: Mauricio García, Ernesto Licona
Stars: Juan Carlos Terreros, Larissa Gomez Rollins, Moy Hinojosa

Rabidondo
Director: Salomón Askenazi
Cinematography: Salomón Askenazi
Script: Salomón Askenazi
Editor: Salomón Askenazi
Music: Unavailable
Stars: Unavailable

El Informe Toledo
Director: Albino Alvarez
Cinematography: Martin Boege, Angel Camacho

Script: Albino Alvarez
Editor: Edna Beatriz Cruz Miranda (post-production assistant)
Music: Steven Brown
Stars: Unavailable

2010

Biutiful
Director: Alejandro González Iñárritu
Cinematography: Rodrigo Prieto
Script: Alejandro González Iñárritu, Armando Bo, Nicolás Giacobone
Editor: Stephen Mirrione
Music/Sound: Gustavo Santaolalla
Stars: Javier Bardem, Maricel Álvarez, Hanaa Bouchaib, Guillermo Estrella

Martín al amanecer/Martin at Dawn
Director: Juan Carlos Carrasco
Cinematography: Aram Díaz
Script: Juan Pablo Cortés, Juan Carlos Carrasco
Editor: Ana García, Juan Carlos Carlos Carrasco
Music/Sound: Agustín Barbabosa
Stars: Rafael Amaro, Diana Bracho, Imelda Castro, Antonio Monroy, Mariana
    Salinas

Revolucíon
Director: Gael García Bernal, Diego Luna, Rodrigo Plá, Gerardo Naranjo, Fer-
    nando Eimbcke, Amat Escalante, Patricia Riggen, Carlos Reygadas . . .
Cinematography: Emiliano Villanueva, Lorenzo Hagerman, Gerardo Barroso,
    Andrea Borbolla, Amat Escalante . . .
Cinematography: Sean Coles, Patrick Murguia, Checco Varese . . .
Script: Laura Santullo, Amat Escalante, Carlos Reygadas, Mariana Chenillo,
    Patricia Riggen . . .
Editor: Agustín Banchero, Lucas Cilintano, Mario Sandoval . . .
Music/Sound: Dario González Valderrama, Andrew Grush . . .
Stars: Adriana Barraza, Mónica Bejarano, Ari Brickman . . .

Sucedió en un día
Director: Issa López, Ignacio Ortiz, Mariana Cahenillo, Daniel Gruener, Beto
    Gómez, Julián Hernandez, Gustavo Lora, Alejandro Lozano
Cinematography: Unavailable
Script: Mariana Chenillo, Gabriel González Meléndez, Francisco Payó González,
    Daniell Gruener, Beto Gómez, Julián Hernández, Sergio Loo, Gustavo Loza,
    Alejandro Lozano, Issa López, Ignacio Ortiz, Ulises Pérez
Editor: Camilo, Abadía, Jorge García, Ricardo Garcia, Felipe Gómez, Adriana
    Martínez, Mario Monroy Nieblas, Lucas Otero, Mario Sandoval
Music/Sound: Arturo Villela
Stars: Irene Azuela, Adriana Barraza, Marius Biegal

También la lluvia / Even the Rain
Director: Icíar Bollaín
Cinematography: Alex Catalán
Script: Paul Laverty
Editing: Ángel Hernández Zoido
Music/Music: Alberto Iglesias
Stars: Gael García Bernal, Luis Tosar and Karra Elejalde Ochoa

The Second Bakery Attack
Director: Carlos Cuarón
Cinematography: Terry Stacey
Script: Carlos Cuarón
Editor: Carlos Armella
Music/Sound: Dave Golden, Jaime Baksht
Stars: Lucas Akoskin, Kirstin Dunst, Brian Geraghty

Abel
Director: Diego Luna
Cinematography: Patrick Murguia
Script: Augusto Mendoza, Diego Luna
Editor: Miguel Schverdfinger
Music/Sound: Jaime Baksht, Ricardo Cabrera
Stars: Chrisopher Ruíz-Esparza, Karina Gidi, José María Yazpik

No eres tú, soy yo
Director: Alejandro Springall
Cinematography: Celiana Cárdenas
Script: Luis Aura, Alejandro Springall
Editor: Jorge García
Music/Sound: Hermino Gutierrez, Andres Franco, Enrique Ojeda
Stars: Eugenio Derbez, Alejandro Barros, Martina García

Post Mortem
Director: Pablo Larraín
Cinematography: Sergio Armstrong
Script: Pablo Larraín
Editor: Andrea Chignoli
Music/Sound: Juan Cristóbal Meza
Stars: Alfredo Castro, Antonia Zegers, Amparo Noguera

Te presento a Laura
Director: Fez Noriega
Cinematography: Jerónimo Denti
Script: Martha Higareda
Editor: Ana Laura Calderón, Michael Courtney
Music/Sound: Martin Thullin, Isabel Muñoz
Stars: Martha Higareda, Kuno Becker, Adriana Barraza

Circo
Director: Aaron Schock
Cinematography: Aaron Schock
Script: Mark Becker, Aaron Schock
Editor: Mark Becker
Music/Sound: Calexico
Stars: Unavailable

Hidalgo–La historia jamás contada
Director: Antonio Serrano
Cinematography: Emiliano Villanueva
Script: Antonio Serrano, Leo Eduardo Mendoza
Editor: Mario Sandoval, Antonio Serrano
Music/Sound: Alejandro Giacomán
Stars: Demían Bichir, Ana de la Reguera, Cecelia Suárez

Pelada
Director: Luke Boughen, Rebekah Fergusson, Gwendolyn Oxenham, Ryan
    White
Cinematography: Rebekah Fergusson, Ryan White
Editor: Jennifer Yulhee Kim
Music/Sound: Kasey Truman
Stars: Unavailable

El mural
Director: Héctor Olivera
Cinematography: Félix Monti
Script: Antonio Armonia, Héctor Olivera, Javier Olivera
Editor: Marcela Sáenz
Music/Sound: Jorge Stavropulos
Stars: Bruno Bichir, Ana Celentano, Carla Peterson, Luis Machín

Seres: Genesis
Director: Angel Mario Huerta
Cinematography: Alejandro Cantú
Script: Armando Guajardo, Angel Mario Huerta, Robert T. Martin Martínez
Editor: Gabriel Ramos
Music/Sound: Marcelo Treviño
Stars: Gonzalo Vega, Manuel Balbi, Alejandra Barros

Sin ella
Director: Jorge Colón
Cinematography: Eduardo Martínez Solares
Script: Jorge Colón, Francisco Sanchez
Editor: Hernan Menendez
Music/Sound: Herminio Gutiérrez
Stars: Alejandro Calva, Luis Arrieta, Fernando Ciangherotti

Somos lo que hay / We Are What We Are
Director: Jorge Michel Grau
Cinematography: Santiago Sanchez
Script: Jorge Michel Grau
Editor: Rodrigo Ríos
Music/Sound: Enrico Chapela
Stars: Francisco Barreiro, Adrián Aguirre, Miriam Balderas

El Infierno / El Narco
Director: Luis Estrada
Cinematography: Damian Garcia
Script: Luis Estrada, Jaime Sampietro
Editor: Mariana Rodríguez
Music/Sound: Michael Brook
Stars: Damián Alcázar, Joaquín Cosio, Ernesto Gómez Cruz

Sin memoria
Director: Sebastián Borensztein
Cinematography: Unavailable
Script: Sebastián Borensztein, Ben Odell
Editor: Unavailable
Music/Sound: Unavailable
Stars: Martha Higareda, Guillermo Iván Dueñas, Pedro Armendáriz Jr.

Las marimbas del infierno / Marimbas from Hell
Director: Julio Hernández Cordón
Cinematography: Julio Hernández Cordón
Script: María Secco
Editor: Lenz Claure
Music/Sound: Antoine Brochu, Alejandro de Icaza, Olivier Peria
Stars: Unavailable

Chicogrande
Director: Felipe Cazals
Cinematography: Damian Garcia
Script: Felipe Cazals
Editor: Óscar Figueroa
Music/Sound: Santiago de la Paz, Neto Gaytán, Samuel Larson
Stars: Damián Alcázar, Juan Manuel Bernal, Bruno Bichir

Marcelino pan y vino
Director: José Luis Gutierrez
Cinematography: Ignacio Prieto
Script: Mikel García Bilbao
Editor: Mayra Mendoza Villa
Music/Sound: Felipe Perez Santiago
Stars: Alejandro Tommasi, Teresa Ruiz, Jorge Andres Fierro

Mandrake
Director: Santiago Limón
Cinematography: Unavailable
Script: Santiago Limón
Editor: Santiago Limón
Music/Sound: Unavailable
Stars: Unavailable

De día y de noche / By Day and By Night
Director: Alejandro Molina
Cinematography: Germán Lammers
Script: Alejandro Molina, Roberto Garza
Editor: Pedro G. García, Roberto Garza, Alejandro Molina
Music/Sound: Jóhann Jóhannsson
Stars: Sandra Echeverría, Fernando Becerril, Juan Carlos Colombo

Deseo
Director: Antonio Zavala Kugler
Cinematography: Esteban de Llaca
Script: Arthur Schnitzler, Antonio Zavala Kugler
Editor: Antonio Zavala Kugler, Franz Zavala
Music/Sound: Lila Downs, Iraida Noriega, Franz Zavala
Stars: Josie Agnessi, Christian Bach, Ari Borovoy

El atentado / The Attempted Dossier
Director: Jorge Fons
Cinematography: Guillermo Granillo
Script: Fernando Javier León Rodríguez, Jorge Fons, Vincente Leñero
Editor: Sigfrido Barjau, Miguel Salgado
Music/Sound: Lucía Álvarez
Stars: Daniel Giménez Cacho, José María Yazpik, Julio Bracho

Pequeños gigantes
Director: Octavio Maya
Cinematography: Octavio Maya
Script: Octavio Maya Guzmán
Editor: Elva
Music/Sound: Victor Garcia Pichardo
Stars: Pedro Cruz, Luis Eduardo, Jose Guadalupe, Martha Higareda, Octavio
   Maya

Brijes/Guardians of the Lost Code (3D)
Director: Benito Fernández
Cinematography: Benito Fernández
Script: Luis Antonio Ávalos
Editor: Diego Fernández, Edith Sanchez
Music/Sound: Juan Manuel Langarica
Stars: José Luis Orozco, José A. Toledano, Miguel Calderón

Sucedió en un día
Director: Mariana Chenillo . . .
Cinematography: Unavailable
Script: Issa Lopéz . . .
Editor: Camilo Abadía, Jorge García, Ricardo García . . .
Music/Sound: Arturo Villela
Stars: Irene Azuela, Adriana Barraza, Marius Biegai . . .

Acorazado
Director: Álvaro Curiel
Cinematography: Germán Lammers
Script: Álvaro Curiel (story and screenplay), Alejandro Lozano (idea)
Editor: Jose Manuel Craviotto
Music/Sound: Ricardo Martín
Stars: Marius Biegai, Camille Natta, Silverio Palacios

Las buenas hierbas / The Good Herbs
Director: María Novaro
Cinematography: Gerardo Barroso
Script: María Novaro
Editor: Sebastián Garza, María Novaro
Music/Sound: Alejandro Icaza
Stars: Úrsula Prueda, Ofelia Medina, Ana Ofelia Murguía

Aqua fria de mar / Cold Water of the Sea
Director: Paz Fabrega
Cinematography: María Secco
Script: Paz Fabrega
Editor: Nathalie Alonso Casale
Music/Sound: Miguel Barbosa
Stars: Luis Carlos Bogantes, Lil Quesada Morúa

El secreto
Director: Gilberto De Anda
Cinematography: Arturo Bidart
Writer: Gilberto De Anda
Editor: Gilberto De Anda
Music/Sound: Gus Reyes
Stars: Christian Bach, Mauricio Islas, Ana Belén Lander, Gabriel Soto, Juan Fer-
    rara, Miguel Pizarro, Germán Roble

Ángel caído
Director: Arturo Anaya
Cinematography: Unavailable
Script: Arturo Anaya
Editor: Daniel Montoya, Mariana Ojeda, Carillo de Albornoz
Music/Sound: Juan Carlos Ertze
Stars: Sebastián Zurita, Humberto Zurita, Laisha Wilkins

180°
Director: Fernando Kalife
Cinematography: Eduardo Flores Torres
Script: Fernando Kalife
Editor: Joesl T. Pashby, Hughes Winborne
Music/Sound: Ángel Illarramendi
Stars: Manuel Garcia-Rulfo, Elizabeth Valdez, Eduardo Blanco

Gaturro
Director: Gustavo Cova
Cinematography: Unavailable
Script: Adriana Lorenzón, Belén Wedeltoft
Editor: Andrés Fernández
Music/Sound: José Caldararo
Stars: Mariano Chiesa, Agustina Gonzalez Cirulnik

Depositarios
Director: Rodrigo Ordoñez
Cinematography: Guillermo Granillo
Script: Rodrigo Ordoñez
Editor: Juan Manuel Figueroa
Music/Sound: Enrique Greiner, Fernando Cámara
Stars: Alejandra Ambrosi, Cesar Ramos, Jose Carlos Montes

Verano de Goliat
Director: Nicolás Pereda
Cinematography: Alejandro Coronado
Script: Nicolás Pereda
Editor: Nicolás Pereda
Music/Sound: Alejandro de Icaza
Stars: Gabino Rodríguez, Teresa Sanchez, Harold Torres

Río de oro / River of Gold
Director: Pablo Aldrete
Cinematography: Lorenzo Hagerman
Script: Pablo Aldrete
Editor: Sebastian Hofmann
Music/Sound: Alejandro de Icaza
Stars: Gonzalo Lebrija, Stephanie Sigman, Kenny Johnston

De la infancia / On Childhoood
Director: Carlos Carrera
Cinematography: Martín Boege
Script: : Carlos Carrera, Fernando Javier León Rodríguez, Silvia Pasternac
Editor: Óscar Figueroa
Music/Sound: Odin Acosta, Raul Atondo
Stars: Damián Alcázar, Benny Emmanuel, Rodrigo Corea

La pantera negra / The Black Panther
Director: Iyari Wertta
Cinematography: Christian Rivera
Script: Unavailable
Editor: Yoame Escamilla, Luciana Jauffred Gorostiza, Francisco X. Rivera
Music/Sound: Unavailable
Stars: Maro Almanda, Enrique Arreola, Marius Biegai

Jean Gentil
Director: Israel Cárdenas, Laura Amelia Guzmán
Cinematography: Unavailable
Script: Israel Cárdenas, Laura Amelia Guzmán
Editor: Unavailable
Music/Sound: José Caldararo
Stars: Jean Remy Gentil, Lys Ambroise, Nadal Walcott

Martha
Director: Marcelino Islas Hernández
Cinematography: Rodrigo Sandoval
Script: Marcelino Islas Hernández
Editor: Rodrigo Téllez
Music/Sound: Ingrid Lowenberg
Stars: Raúl Adalid, Berenice Avilés, Carlos Ceja

El Baile de San Juan
Director: Francisco Athié
Cinematography: Ramón F. Suárez
Script: Francisco Athié
Editor: Roger Ikhlef, Samuel Larson
Music/Sound: Jordi Savall
Stars: José María de Tavira, Marcello Mazzarella, Pedro Armendáriz Jr.

Thank You for Not Smoking
Director: Fernando Perezgil
Cinematography: Alan Vidali
Script: Fernando Perezgil, Gerardo Moreno
Editor: Andrei Gutierrez
Music/Sound: Alexis Pozos
Stars: Issac Bravo, Monica Rojas, Luis Romano

Matinée
Director: Ana Laura Rascón
Cinematography: Unavailable
Script: Paula Rendón
Editor: Marcelo Quiñones
Music/Sound: Jaime González
Stars: Everardo Arzate, Alejandra Barros

El efecto tequila
Director: Leon Serment
Cinematography: Ramon Orozco
Script: Reyes Bercini, Patricio Saiz, Leon Serment
Editor: Óscar Figueroa
Music/Sound: Alejandro Giacomán
Stars: Eduardo Victoria, Karla Souza, José Alonso

Héroes verdaderos
Director: Carlos Kuri
Cinematography: Unavailable
Script: Carlos Kuri, Riley Roca
Editor: Armando Avilez
Music/Sound: Raúl Carballeda
Stars: José Lavat, Víctor Trujillo, Jaqueline Andere

AAA, la película: Sin límite en el tiempo
Director: Alberto Rodriguez
Cinematography: Unavailable
Script: David Hernández Miranda
Editor: Roberto Bolado
Music/Sound: Leoncio Lara
Stars: César Arias, Jorge Badillo, Manuel Campuzano

Borrar de la memoria
Director: Alfredo Gurrola
Cinematography: Juan Bernardo Sánchez Mejía
Script: Rafael Avina
Editor: Luis Alonso Cortés, Alfredo Gurrola
Music/Sound: Alfredo Santa Ana
Stars: René Campero, Kariam Castro, Alejandro Cuétara

Desafío
Director: Julio Bracho and Jorge Luquín
Cinematography: Alberto Casillas, Ernesto Herrera
Script: Julio Bracho, Catalina Maria Irwin, Monobloc
Editor: Freddy Noriega
Music/Sound: Antonio Tranquilino
Stars: Ari Brickman, Rocío Verdejo, Marina de Tavira

Him: Más allá de la luz
Director: Frank Darier-Baziere
Cinematography: Las Herrmann
Script: Frank Darier-Baziere
Editor: Frank Darier-Baziere
Music/Sound: Pablo Arellano
Stars: Guillermo Larrea, Marcela Ruiz Esparza, Nando Estevane

Amor, sal y pimiento / Love, Salt and Pepper
Director: J. Luis Rivera
Cinematography: J. Luis Rivera
Script: J. Luis Rivera
Editor: Amado Miranda
Music/Sound: Jonathan Sales Ocañes
Stars: Carolina Valdés, Jorge Mendoza, Alexsander Sauvinet

Contraluz / Backlighting
Director: Kenia González
Cinematography: Ernesto Caleb Castillo
Script: Ernesto Caleb Castillo, Kenia González
Editor: Ernesto Caleb Castillo, Manuel Fregoso, Kenia González
Music/Sound: Brad Kane
Stars: Sebastián Aguirre, Irán Castillo, Diego Llorente

Frontera
Director: Jesse Estrada
Cinematography: James Rodriguez
Script: Jesse Estrada
Editor: Jon Vasquez
Music/Sound: Damian Rodriguez
Stars: Todd Allen, Fernando Allende, Carlos Humberto Camacho

Seguir siendo: Café Tacvba
Director: Ernesto Contreras, José Manuel Cravioto
Cinematography: Ernesto Contreras, José Manuel Craviotto
Script: Tonatiúh Martínez
Editor: Ernesto Contreras, José Manuel Craviotto, Pedro Jiménez
Music/Sound: Raul Atondo
Stars: Unavailable

Confession of a Gangster
Director: Kenneth Castillo
Cinematography: Mike Testin
Script: Kenneth Castillo
Editor: Daniel Carvajal
Music/Sound: Omar De Santiago, Joe Kraemer, R Musiq
Stars: Vanessa Alderete, Ivan Basso, Yeniffer Behrens

Sex express coffee
Director: Óscar Gonzalez
Cinematography: Unavailable
Script: Óscar Gonzalez
Editor: Unavailable
Music/Sound: Unavailable
Stars: Ricardo Bonno, Fernando Conagra, Diego de Erice

Rock Marí
Director: Chava Cartas
Cinematography: Luis Ávilla
Script: Luis Aguilar, Adrían Coy, Arnulfo Padilla
Editor: Ángel Sebastián Cortés
Music/Sound: Gabriel Coll Barberies
Stars: Mariane Güereña, Damian Núñez, Dolores Heredia

El mar muerto
Director: Ignacio Ortiz
Cinematography: Santiago Navarrete
Script: Ignacio Ortiz
Editor: Sigrido Barjau and Edson Ramírez
Music/Sound: Unavailable
Stars: Joaquín Cosio, Aida López, Ana Ofeolia.

A tiro de piedra / A Stone's Throw Away
Director: Sebastián Hiriart
Cinematography: Sebastián Hiriart
Script: Sebastián Hiriart, Gabino Rodríguez
Editor: Pedro G. García
Music/Sound: Emiliano González de León, Emiliano Motta
Stars: Gabino Rodríguez, Rogelio Medina, Alejadra España

Te extraño / I Miss You
Director: Fabián Hofman
Cinematography: Alberto Anaya
Script: Diana Cardozo
Editor: Miguel Schverdfinger
Music/Sound: Lena Esquenazi
Stars: Carmen Beato, Sofía Espinosa, Álvaro Guerrero

Goliath
Director: Jaime Fidalgo
Cinematography: Unavailable
Script: Jaime Fidalgo, Alejandro Piña
Editor: Jaime Fidalgo
Music/Sound: Fernando De La Huerta
Stars: Fernando De La Huerta, Mariana de Lira, Eduardo "Rana" Gutiérrez

Fragmentos Sobre El Vertigo
Director: Lola Ovando
Cinematography:
Script: Lola Ovando
Editor: Victor Velázquez
Music/Sound: Pablo Mondragón
Stars: Karla Aridne, Marta Aura, Fernando Becerril

La brujula la lleva el muerto
Director: Arturo Pons
Cinematography: Luis David Sansans
Script: Arturo Pons
Editor: Paloma López
Music/Sound: Eduardo Castillo
Stars: Gael Sánchez, Pedro Gamez, Vicky de Fuentes

Musth / Follow Me Down
Director: Mauricio T. Valle
Cinematography: Niels Buchholzer
Script: Mauricio T. Valle
Editor: Jorge Macaya
Music/Sound: Al Rey, Rodolfo Romero
Stars: Gabriela de la Garza, Eduardo Arroyuelo, Alejandro Camacho

Preludio
Director: Eduardo Lucatero
Cinematography: Alejandro Perez Gavilan, Fido Pérez-Gavilán
Script: Eduardo Lucatero
Editor: Unavailable
Music/Sound: Unavailable
Stars: Ana Serradilla, Luis Arrieta, Tiaré Scanda

La mano de Satán
Director: Óscar González Iñiguez
Cinematography: Israel Moreno
Script: Óscar González Iñiguez
Editor: Unavailable
Music/Sound: Adrian Gutierrez
Stars: Ricardo Bonno, Rodrigo Calvo, Natalia Garay

Clean Is Good
Director: Carlos Matiella
Cinematography: Eduardo Filippini
Script: Carlos Matiella
Editor: Carlos Matiella
Music/Sound: Carlos Cendejas, Yonny Roldan, Armando Gudiño
Stars: Constantino Caso, Diego Matiella

Illegal
Director: Hector Mata
Cinematography: Hector Mata
Script: Unavailable
Editor: Hector Mata
Music/Sound: Unavailable
Stars: Unavailable

El Intrugo / The Intruder
Director: Carlos Algara, Carlos Ramírez
Cinematography: Marissa Juarez-Barrera
Script: Carlos Algara, Carlos Ramirez
Editor: Carlos Algara
Music/Sound: Gerardo Garza Chetes
Stars: Alejandro Algara, Oliver Cantú Lozano, Sofía Garza Guerra

Martín al amanecer
Director: Juan Carlos Carrasco
Cinematography: Aram Diaz
Script: Juan Pablo Cortes, Juan Carlos Carrasco
Editor: Ana Garcia
Music/Sound: Agustin Barbabosa
Stars: Rafael Amaro, Diana Bracho, Imelda Castro

El vástago
Director: Mauricio Calderón
Cinematography: Jhasua A. Camarena
Script: Mauricio Calderón
Editor: Mauricio Calderón, Christopher Casillas
Music/Sound: Jose Juan Mendoza Gonzalez
Stars: Eduardo Covarrubias, Abril Iñiguez, Yosi Lugo

0.56% ¿Qué le pasó a Mexico?
Director: Lorenzo Hagerman
Cinematography: Lorenzo Hagerman
Script: Lynn Fainchtein, Lorenzo Hagerman
Editor: Lorenzo Hagerman
Music/Sound: Camilo Frodeval, Ricardo y Tambuco Gallardo, Raul Vizzi, Javier
    Álvarez
Stars: Felipe Calderón Hinojosa, Andrés Manuel López Obrador, Elena Ponia-
    towska

1/20
Director: Gerardo del Castillo Ramierez
Cinematography: Sergio Escudero Martinez
Script: Matthue Roth
Editor: Laura Tresserras Ridao
Music/Sound: Georgina Marinez-Sunol, Matthew Pierce
Stars: Anabelle Munro, Ilfenesh Hadera, Will Shepherd

Tierra madre
Director: Dylan Verrechia
Cinematography: Dylan Verrechia
Script: Dylan Verrechia, Aidee Gonzalez
Editor: Dylan Verrechia

Music/Sound: Dylan Verrechia
Stars: Aidee Gonzalez, Rosalba Valenzuela, Yesenia Espinoza

18 Cigarrillos y medio
Director: Marcelo Tolces
Cinematography: Kenji Katori
Script: Marcelo Tolces
Editor: Yibran Assaud
Music/Sound: Pedro Gonzalez, Kiyoshi Osawa, Gabriel Reyna
Stars: Natalia Herrero, Alejandro Hirschfeld, Hernán Melgarejo

Cefalópodo / Cephalopod
Director: Rubén Imaz
Cinematography: Gerardo Barroso
Script: Rubén Imaz
Editor: Mariana Rodríguez
Music/Sound: Julian Caparros, Salvador Félix
Stars: Unax Ugalde, Alejandra Ambrosi, José Ángel Bichir

Angus Dei: Lamb of God
Director: Alejandra Sánchez
Cinematography: Pablo Ramírez, Érika Licea
Script: Alejandra Sánchez
Editor: Ana García
Music/Sound: Ana García, Tareke Ortiz
Stars: Jesús Romero Colín

El Vigilante
Director:Daniel Galileo Alvarez, Andres Delsol
Cinematography: Emilio Salinas
Script: Andres Delsol, Andres Delsol
Editor: Daniel Galileo Alvarez
Music/Sound: Ana Paula Enriquez, Daniel Maurer
Stars: Miguel Couturier, Mitzi Elizalde, Luis Fonseca

Cosas feas
Director: Isaac Ezban
Cinematography: Francisco Ohem
Script: Isaac Ezban
Editor: Isaac Ezban
Music/Sound: Fernando Alanis, Fabian Arellano
Stars: Carlos Aragón, Iván Arriaga, Mijael Askenazi

Grandes finales de telenovelas
Director: Juan Carlos Munoz
Cinematography: Unavailable
Script: Pablo Zuack
Editor: Unavailable

Music/Sound: Unavailable
Stars: Lucero, Helena Rojo, Diana Bracho . . .

La máquina del tiempo
Director: Abe Rosenberg
Cinematography: Joseph Hemsani
Script: Abe Rosenberg
Editor: Joseph Hemsani
Music/Sound: Ilan Bar-Lavi
Stars: Eitan Ben-Ari, Efraín Fishbein, Mariana Peñalva

Hermoso Silencio
Director: Jorge A. Jimenez
Cinematography: Philip Roy
Script: Jorge A. Jimenez
Editor: Zach Humphreys
Music/Sound: Unavailable
Stars: Jorge A. Jimenez, Carmen Salinas and Brad Maule

29
Director: Carlos Armella
Cinematography: Diego Rodriguez
Script: Carlos Armella
Editor: Carlos Armella
Music/Sound: Carlos Mier
Stars: Patricia Meneses and Noé Velázquez

Ser
Director: Carolina Duarte
Cinematography: Luis Oliver
Script: Carolina Duarte
Editor: Luis Eduardo Case
Music/Sound: Manuel Castillo
Stars: Daniel Almeida, América Barrón, Alicia Encinas

En algún lugar
Director: Mauricio Palos
Cinematography: Mauricio Palos
Script: Andrés Eichelmann Kaiser, Mauricio Palos
Editor: Andrés Eichelmann Kaiser
Music/Sound: Omar Torres
Stars: Unavailable

Rojo (La sangre que derramaron nuestros héroes)
Marissa Rivera Bolaños
Director: Marissa Rivera Bolaños
Cinematography: Greta Zozula
Script: Marissa Rivera Bolaños, Rodrigo Quintero

Editor: Marissa Rivera Bolaños
Music/Sound: Marissa Rivera Bolaños, Retsu Motoyoshi
Stars: Edgar Aguirre, Damián Rodríguez Cuevas, Aldo Estrada

Busco empleo
Director: Francisco Valle
Cinematography: Vidblaín Balvás
Script: Francisco Valle
Editor: Martin Bautista, Francisco Valle
Music/Sound: Pamela Hersch
Stars: Alyosha Barreiro, Carlos Ceja, Laura de Ita

Emma
Director: Masha Kostiurina
Cinematography: Pierre Saint-Martin
Script: Masha Kostiurina
Editor: Enrique Vázquez
Music/Sound: Juan Pablo Villa
Stars: Silvia Contreras, Marcia Coutiño, Paola Jiménez

G.
Director: J. Xavier Velasco
Cinematography: Felipe Perez-Burchard
Script: J. Xavier Velasco
Editor: J. Xavier Velasco
Music/Sound: Alejandro Bonilla
Stars: Arturo Farfán and Yekk Muzik

Naco es chido
Director: Sergio Arau
Cinematography: Gerardo Barroso
Script: Sergio Arau, Tihui Arau, Francisco Barrios, Armando Vega Gil
Editor: Sebastian Hofmann, Adrian Salinas
Music/Sound: Saúl Almaráz
Stars: Sergio Arau, Yareli Arizmendi and Flavia Atencio

Mexicali
Director: Max Herrlander, Juan Palacio
Cinematography: Julio Torres
Script: Max Herrlander, Juan Palacio
Editor: Max Herrlander, Juan Palacio
Music/Sound: Russell Burn, Gustaf Heden
Stars: Boxer, Jezabel Franco, Max Herrlander, Wendy Lopez

The Man
Director: Sébastien Guerra
Cinematography: Sébastien Guerra
Script: Juan Pablo Campa

Editor: Unavailable
Music/Sound: Ismael Plascencia
Stars: Juan Pablo Campa

Vuelve a la vida
Director: Carlos Hagerman
Cinematography: John Grillo
Script: John Grillo, Carlos Hagerman
Editor: Valentina Leduc Navarro
Music/Sound: Rigo Dominguez, Mariano Mercerón
Stars: Roberto Balderas, John Grillo and Alejandro Martinez

The Gray Strip
Director: Jorge Meraz
Cinematography: Jorge Marcial
Script: Unavailable
Editor: Jorge Meraz
Music/Sound: Jorge Meraz
Stars: Jorge Ramos Herrera, Francisco Adame, Manuel Adame

Clankety, Clank
Director: Maurico Leiva-Cock
Cinematography: Pedro Gómez Millán
Script: Mauricio Leiva-Cock, Daniel Shea Zimbler
Editor: Michael Garber, Mauricio Leiva-Cock
Music/Sound: Sebastien Carew-Reid
Stars: Tom Fenaughty, George Gully, Kevin Kutch

Todo, en fin, el silencio lo ocupaba
Director: Nicolás Pereda
Cinematography: Gerardo Barroso, Lisa Tillinger, Alejandro Coronado
Script: Unavailable
Editor: Nicolás Pereda
Music/Sound: Marcela Rodríguez, Nicolás Pereda
Stars: Jesusa Rodríguez

Poco es nada
Director: Gustavo Mora
Cinematography: Gustavo Mora
Script: Unavailable
Editor: Gustavo Mora
Music/Sound: Steven Brown
Stars: Yanitza Acevedo, Martha Bolaños, Benito Cardenas

Amaneceres oxidados
Director: Diego Cohen
Cinematography: Aram Diaz
Script: Diego Cohen

Editor: Pedro G. García
Music/Sound: Uriel Villalobos, Abigail Váquez
Stars: Ari Brickman, Alan Chávez, Armando Hernández

Ernesto
Director: Fernando Méndez
Cinematography: Unavailable
Script: Montserrat Ocampo
Music/Sound: Unavailable
Stars: Guillermo Ayala

Catarsis
Director: Julián Robles
Cinematography: Andrés León Becker
Script: Julián Robles
Editor: Unavailable
Music/Sound: Unavailable
Stars: Sergio Bustamante, Helena Rojo, Arturo Beristáin

Secuestro y muerte
Director: Rafael Filippelli
Cinematography: Fernando Lockett
Script: Beatriz Sarlo, David Oubiña, Mariano Llinás
Editor: Alejo Moguillansky
Music/Sound: Gabriel Chwojnik
Stars: Enrique Piñeyro, Alberto Ajaka, Esteban Bigliardi, Agustina Muñoz,
    Matías Umpiérrez

Igualdad
Director: René Herrera
Cinematography: Carlos Hidalgo
Script: Olga Varela, René Herrera
Editor: Alejandro Aguirre
Music/Sound: Francisco Albisua
Stars:Moises Arizmendi, María Aura, Rocío Verdejo

Erase Una Vez En Durango
Director: Juan Antonio de la Riva
Script: Alejandro Parodi, Juan Antonio de la Riva
Cinematograph: Arturo de la Rosa
Editor: Óscar Figueroa
Music/Sound: Manuel Montaño , Gabriel Coll, Antonio Avitia
Stars: Lumi Cavazos, Jorge Galván, Iñaki Goci

Serial comic no.1 fijacion
Director: César Ámigo Aguilar
Cinematography: Xavier Xequé
Script: César Ámigo Aguilar (story), Montserrat Pérez (screenplay)

Editor: Erik Mariñelarena Herrera
Music/Sound: Pedro Escarcega
Stars: Fernanda Borches, Esteban Monroy, Miguel A. Reina Gómez Maganda

Tin Tan
Director: Francesco Taboada Tabone
Cinematography: Francesco Taboada Tabone
Script: Aldo Jiménez Tabone (screenplay)
Editor: Aldo Jiménez Tabone, Francesco Taboada Tabone
Music/Sound: Unavailable
Stars: Gaspar Henaine, Yolanda Montes and Silvia Pinal

Amaren ideia
Director: Maider Oleaga
Cinematography: Bernardo Jasso
Script: Maider Oleaga
Editor: Enara Goikoetxea, Maider Oleaga
Music/Sound: Iñaki Salvador

Peoria
Director: Andres Clariond
Cinematography: Héctor Ortega
Script: Andres Clariond
Editor: Yibran Assaud
Music/Sound: Pedro Gonzalez, Kiyoshi Osawa, Gabriel Reyna
Stars: Joel Bryant, Reynaldo Perez, Angela Perri

New Children/New York
Director: Gisela Sanders Alcántara
Cinematography: Dan Akiba
Script: Gisela Sanders Alcántara, Lauren Mucciolo
Editor: Andrea Chignoli
Music/Sound: Yaramir Caban, Camila Celin, Maya Martinez
Stars: Desiree Camacho, Fausto El Piro, Emanuel Loarca

Atrocious
Director: Fernando Barreda Luna
Cinematography: Ferrán Castera Mosquera
Script: Fernando Barreda Luna
Editor: Fernando Barreda Luna
Music/Sound: Octavio Flores, Perez Berk, Jorge Jaime Pikis
Stars: Cristian Valencia, Clara Moraleda, Chus Pereiro

Los dos Pérez
Director: Adolfo Dávila
Cinematography: Miguel Lopez
Script: Roberto Bonelli, Alexander Dahm, Adolfo Dávila
Editor:Alexander Dahm
Music/Sound: Carlos Cendeja
Stars: Damián Alcázar, Martha Higareda, Julia Urbina

La Region que Recuerda: Ecos de la Revolucion Mexicana en Namiquipa
Director: Clementina Campos
Cinematography: Clementina Campos
Script: Clementina Campos
Editor: Dorian Neyra.
Music/Sound: Dorian Neyra.
Stars: Martha Aguila, Martin Aguilar, Rolando Alderete

La princesa y el caracol
Director: Bernardo Rugama
Cinematography: Juan Castillero
Script: Bernardo Rugama
Editor: César O.G. Valdez
Music/Sound: Juan Pablo Miramontes
Stars: Maryfer Santillan

Redención
Director: Juan Pablo Cortes, José Antonio Hernández
Cinematography: Aram Diaz
Script: Juan Pablo Corted, José Antonio Hernández
Editor: Juan Pablo Cortes, José Antonio Hernández
Music/Sound: Uriel Villalobos, Abigail Váquez
Stars: Donal Cortés, Rafael Cortés and Erika de la Llave

Dreaming in a Time of Hate
Director: Oscar Arvizo
Cinematography: Unavailable
Script: Oscar Arvizo
Editor: Jason Peri
Music/Sound: Unavailable
Stars: Sofia Ruiz, Julio Mazariego and Eliezer Ortiz

Lluvia de ideas
Director: Adolfo Dávila
Cinematography: Miguel Lopez
Script: Adolfo Dávila
Editor: Alexander Dahm
Music/Sound: Unavailable
Stars: Julian Pablo Dominguez, Martha Higareda, Mauricio Llera

Embargado
Director: António Ferreira
Cinematography: Luís Pedro Madeira
Script: Filipe Costa, Cláudia Carvalho and Pedro Diogo
Editor: António Ferreira, Tiago Sousa
Music/Sound: Paulo Castilho
Stars: José Saramago, Tiago Sousa

Notes

✵

Lights, Camera, Action

1. John Hopewell, "Latin Filmmaker on a Roll," *Variety,* February 23, 2009, 7.

2. Paul Julian Smith, "Paul Julian Smith Reports on a Rich Crop of Home-grown Films," *Film Quarterly* 63, no. 3 (2010): 18.

3. See Octavio Paz, *The Labyrinth of Solitude: Life and Thought in Mexico,* trans. Lysander Kemp (New York: Grove Press, 1961); and José Vasconcelos, *Cosmic Race: A Bilingual Edition,* trans. and annotated Didier T. Jaén (Baltimore: Johns Hopkins University Press, 1997), especially pronouncements such as "por mi raza hablará el espíritu" (Through my race spirit shall speak).

4. Paulo Antonio Paranaguá, ed., *Mexican Cinema,* trans. Ana M. López (London: British Film Institute, 1995).

5. Rogelio Agrasánchez, Jr., *Mexican Movies in the United States: A History of the Films, Theaters, and Audiences, 1920–1960* (Jefferson, N.C.: McFarland, 2006).

6. Doyle Greene, *Mexploitation Cinema: A Critical History of Mexican Vampire, Wrestler, Ape-Man and Similar Films, 1957–1977* (Jefferson, N.C.: McFarland & Co., 2005).

7. Jason Wood, *The Faber Book of Mexican Cinema* (London: Faber and Faber, 2006); Jason Wood, *Talking Movies: Contemporary World Filmmakers in Interview* (London: Wallflower, 2006).

8. Jethro Soutar, *Gael García Bernal and the Latin American New Wave* (London: Portico, 2008).

9. Soutar, *Gael García Bernal,* ii.

10. R. Hernandez-Rodriguez, *Splendors of Latin Cinema* (Santa Barbara: Praeger, 2010), 47.

11. Paul Julian Smith, *Amores Perros* (London: British Film Institute, 2002), 8.

12. John King, *Magical Reels* (London: Verso, 1990).

13. Carlos J. Mora, *Mexican Cinema: Reflections of a Society, 1896–2004,* 3d ed. (Jefferson, N.C.: McFarland, 2005).

14. Scott L. Baugh, "Developing History/Historicizing Development in Mexican *Nuevo Cine* Manifestoes around *'la Crisis,'*" *Film and History* 34, no. 2 (2004): 25–37.

15. Timothy Dugdale, "The French New Wave: New Again," in *New Punk Cinema,* ed. Nicholas Rombes (Edinburgh: Edinburgh University Press, 2005), 67.

16. Dugdale, "French New Wave," 70.

17. Andrea Noble, *Mexican National Cinema* (New York: Routledge, 2005).

18. Sergio de la Mora, *Cinemachismo: Masculinities and Sexuality in Mexican Film* (Austin: University of Texas Press, 2006).

19. Miriam Haddu, *Contemporary Mexican Cinema, 1989–1999: History, Space, and Identity* (Lewiston, N.Y.: Edwin Mellen, 2007), 5.

20. Haddu, *Contemporary Mexican Cinema,* 230.

21. Elissa J. Rashkin, *Women Filmmakers in Mexico: The Country of Which We Dream* (Austin: University of Texas Press, 2001), 220.

22. Rashkin, *Women Filmmakers,* 220.

23. Charles Ramírez Berg, *Cinema of Solitude: A Critical Study of Mexican Film, 1967–1983* (Austin: University of Texas Press, 1992), 2.

24. See Charles Ramírez Berg, "The Indian Question," in *New Latin American Cinema: Theory, Practices, and Transcontinental Articulations,* ed. Michael T. Martin, 76–93 (Detroit: Wayne State University Press, 1997).

25. Charles Ramírez Berg, *Latino Images in Film: Stereotypes, Subversion, and Resistance* (Austin: University of Texas Press, 2002).

26. David William Foster, *Mexico City in Contemporary Mexican Cinema* (Austin: University of Texas Press, 2002).

27. Emily Hind, "*Provincia* in Recent Mexican Cinema, 1989–2004," *Discourse* 26, nos. 1–2 (2004): 26.

28. Freya Schiwy, *Indianizing Film: Decolonization, the Andes, and the Question of Technology* (Newark, N.J.: Rutgers University Press, 2009), 649.

29. Laura Podalsky, "The Young, the Damned, and the Restless," *Framework: The Journal of Cinema and Media* 49, no. 1 (2008): 144–60.

30. Celestino Deleyto and María del Mar Azcona, *Alejandro González Iñárritu* (Urbana: University of Illinois Press, 2010), 3.

31. Deleyto and del Mar Azcona, *Alejandro González Iñárritu,* 6.

32. Paul Julian Smith, "Transatlantic Traffic in Recent Mexican Films," *Journal of Latin American Cultural Studies* 12, no. 3 (2003): 389–400.

33. Catherine Grant and Annette Kuhn, eds., *Screening World Cinema* (New York: Routledge, 2006).

The Nuts and Bolts of Mexican Film

1. Seymour Chatman, "What Novels Can Do That Films Can't (and Vice Versa)," in *Literary Theories in Praxis,* ed. Shirley F. Staton, 159–69 (Philadelphia: University of Pennsylvania Press, 1987).

2. Jennifer Van Sijll, *Cinematic Storytelling: The Hundred Most Powerful Film Conventions Every Filmmaker Must Know* (Studio City, Calif.: Michael Wiese Productions, 2005), 236.

3. Vsevolod Pudovkin, "On Editing," in *Film Technique and Film Acting,* ex-

cerpted in *Film and Criticism,* ed. Leo Braudy and Marshall Cohen, 7th ed. (Oxford and New York: Oxford University Press, 2009), 7.

4. Pudovkin, "On Editing," 9.

5. Pudovkin, "On Editing," 10.

6. Pudovkin, "On Editing," 11.

7. Victor Shklovsky, "The Semantics of Cinema," in *The Film Factory: Russian and Soviet Cinema in Documents,* ed. and trans. Richard Taylor (Cambridge, Mass.: Harvard University Press, 1988), 133.

8. Colin McGinn, *The Power of Movies* (New York: Random House, 2005), 127.

9. David Bordwell, *Narration in the Fiction Film* (Madison: University of Wisconsin Press, 1985), 62.

10. Tatiana Lipkes, "Carlos Reygadas," *La Tempestad* 8, no. 53 (2007): 77.

11. José Teodoro, "On Earth as It Is in Heaven," *Film Comment* 45, no. 1 (2009): 50.

Hecho a Mano . . . Hecho por *Homo sapiens*

1. Alison Gopnik, *Philosophical Baby: What Children's Minds Tell Us about Truth, Love, and the Meaning of Life* (New York: Farrar, Straus and Giroux, 2009), 103–4.

2. Kristin Thompson, *Breaking the Glass Armor: Neoformalist Film Analysis* (Princeton, N.J.: Princeton University Press, 1988), 41.

3. Yadin Dudai, "Enslaving Central Executives: Toward a Brain Theory of Cinema," *Projections* 2, no. 2 (2008): 35.

4. Dudai, "Enslaving Central Executives," 35.

5. Dudai, "Enslaving Central Executives," 35.

6. Ira Konigsberg, "Film Studies and the New Science," *Projections* 1, no. 1 (2007): 5.

7. David Bordwell, *Poetics of Cinema* (New York, London: Routledge, 2009), 123.

8. Bordwell, *Poetics of Cinema,* 123.

9. Thompson, *Breaking the Glass Armor,* 35.

10. Celestino Deleyto and María del Mar Azcona, *Alejandro González Iñárritu* (Urbana: University of Illinois Press, 2010), 30.

11. J. M. Zacks, N. K. Speer, and J. R. Reynolds, "Segmentation in Reading and Film Comprehension," *Journal of Experimental Psychology: General* 138 (2009): 308.

12. Jens Eder, "Feelings in Conflict: *A Clockwork Orange* and the Explanation of Audiovisual Emotions.," *Projections* 2, no. 2 (2008): 72.

13. Eder, "Feelings in Conflict," 72, emphasis in the original.

14. Eder, "Feelings in Conflict," 77–78.

15. Patrick Colm Hogan, "Projection, Violations of Continuity, and Emotion in the Experience of Film," *Projections* 1, no. 1 (2007): 41.

16. Hogan, "Projection," 41.

17. Hogan, "Projection," 47.

18. Hogan, "Projection," 48.

19. Jeff Smith, "Movie Music as Moving Music: Emotion, Cognition, and the Film Score," in *Passionate Views: Film, Cognition, and Emotion,* ed. Carl Plantinga and Greg M. Smith, 146–66 (Baltimore: Johns Hopkins University Press, 1999).

20. Isabelle Peretz and John Sloboda, "Music and the Emotional Brain," *Neurosciences and Music: Annals New York Academy of Sciences* 1060 (December 2005): 410.

21. Carl Plantinga, "I Followed the Rules, and They All Loved You More": Moral Judgment and Attitudes toward Fictional Characters in Film," *Midwest Studies in Philosophy* 34, no. 1 (2010): 51.

22. Anne Bartsch, "Meta-emotion: How Films and Music Videos Communicate Emotions about Emotions," *Projections* 2, no. 1 (2008): 48.

23. Patrick Colm Hogan, *Understanding Indian Cinema: Culture, Cognition, and Cinematic Imagination* (Austin: University of Texas Press, 2008), 198.

24. Carl Plantinga, *Moving Viewers: American Film and the Spectator's Experience* (Berkeley: University of California Press, 2009), 122.

25. Beatrice de Gelder, "Toward the Neurobiology of Emotional Body Language," *Nature* 7 (March 2006): 243.

26. de Gelder, "Toward the Neurobiology," 246–47.

27. de Gelder, "Toward the Neurobiology," 247.

28. de Gelder, "Toward the Neurobiology," 248.

29. de Gelder, "Toward the Neurobiology," 248.

30. Stephen Prince, "Psychoanalytic Film Theory," in *Post-Theory: Reconstructing Film Studies,* ed. David Bordwell and Noël Carroll (Madison: University of Wisconsin Press, 1996), 81.

31. Hogan, *Understanding Indian Cinema,* 6.

32. Plantinga, *Moving Viewers,* 62.

33. Plantinga, *Moving Viewers,* 62.

34. Hogan, *Understanding Indian Cinema,* 200–201.

35. Eder, "Feelings in Conflict," 71.

36. Eder, "Feelings in Conflict," 71.

37. Plantinga, *Moving Viewers,* 33.

38. Seth Duncan and Lisa Feldman Barrett, "Affect Is a Form of Cognition: A Neurobiological Analysis," *Cognition and Emotion* 21 (2007): 1193.

39. Hogan, *Understanding Indian Cinema,* 6.

40. Matthew Gervais and David Sloan Wilson, "The Evolution and Functions of Laughter and Humor: A Synthetic Approach," *Quarterly Review of Biology* 80, no. 4 (2005): 398.

41. Gervais and Wilson, "Evolution and Functions," 398.

42. Gervais and Wilson, "Evolution and Functions," 398.

43. Mathew Hurley, Daniel C. Dennett, and Reginald B. Adams Jr., *Inside Jokes: Using Humor to Reverse-Engineer the Mind* (Cambridge, Mass.: MIT Press, 2011), 261.

44. Hurley, Dennett, and Adams, *Inside Jokes,* 262.

45. Andrea Samson, Stefan Zysset, and Oswald Huber, "Cognitive Humor

Processing: Different Logical Mechanisms in Nonverbal Cartoons—an fMRI Study," *Social Neuroscience* 3, no. 2 (2008): 125–40.

46. Hurley, Dennett, and Adams, *Inside Jokes,* 265.

47. Hurley, Dennett, and Adams, *Inside Jokes,* 265.

48. Hurley, Dennett, and Adams, *Inside Jokes,* 275.

49. Hurley, Dennett, and Adams, *Inside Jokes,* 271.

50. Hurley, Dennett, and Adams, *Inside Jokes,* 276.

51. Herbert Lindenberger, "Arts in the Brain: What Might Neuroscience Tell Us?," in *Toward a Cognitive Theory of Narrative Acts,* ed. Frederick Luis Aldama (Austin: University of Texas Press, 2010), 34.

52. Plantinga, *Moving Viewers,* 117.

53. Plantinga, *Moving Viewers,* 44.

U.S.-Mexico Crossings, Trends, and Backdrops

1. Clara E. Rodríguez, *Heroes, Lovers, and Others: The Story of Latinos in Hollywood* (Washington, D.C.: Smithsonian Books, 2004), 2.

2. William Nericcio, *Tex[t]-Mex: Seductive Hallucinations of the "Mexican" in America* (Austin: University of Texas Press, 2007), 108.

3. A. O. Scott, "The World Is Watching, Not Americans," *New York Times,* January 21, 2007, http://www.nytimes.com/2007/01/21/movies/21scot.html?ref=movies.

4. Scott, "The World Is Watching."

5. Zuzana M. Pick, *Constructing the Image of the Mexican Revolution: Cinema and the Archive* (Austin: University of Texas Press, 2010), 5.

6. Pick, *Constructing the Image,* 233.

7. Charles Ramírez Berg, *Latino Images in Film: Stereotypes, Subversion, and Resistance* (Austin: University of Texas Press, 2002), 199.

8. Camilla Fojas, *Border Bandits: Hollywood on the Southern Frontier* (Austin: University of Texas Press, 2008), 19.

9. Fojas, *Border Bandits,* 95.

10. John King, *Magical Reels* (London: Verso, 1990), 16.

11. King, *Magical Reels,* 17.

12. Rodríguez, *Heroes,* 145.

13. Katarzyna Marciniak, *Alienhood: Citizenship, Exile, and the Logic of Difference* (Minneapolis: University of Minnesota Press, 2006), 7.

Contexts, Critiques, Distribution, Exhibition, and Obstacles

1. Jason Wood, *The Faber Book of Mexican Cinema* (London: Faber and Faber, 2006), 172.

2. Jethro Soutar, *Gael García Bernal and the Latin American New Wave* (London: Portico, 2008), 55.

3. Soutar, *Gael García Bernal,* 55.

4. Jason Wood, *Talking Movies: Contemporary World Filmmakers in Interview* (London: Wallflower, 2006), 196.

5. Anne Marie Stock, "Authentically Mexican? Mi Querido Tom Mix and Cronos Reframe Critical Questions," in *Mexico's Cinema: A Century of Film and Filmmakers,* ed. Joanne Hershield and David Maciel (Wilmington, Del.: Scholarly Research Books, 1999), 268.

6. Laura Podalsky, "The Young, the Damned, and the Restless," *Framework: The Journal of Cinema and Media* 49, no. 1 (2008): 145.

7. Podalsky, "The Young," 145.

8. Laura Podalsky, "Out of Depth: The Politics of Disaffected Youth in Contemporary Latin American Cinema," in *Youth Culture in Global Cinema,* ed. Timothy Shary and Alexandra Seibel (Austin: University of Texas Press, 2007), 109.

9. Rita González, Jesse Lerner, and Isabelle Marmasse, *Mexperimental Cinema: Sixty Years of Avant-Garde Media Arts from Mexico* (Santa Monica, Calif.: Smart Art, 1998), 43.

10. Eli Zaretsky, *Capitalism, the Family, and Personal Life* (New York: Harper and Row, 1976), 71.

11. David Agren, "Mexico: Death Toll from Drug-Related Violence Is Thousands Higher Than Was Reported Earlier," *New York Times,* August 3, 2010, http://www.nytimes.com/2010/08/04/world/americas/04forbriefs-MEXICO.html.

12. Roy Armes, *Thirdworld Filmmaking and the West* (Berkeley: University of California Press, 1987), 37.

13. Soutar, *Gael García Bernal,* 44.

14. Armes, *Thirdworld Filmmaking,* 41.

15. Quoted in Wood, *Faber Book,* 40.

16. Quoted in Wood, *Faber Book,* 40.

17. See Victor "EL TLC: La Otra Conquista," *Ugalde, Industrias Culturales y TLC: Impactos y retos de la apertura* (Mexico: Fronteras Comunes, 2008), 85–105.

18. Paul Julian Smith, "Paul Julian Smith Reports on a Rich Crop of Homegrown Films," *Film Quarterly* 63, no. 3 (2010): 18.

19. David Bordwell, *Poetics of Cinema* (New York and London: Routledge, 2009), 28.

Refrito and Buena Onda Films Put to the Test

1. Nuala Finnegan, "'So What's Mexico Really Like?' Framing the Local, Negotiating the Global in Alfonso Cuarón's *Y tu Mamá También,*" in *Contemporary Latin American Cinema: Breaking into the Global Market,* ed. Deborah Shaw (New York: Rowman and Littlefield, 2007), 30.

2. Finnegan, "So What's Mexico Really Like?," 38.

3. Jennifer Van Sijll, *Cinematic Storytelling: The Hundred Most Powerful Film Conventions Every Filmmaker Must Know* (Studio City, Calif.: Michael Wiese Productions, 2005), 238.

4. Van Sijll, *Cinematic Storytelling,* 238.

5. Celestino Deleyto and María del Mar Azcona, *Alejandro González Iñárritu* (Urbana: University of Illinois Press, 2010), 24.

6. Deleyto and Mar Azcona, *Alejandro González Iñárritu,* 53.

7. Deleyto and Mar Azcona, *Alejandro González Iñárritu,* 62.

8. Deleyto and Mar Azcona, *Alejandro González Iñárritu,* 62.

9. Deleyto and Mar Azcona, *Alejandro González Iñárritu,* 94.

10. Deleyto and Mar Azcona, *Alejandro González Iñárritu,* 97.

11. Deleyto and Mar Azcona, *Alejandro González Iñárritu,* 119.

12. Deleyto and Mar Azcona, *Alejandro González Iñárritu,* 119.

13. Deleyto and Mar Azcona, Alejandro González Iñárritu, 100–101.

14. Lisa Hirsch, "Emmanuel Lubezki," *Daily Variety* 290, no. 50: A8.

15. Jorge Ayala Blanco, *La fugacidad del cine mexicano* [The ephemerality of Mexican cinema] (Mexico City: Océano, 2001), 485.

16. Tom Huntington, "Of Steadicams and Skycams: Filmmakers Have Long Sought the Means to Add a Little Kinetic Energy to Their Moving Images," *American Heritage of Invention and Technology* 24, no. 1 (2009): 32.

17. Isabelle Peretz and John Sloboda, "Music and the Emotional Brain," *Neurosciences and Music: Annals, New York Academy of Sciences* 1060 (December 2005): 410.

18. Jeff Smith, "Movie Music as Moving Music: Emotion, Cognition, and the Film Score." In *Passionate Views: Film, Cognition, and Emotion,* edited by Carl Plantinga and Greg M. Smith (Baltimore: Johns Hopkins University Press, 1999), 161.

19. Patrick Colm Hogan, *Understanding Indian Cinema: Culture, Cognition, and Cinematic Imagination* (Austin: University of Texas Press, 2008), 200.

20. Jonathan Frome, "Representation, Reality, and Emotions across Media." *Film Studies: An International Review* 8 (Summer 2006), 18.

21. Patrick Colm Hogan, "Epilogue of Suffering," *SubStance* 30, nos. 1–2 (2001): 134.

Bubblegums That Pop; Refritos That Go "Ah"

1. Elissa J. Rashkin, *Women Filmmakers in Mexico: The Country of Which We Dream* (Austin: University of Texas Press, 2001), 116.

Works Cited

Agrasánchez, Rogelio, Jr. *Mexican Movies in the United States: A History of the Films, Theaters, and Audiences, 1920–1960*. Jefferson, N.C.: McFarland, 2006.

Agren, David. "Mexico: Death Toll from Drug-Related Violence Is Thousands Higher Than Was Reported Earlier." *New York Times,* August 3, 2010, http://www.nytimes.com/2010/08/04/world/americas/04forbriefs-MEXICO.html.

Armes, Roy. *Thirdworld Filmmaking and the West*. Berkeley: University of California Press, 1987.

Ayala Blanco, Jorge. *La fugacidad del cine mexicano* [The ephemerality of Mexican cinema]. Mexico City: Océano, 2001.

Bartsch, Anne. "Meta-emotion: How Films and Music Videos Communicate Emotions about Emotions." *Projections* 2, no. 1 (2008): 45–59.

Baugh, Scott L. "Developing History/Historicizing Development in Mexican Nuevo Cine Manifestoes around '*la Crisis*.'" *Film and History* 34, no. 2 (2004): 25–37.

Berg, Charles Ramírez. *Cinema of Solitude: A Critical Study of Mexican Film, 1967–1983*. Austin: University of Texas Press, 1992.

Berg, Charles Ramírez. "The Indian Question." In *New Latin American Cinema: Theory, Practices, and Transcontinental Articulations,* edited by Michael T. Martin, 76–93. Detroit: Wayne State University Press, 1997.

Berg, Charles Ramírez. *Latino Images in Film: Stereotypes, Subversion, and Resistance*. Austin: University of Texas Press, 2002.

Bordwell, David. *Narration in the Fiction Film*. Madison: University of Wisconsin Press, 1985.

Bordwell, David. *Poetics of Cinema*. New York and London: Routledge, 2009.

Chatman, Seymour. "What Novels Can Do That Films Can't (and Vice Versa)." In *Literary Theories in Praxis,* edited by Shirley F. Staton, 159–69. Philadelphia: University of Pennsylvania Press, 1987.

Cohen, Annabel. "Film Music: Perspectives from Cognitive Psychology." In *Music and Cinema,* edited by James Buhler, Caryl Flinn, and David Neumeyer, 360–78. Hanover, N.H.: Wesleyan University Press, 2000.

de Gelder, Beatrice. "Toward the Neurobiology of Emotional Body Language." *Nature* 7 (March 2006): 242–49.

de la Mora, Sergio. *Cinemachismo: Masculinities and Sexuality in Mexican Film.* Austin: University of Texas Press, 2006.

Deleyto, Celestino, and María del Mar Azcona. *Alejandro González Iñárritu.* Urbana: University of Illinois Press, 2010.

Donnelly, K. J. *The Spectre of Sound: Music in Film and Television.* London: British Film Institute, 2005.

Dudai, Yadin. "Enslaving Central Executives: Toward a Brain Theory of Cinema." *Projections* 2, no. 2 (2008): 21–42.

Dugdale, Timothy. "The French New Wave: New Again." In *New Punk Cinema,* edited by Nicholas Rombes, 56–71. Edinburgh: Edinburgh University Press, 2005.

Duncan, Seth, and Lisa Feldman Barrett. "Affect Is a Form of Cognition: A Neurobiological Analysis." *Cognition and Emotion* 21 (2007): 1184–211.

Eder, Jens. "Feelings in Conflict: *A Clockwork Orange* and the Explanation of Audiovisual Emotions." *Projections* 2, no. 2 (2008): 66–84.

Feagin, Susan L. "Time and Timing." In *Passionate Views: Film, Cognition, and Emotion,* edited by Carl Plantinga and Greg M. Smith, 168–79. Baltimore: Johns Hopkins University Press, 1999.

Finnegan, Nuala. "'So What's Mexico Really Like?' Framing the Local, Negotiating the Global in Alfonso Cuarón's *Y tu Mamá También.*" In *Contemporary Latin American Cinema: Breaking into the Global Market,* edited by Deborah Shaw, 29–50. New York: Rowman and Littlefield, 2007.

Fojas, Camilla. *Border Bandits: Hollywood on the Southern Frontier.* Austin: University of Texas Press, 2008.

Foster, David William. *Mexico City in Contemporary Mexican Cinema.* Austin: University of Texas Press, 2002.

Frome, Jonathan. "Representation, Reality, and Emotions across Media." *Film Studies: An International Review* 8 (Summer 2006): 12–25.

Gervais, Matthew, and David Sloan Wilson. "The Evolution and Functions of Laughter and Humor: A Synthetic Approach." *Quarterly Review of Biology* 80, no. 4 (2005): 395–430.

González, Rita, Jesse Lerner, and Isabelle Marmasse. *Mexperimental Cinema: Sixty Years of Avant-Garde Media Arts from Mexico.* Santa Monica, Calif.: Smart Art, 1998.

Gopnik, Alison. *Philosophical Baby: What Children's Minds Tell Us about Truth, Love, and the Meaning of Life.* New York: Farrar, Straus and Giroux, 2009.

Grant, Catherine, and Annette Kuhn, eds. *Screening World Cinema.* New York: Routledge, 2006.

Greene, Doyle. *Mexploitation Cinema: A Critical History of Mexican Vampire, Wrestler, Ape-Man, and Similar Films, 1957–1977.* Jefferson, N.C.: McFarland, 2005.

Haddu, Miriam. *Contemporary Mexican Cinema, 1989–1999: History, Space, and Identity.* Lewiston, N.Y.: Edwin Mellen, 2007.

Hernandez-Rodriguez, R. *Splendors of Latin Cinema.* Santa Barbara: Praeger, 2010.

Hind, Emily. "*Provincia* in Recent Mexican Cinema, 1989–2004." *Discourse* 26, nos. 1–2 (2004): 26–45.

Hogan, Patrick Colm. "Epilogue of Suffering." *SubStance* 30, nos. 1–2 (2001): 119–43.

Hogan, Patrick Colm. "Projection, Violations of Continuity, and Emotion in the Experience of Film." *Projection* 1, no. 1 (2007): 41–58.

Hogan, Patrick Colm. *Understanding Indian Cinema: Culture, Cognition, and Cinematic Imagination.* Austin: University of Texas Press, 2008.

Hopewell, John. "Latin Filmmaker on a Roll." *Variety,* February 23, 2009, 7.

Huntington, Tom. "Of Steadicams and Skycams: Filmmakers Have Long Sought the Means to Add a Little Kinetic Energy to Their Moving Images." *American Heritage of Invention and Technology* 24, no. 1 (2009): 24–32.

Hurley, Mathew, Daniel C. Dennett, and Reginald B. Adams Jr. *Inside Jokes: Using Humor to Reverse-Engineer the Mind.* Cambridge, Mass.: MIT Press, 2011.

James, P. D. *Children of Men.* New York: Warner, 1992.

King, John. *Magical Reels.* London: Verso, 1990.

Konigsberg, Ira. "Film Studies and the New Science." *Projections* 1, no. 1 (2007): 1–24.

Lindenberger, Herbert. "Arts in the Brain: What Might Neuroscience Tell Us?" In *Toward a Cognitive Theory of Narrative Acts,* edited by Frederick Luis Aldama, 13–35. Austin: University of Texas Press, 2010.

Lipkes, Tatiana. "Carlos Reygadas." *La Tempestad* 8, no. 53 (2007): 76–77.

Marciniak, Katarzyna. *Alienhood: Citizenship, Exile, and the Logic of Difference.* Minneapolis: University of Minnesota Press, 2006.

Marx, Karl. *Capital: A Critique of Political Economy.* Harmondsworth: Penguin, 1978.

McGinn, Colin. *The Power of Movies.* New York: Random House, 2005.

Mora, Carlos J. *Mexican Cinema: Reflections of a Society, 1896–2004.* 3d ed. Jefferson, N.C.: McFarland, 2005.

Nericcio, William. *Tex[t]-Mex: Seductive Hallucinations of the "Mexican" in America.* Austin: University of Texas Press, 2007.

Noble, Andrea. *Mexican National Cinema.* New York: Routledge, 2005.

Paz, Octavio. *The Labyrinth of Solitude: Life and Thought in Mexico.* Translated by Lysander Kemp. New York: Grove Press, 1961.

Peretz, Isabelle, and John Sloboda. "Music and the Emotional Brain." *Neurosciences and Music: Annals, New York Academy of Sciences* 1060 (December 2005): 409–11.

Pick, Zuzana M. *Constructing the Image of the Mexican Revolution: Cinema and the Archive.* Austin: University of Texas Press, 2010.

Plantinga, Carl. "I Followed the Rules, and They All Loved You More": Moral Judgment and Attitudes toward Fictional Characters in Film." *Midwest Studies in Philosophy* 34, no. 1 (2010): 34–51.

Plantinga, Carl. *Moving Viewers: American Film and the Spectator's Experience.* Berkeley: University of California Press, 2009.

Podalsky, Laura. "Migrant Feelings: Melodrama, *Babel,* and Affective Communities." *Studies in Hispanic Cinemas* 7, no. 1 (2010): 47–58.

Podalsky, Laura. "The Young, the Damned, and the Restless." *Framework: The Journal of Cinema and Media* 49, no. 1 (2008): 144–60.

Podalsky, Laura. "Out of Depth: The Politics of Disaffected Youth in Contemporary Latin American Cinema." In *Youth Culture in Global Cinema,* edited by Timothy Shary and Alexandra Seibel, 109–30. Austin: University of Texas Press, 2007.

Pranaguá, Paulo Antonio, ed. *Mexican Cinema.* Translated by Ana M. López. London: British Film Institute, 1995.

Prince, Stephen. "Psychoanalytic Film Theory." In *Post-Theory: Reconstructing Film Studies,* edited by David Bordwell and Noël Carroll, 80–88. Madison: University of Wisconsin Press, 1996.

Pudovkin, Vsevolod. "On Editing." In *Film Technique and Film Acting. Excerpted in Film and Criticism,* edited by Leo Braudy and Marshall Cohen, 7th ed., 7–12. Oxford and New York: Oxford University Press, 2009.

Rashkin, Elissa J. *Women Filmmakers in Mexico: The Country of Which We Dream.* Austin: University of Texas Press, 2001.

Rodríguez, Clara E. *Heroes, Lovers, and Others: The Story of Latinos in Hollywood.* Washington, D.C.: Smithsonian Books, 2004.

Rohter, Larry. "Gustavo Santaolalla: His Film Scores are Spare, His Tango Newfangled." *New York Times,* August 15, 2008. http://www.nytimes.com/2008/08/15/arts/15iht-15gus.15318500.html?pagewanted=all.

Samson, Andrea, Stefan Zysset, and Oswald Huber. "Cognitive Humor Processing: Different Logical Mechanisms in Nonverbal Cartoons—an fMRI Study." *Social Neuroscience* 3, no. 2 (2008): 125–40.

Schiwy, Freya. *Indianizing Film: Decolonization, the Andes, and the Question of Technology.* Newark, N.J.: Rutgers University Press, 2009.

Scott, A. O. "The World Is Watching, Not Americans." *New York Times,* January 21, 2007. http://www.nytimes.com/2007/01/21/movies/21scot.html?ref=movies.

Shklovsky, Victor. "The Semantics of Cinema." In *The Film Factory: Russian and Soviet Cinema in Documents,* edited and translated by Richard Taylor, 129–34. Cambridge, Mass.: Harvard University Press, 1988.

Smith, Jeff. "Movie Music as Moving Music: Emotion, Cognition, and the Film Score." In *Passionate Views: Film, Cognition, and Emotion,* edited by Carl Plantinga and Greg M. Smith, 146–66. Baltimore: Johns Hopkins University Press, 1999.

Smith, Paul Julian. *Amores Perros.* London: British Film Institute, 2002.

Smith, Paul Julian. "Paul Julian Smith Reports on a Rich Crop of Homegrown Films." *Film Quarterly* 63, no. 3 (2010): 18–22.

Smith, Paul Julian. "Transatlantic Traffic in Recent Mexican Films." *Journal of Latin American Cultural Studies* 12, no. 3 (2003): 389–400.

Soutar, Jethro. *Gael García Bernal and the Latin American New Wave.* London: Portico, 2008.

Steinbeck, John. *Viva Zapata: The Original Screenplay.* New York: Penguin, 1975.

Stock, Anne Marie. "Authentically Mexican? Mi Querido Tom Mix and Cronos Reframe Critical Questions." In *Mexico's Cinema: A Century of Film and Filmmakers,* edited by Joanne Hershield and David Maciel, 267–86. Wilmington, Del.: Scholarly Research Books, 1999.

Tegel, Simeon. "Mexico Hits B.O. Jackpot." *Variety,* March 27–April 2, 2000, 38.

Teodoro, José. "On Earth as It Is in Heaven." *Film Comment* 45, no. 1 (2009): 48–51.

Thompson, Kristin. *Breaking the Glass Armor: Neoformalist Film Analysis.* Princeton, N.J.: Princeton University Press, 1988.

Ugalde, Victor. "El TLC: La otra conquista," *Industrias Culturales y TLC: Impactos y re tos de la apertura* (Mexico: Fronteras Comunes, 2000): 85–105.

Van Sijll, Jennifer. *Cinematic Storytelling: The Hundred Most Powerful Film Conventions Every Filmmaker Must Know.* Studio City, Calif.: Michael Wiese Productions, 2005.

Vasconcelos, José. *Cosmic Race: A Bilingual Edition.* Translated and annotated by Didier T. Jaén. Baltimore: Johns Hopkins University Press, 1997.

Wood, Jason. *The Faber Book of Mexican Cinema.* London: Faber and Faber, 2006.

Wood, Jason. *Talking Movies: Contemporary World Filmmakers in Interview.* London: Wallflower, 2006.

Zacks, J. M., N. K. Speer, and J. R. Reynolds. "Segmentation in Reading and Film Comprehension." *Journal of Experimental Psychology: General* 138 (2009): 307–27.

Zaretsky, Eli. *Capitalism, the Family, and Personal Life.* New York: Harper and Row, 1976.

Index

queer art-house, 1
queer cinema, 6
Quinn, Anthony (Rudolfo Oaxaca), 68
Quintana Roo, Mexico, 26

Raczynski, Kristoff: *Amores perros,* 37
Ramirez, Arcelia: *Perfume de violetas,* 128
Ramírez Berg, Charles, 72, 74; *Cinema of Solitude,* 6; *Latino Images,* 7; *Latino Images in Film,* 75
Ramírez Suárez, Jorge: *Conejo en la luna/Rabbit on the Moon,* 82
Ramos, Sam, 3
Rashkin, Elissa, 127; *Women Filmmakers in Mexico,* 6
reality effect function, 59–60
refrito films, 19, 86, 90–96; adult-oriented, 121. *See also* Arau, Alfonso: *Zapata: El sueño del héroe;* Colón, Jorge: *Cansada de besar sapos/Tired of Kissing Frogs;* Sariñana, Fernando: Todo el poder; Serrano, Antonio: *Sexo, pudor y lágrimas*
Remedios, Honduras, 18
Retes, Gabriel: *El bulto,* 6
Reygadas, Carlos: *Batalla en el cielo/Battle in Heaven,* 20, 21, 46; *Luz silenciosa/Silent Night,* 20, 21
Richards, Keith: "Ruby Tuesday," 116
Richardson, Tony: *The Border,* 72
Riggen, Patricia: *La misma luna/Under the Same Moon,* 12–13, 63, 65
Ripstein, Arturo, 10, 77
Rivera, Alex: *Sleep Dealer,* 2
Rivera, Antonia: *Buscando a Leti,* 64
Rivera, Carolina: *Amor xtremo,* 87
RKO, 5, 149
Roberts, Julia: *The Mexican,* 72
Rodarte, Miguel: *El tigre de Santa Julia/The Tiger of Santa Julia,* 87
Rodríguez, Clara E., 74, 75; *Heroes, Lovers, and Others,* 68
Rodriguez, Freddy: *Harsh Times,* 74

Rodríguez, Gabino: *La niña en la piedra,* 130
Rodriguez, Robert: *Desperado,* 69; *From Dusk Till Dawn,* 69; *Spy Kids,* 68
Rodríguez-López, Omar: *El búfalo de la noche,* 77
Rohter, Larry, 40
Rojo, Maria: *Perfume de violetas,* 128
Roland, Gilbert, 68
Rolling Stones, 112; "Ruby Tuesday," 116
Rotberg, Dana, 77
Roth, Celia: *La hija del caníbal/Lucía Lucía / The Daughter of Canibal,* 123
rural, 7, 65, 71, 84, 91, 96

Saenz, Luisa: *40 días/40 Days,* 62
Sahmi, Wahiba: *Babel,* 106
Salcés, Carlos: *Zurdo,* 2
Salinas, Jorge: *Sexo, pudor y lágrimas,* 92
Salinas de Gortari, Carlos, 6, 80
Salles, Walter, 7
Sánchez, Eva Lopéz: *La última y nos vamos/One More and We Leave,* 86
Sánchez-Gijón, Aitana: *Sin dejar huella/Without a Trace,* 65
Sanchez Parra, Gustavo: *Amores perros,* 34
Santaolalla, Gustavo: *Amores perros,* 40; *Babel,* 105
Santullo, Laura: *La zona/The Zone,* 132
Sariñana, Carlos: *Amor xtremo,* 87
Sariñana, Fernando
    Amar te duele/Loving You Hurts, 121–22, 133
    cameras, 10
    emotion, 139
    music, 40–41, 87
    Amor xtremo, 87
    El segundo aire/A Second Chance, 96
    Ninas mal/Bad Girls, 87
    Todo el poder, 85, 88, 94–96
Sariñana, Ximena: *Amor xtremo,* 87
Sarris, Andrew, 143
Scanda, Tiaré: *De ida y vuelta/Back and*